Writing Revolution

AESTHETICS
AND
POLITICS
IN
HAWTHORNE,
WHITMAN,
AND
THOREAU

Writing Revolution

Peter J. Bellis

The University of Georgia Press

Athens and London

© 2003 by the University of Georgia Press

Athens, Georgia 30602

All rights reserved

Set in Berthold Baskerville by Bookcomp, Inc.

Printed and bound by Thomson-Shore

The paper in this book meets the guidelines for
permanence and durability of the Committee on
Production Guidelines for Book Longevity of the
Council on Library Resources.

Printed in the United States of America

07 06 05 04 03 C 5 4 3 2 1

Library of Congress Cataloging-in-Publication Data

Bellis, Peter J.

Writing revolution: aesthetics and politics in Hawthorne,
Whitman, and Thoreau / Peter J. Bellis.

p. cm.

Includes bibliographical references and index.

ISBN 0-8203-2392-6 (hardcover : alk. paper)

1. American literature – 19th century – History and criticism.

2. Politics and literature – United States – History – 19th century.

3. Hawthorne, Nathaniel, 1804–1864 – Political and social views.

4. Thoreau, Henry David, 1817–1862 – Political and social views.

5. Revolutionary literature, American – History and criticism.

6. Whitman, Walt, 1819–1892 – Political and social views.

7. Hawthorne, Nathaniel, 1804–1864 – Aesthetics.

8. Thoreau, Henry David, 1817–1862 – Aesthetics.

9. Whitman, Walt, 1819–1892 – Aesthetics.

10. Aesthetics, American.   I. Title: Aesthetics and politics
in Hawthorne, Whitman, and Thoreau.   II. Title.

PS217.P64 B45   2003

810.9'358 – dc21   2002006742

British Library Cataloging-in-Publication Data available

CONTENTS

ACKNOWLEDGMENTS

This book began in the classroom, in exchanges with students, and it has grown in conversations with friends and colleagues over the years. The project has been aided by a Max Orovitz Summer Research Award and by sabbatical grants from the University of Miami, for which I am very grateful.

It has also been supported, in less tangible but more important ways, by a number of colleagues who have read and commented on portions of the manuscript; among them, I especially wish to thank Joe Alkana, Russ Castronovo, and John Paul Russo, whose challenges and contributions have strengthened the book immensely. I am also indebted to Alison Waldenberg, Erin McElroy, and the staff of the University of Georgia Press.

Portions of chapters 1, 2, and 4 have appeared in *ESQ* (41, no. 2 [1995]: 97–119), *Studies in the Novel* (26 [1994]: 199–217), and *Centennial Review* (43, no. 1 [1999]: 71–94), respectively.

Most of all, I want to thank my family, who have helped me to keep this project in perspective and in its place. Miriam, Katie, and Alex–this book, like everything else, is for you.

Writing Revolution

⌒

The Eighteenth Brumaire and the Magic Lantern

My objective here, put in its broadest terms, is to think about the ways in which literature can engage with or act upon the world. No act of representation, whether political or discursive, is ever simple; each transforms or displaces its object in some fashion. But representations — and *aesthetic* representations in particular — are nevertheless often consigned to second-order or derivative status in relation to their "originals."

In literary studies, formalist and deconstructive readings have been under attack for some years now, charged with isolating texts as distinctive aesthetic or linguistic objects from their social and historical contexts. But historicist and cultural approaches have often responded by simply reversing the picture, reducing texts to no more than superstructural effects of historical or ideological forces — a kind of "thick propaganda," in Sacvan Bercovitch's phrase.[1] What I hope to explore here is a middle ground, a terrain on which discourse can interact with its social and cultural context. How, I mean to ask, might it be possible for literary discourse to intervene in and help to shape the realms of history and politics?[2]

1

I have chosen to approach these issues through the work of three nineteenth-century American writers – Nathaniel Hawthorne, Walt Whitman, and Henry David Thoreau – all of whom write in response to the same historical moment. Georg Lukacs describes the early nineteenth century as a time when "it was possible for writers to grasp their own present as *history*."[3] Hawthorne, writing in the period before and after the failed revolutions of 1848, stands at a crucial historical juncture, at the end of what Lukacs sees as the great period of realism, before "bourgeois ideology . . . dehistoricizes reality."[4] Indeed, Hawthorne's historical self-consciousness makes it difficult to speak of "historicizing" or "rehistoricizing" his work, for his project is, in a sense, already an examination of the relation between text and historical context. His romance brings together the imaginary and the actual, the aesthetic and the historical – not to aestheticize or neutralize history and politics, but to undertake an imaginative entry into their territory.

Whitman, on the other hand, begins his poetic career with an attempt to move beyond such ideas of mediation and interconnection, to make a revolutionary break with representation altogether. His vision in 1855 is of a poetry of democratic inclusion, in which things themselves are made present to the reader with an immediacy that transcends language itself. They come at the problem from different directions, but both Hawthorne and Whitman would move from the aesthetic or imaginary into a new realm – either the neutral territory of romance, or the transformative verbal space of a new American poetry.

Thoreau's work contrasts with Hawthorne's and Whitman's in that it both affirms and denies the possibility of such a space. *Walden* begins as a project based on mediation – between town and nature, between the reader and the pond. On such a middle ground, Thoreau proposes, human and natural history might be reconnected, yielding both an unalienated labor and a critique of the status quo. But in his abolitionist essays of the 1850s, written both during and after *Walden,* Thoreau abandons political and verbal representation as inadequate to the moral crisis of slavery. If Whitman can envision a transcendence of mediation, Thoreau finally anticipates only an apocalyptic violence, one that exceeds and annihilates both the discursive and the political.

Each of these writers stands at a different point on the political and artistic spectrum, and each has different objectives. But three white men from New York and New England obviously cannot represent the full range of voices in antebellum American writing. James Fenimore Cooper, Catherine Sedgwick, and William Gilmore Simms also work with historical materials, for example, and both Herman Melville and Frederick Douglass experiment with different forms and genres in addressing political and social issues. This book is not intended, then, as a thorough survey of the period; it is oriented instead toward the consideration of a particular issue—the relation between literature and politics—and I have taken Hawthorne, Whitman, and Thoreau as my subjects because they offer contrasting and instructive approaches to the problem.

The following chapters are, I think, best regarded as a set of linked essays rather than a single extended argument. Generally speaking, they follow a pattern of exploration and then return, an expansion of possibilities followed by an acknowledgement of limits—the rhythm, I suspect, of all engagement between the aesthetic and the political.

In a sense, Thoreau's later writing reconfirms an opposition between aesthetics and history, discourse and action, returning us to the point at which Hawthorne began. One way, perhaps, in which to step outside this circle is to approach the issue through another text of the 1850s, one whose perspective is both historical and theoretical: Karl Marx's "Eighteenth Brumaire of Louis Bonaparte," first published in New York in 1851, focuses directly on the relation between representation and revolution. It is at once a slashing piece of political journalism and an effort to project the terms in which social revolution might be described.

I turn to Marx at this point for several reasons. First of all, his work provides the general ground for many of today's critiques of aesthetic production—as either ideologically determined or otherwise incompatible with revolutionary action. Second, however, if we focus on the "Eighteenth Brumaire" in particular, as an exemplary precursor of such critiques, we will find that it actually complicates and problematizes their perspective in important ways, for the essay ends by entangling action and discourse instead of separating and opposing them.

Marx builds his essay upon an opposition between the French Revolution of 1789–an event of real "world-historical" importance in his
terms–and the bourgeois revolution of 1848–51.[5] The emptiness of the
latter is repeatedly figured in terms of theatricality, as an aestheticized
performance that in fact obstructs or precludes true revolutionary action.

Parliamentary representation under the bourgeois republic takes place
on a public "political stage"–this conceit recurs a dozen times or more
in the course of the essay (442, 457, and elsewhere). The National Assembly "performs on the boards," but in a "piece [that] is not played
twice" (449). The "French bourgeoisie itself played the most complete
comedy, but in the most serious manner," Marx observes, "and was itself
half deceived, half convinced by the solemnity of its own principal and
state actions" (480). Louis Napoleon's victory is made possible because
he, on the other hand, "took the comedy as plain comedy," as theatrical
performance rather than historically significant action (480).

Again and again such theater is revealed as empty verbiage, as calls
to arms are substituted for real resistance (463). In the bourgeois revolution, "the phrase [goes] beyond the content," while in the "social revolution," "the content goes beyond the phrase" (439). Proletarian revolution, by definition, exceeds representation; it "cannot draw its poetry
from the past, but only from the future," from a form it will itself create (439). Bourgeois revolutions are matters of swiftly passing "dramatic
effects," but proletarian ones "criticise themselves constantly, interrupt
themselves continually in their own course, come back to the apparently
accomplished in order to begin it afresh" (439). True revolution brings
with it an interrogation and supercession of all pre-existing forms of representation, both political and discursive.

Nowhere is this gap between revolution and its representation registered more forcefully, however, than in the pages of the "Eighteenth
Brumaire" itself. Marx's writing is overtly rhetorical throughout, con-
sistently–even compulsively–figurative and allusive. His description of
proletarian revolutions, for instance, continues in this way: "[they] deride
with unmerciful thoroughness the inadequacies, weaknesses and paltri-
nesses of their first attempts, seem to throw down their adversary only in

order that he may draw new strength from the earth and rise again more gigantic before them, recoil ever and anon from the indefinite prodigiousness of their own aims" (439–40). The length and complexity of this sentence suggests an effort to mimic the halting and indirect progression of the revolution itself, but Marx's allusion to Antaeus is precisely the kind of gesture toward the past that he associates with bourgeois revolution. And, as if to further emphasize the difference, Marx concludes his paragraph with a quotation from Aesop, one that bears within it an echo of Hegel. Marx's own language thus remains within the rhetorical or figurative realm of bourgeois representation, even as he attempts to sketch out an alternative to it.

There are moments in the essay at which Marx seems to contradict or modify his initial opposition. The parliamentary republic, he acknowledges, does force the bourgeoisie to "confront the subjugated classes and contend against them without intermediation," thus revealing the true class nature of the long-term conflict (460). If, in the February Revolution of 1848, "the social republic appeared as a phrase," that phrase is not an empty one–it is, in this case, "a prophecy" (510). Just as "Men make their own history, but they do not make it just as they please," so too, representation is not empty and without consequences, but those consequences may be discernible only in retrospect (437).

There is, then, no sustainable opposition between an idealized and pure revolutionary praxis and an empty realm of merely discursive performance. Late in the "Eighteeenth Brumaire," when Marx discusses the French peasantry, he argues that a state built on a system of peasant small holdings must collapse, and this is how "the proletarian revolution obtains that chorus without which its solo song in all peasant nations becomes a swan song" (521). The revolution must take or be given form (a song), and must thus remain within the realm of representation and interpretation (solo song vs. swan song). As Stephen Greenblatt puts it, "social actions are themselves always embedded in systems of public signification, always grasped, even by their makers, in acts of interpretation."[6] Even in Marx, then, politics and discourse, history and the aesthetic, remain in an uneasy tension, incommensurable on the one hand, inseparable on the other. The French parliamentary republic may not be a "neutral territory," but it is a "staging point" for both real historical action and illusion.[7]

The contemporary Americanist whose work follows most directly from Marx's analysis is, perhaps, Sacvan Bercovitch. For him, representing politics or history in any form only neutralizes them, reducing revolutionary praxis to mere discourse. By committing himself to writing – to discourse about change – an author has already accepted the pluralist conception of mediated or incremental reform. Bercovitch thus echoes Marx in positing an opposition between discourse, which seems inevitably to be co-opted or redefined by liberal ideology, and revolutionary action, which he locates outside or beyond such ideological constraints.

Aesthetic representation, he argues, can never free itself from its ideological context; it is, instead, doubly bound to it, unable to envision or express alternatives to the hegemonic order. Dissent becomes a matter of merely interpretive conflict, confined to the level of discourse alone. One ground for the formalist valorization of the literary or aesthetic – its ostensible self-consciousness about its own form and contents – would seem, from Bercovitch's political perspective, to be its most conservative aspect. Such an awareness of the problems of *representing* social change means that representation becomes the primary issue, and the impetus toward change is lost. Aesthetic self-consciousness only roots both text and reader even more firmly in the realm of discourse, and thus within the limits of the pluralist status quo.[8]

Richard Terdiman, discussing what he terms "symbolic resistance" in nineteenth-century France, would agree with Bercovitch that "programmatic revolutionary discourse" was dying out by midcentury.[9] Such an essentially "performative" counterdiscourse was, he says, no longer possible after 1848, given the increasing force of middle-class hegemony.[10] But the result, in his view, was a redirection, not just a co-optation, of revolutionary energy – into a drive toward literary or "textual revolution," in which "the esthetic" became "a mode of struggle" and "ideological resistance."[11] America, I would suggest, experienced the revolutionary crises of 1848 largely secondhand, and such oppositional energies remained alive and unspent through the 1850s, as intensifying struggles over race and class prevented such a hegemonic enclosure. A performative, trans- forming impulse is still central to the work of all the writers I discuss here, and most especially to the early Whitman.

Evan Carton has approached the nineteenth-century romance from a more optimistic perspective than Bercovitch, describing it as a "self- consciously dialectical . . . rhetorical performance," an "enterprise . . . by which one might resist . . . both the complete alienation and the com- plete identification of imagination and world." [12] His concern is primarily with what one might call the "poetics" of the romance, the theoretical and rhetorical grounding of its claims for representational authority. But what I find most suggestive in Carton's formulation is the idea of romance as *resistance,* resistance to absorption by either the imaginary or the ac- tual, to determination by either internal aesthetic demands or external political ones—or to co-optation by the pluralist hegemony Bercovitch describes. Paul de Man speaks of "textual instances that are irreduceable to grammar or to historically determined meaning," and calls these the "rhetorical dimensions of a text." [13] But the same theory that shows the necessity of a rhetorical reading, he continues, must also "avoid and re- sist" it: "Nothing can overcome the resistance to theory since theory *is* itself this resistance." [14] For Hawthorne, I would argue, the romance's his- torical and rhetorical self-consciousness works in just this way—to resist co-optation by any hegemonic discourse or totalizing representation.

This notion of a resistance or tension internal to the literary work does not mean simply a devaluation or marginalization of the force of ideology and politics. It is central, for example, to the analysis of Pierre Macherey, who defines "literary discourse" as "a contestation of language": "the book," he says, "gives an implicit critique of its ideological content, if only because it resists being incorporated into the flow of ideology in order to give a *determinate representation* of it." [15] The primary mode of this resistance, according to Macherey, is "the multiplicity of [the work's] meanings"; criticism "measures the *distance* which separates the *various* meanings." [16] Such multiplicity or ambiguity of meaning, which bears a clearly conservative valence for Bercovitch, can just as easily carry a pro- gressive charge—it is Marxist proletarian revolutions, we may recall, that "criticize themselves . . . interrupt themselves . . . [and] begin . . . afresh" (439). "The reality of any hegemony," Raymond Williams reminds us, is that "it is never either total or exclusive. . . . It is also continually resisted, limited, altered, challenged by pressures not at all its own."[17] Literary texts have the potential to do far more than simply demonstrate their own ideological enclosure; the writers I discuss would all strike through such limits into the realm of social and political action. For them, the depiction of historical or social change within the literary text brings aesthetic discourse into direct contact with the political. And insofar as their work succeeds in redefining the relation between text and reader, it also alters that between the reader and his world—placing him in a different relation to ideology as both an interpretive and a political subject.

If aesthetic representations are always also political, so—as my reading of the "Eighteenth Brumaire" suggests—political actions must also involve processes of representation (and, inevitably, interpretation as well). Homi Bhabha insists on this interrelation when he speaks of writing as "a productive matrix which defines the 'social' and makes it available as an object of/for action. Textuality is not simply a second-order ideological expression or a verbal symptom of a pre-given ideological subject."[18] I would argue, then, following Bhabha and Greenblatt, that one cannot isolate or define separate realms of discourse and action; one must look instead to the sites and forms of their interaction. Both Hawthorne's romance, with its interpenetration of actual and imaginary, historical and aesthetic, and Whitman's poetry, with its fluid and expansive textual space, are among those sites.

The view implicit in Hawthorne's romance, and the one I wish to suggest here, is that the relation between cultural and public, aesthetic and political, is a matter of continual reconstruction and negotiation, in which ideology plays an inescapable—but not fully determining—role. I take the idea of a "negotiation" from Bhabha, who uses it to describe the link between critical theory and political action. When Bhabha describes the work of theoretical critique, his terms are much like those Hawthorne uses to define the romance: "The language of critique is effective," Bhabha says, "to the extent to which it overcomes the given grounds of opposition and opens up a space of 'translation': a place of hybridity," in which a new "political object . . . *neither the one nor the Other,*" can be constructed.[19] Bhabha, along with other theorists, such as Ernesto Laclau and Chantal Mouffe, seeks to position his work in a space *between* theory and politics.[20]

Hawthorne's approach is, one might say, from the "right" and Whitman's from the "left." But the former's "hybrid" genre of romance comes into being in a space not unlike the one Bhabha describes, in which ostensible opposites – discourse and action, aesthetics and politics – meet and interpenetrate. And the latter's poetic territory is one in which distinctions between "one" and "Other," words and things, break down entirely.

According to Bercovitch, antebellum American writers could see dissent only in individual terms; as he puts it in discussing *The Scarlet Letter,* "To endorse Hester as radical is to believe that social change follows from self-realization, not vice versa; that true revolution is therefore an issue of individual growth rather than group action" (*Office,* 125). Dissent is neutralized once again, because it can only be expressed in the terms offered by the dominant culture. If the goal is "self-realization," then "such categories as race, class, and gender [are defined] as social 'limitations,' to be transcended en route to representative individualism" (*Office,* 146). For Bercovitch's Hawthorne, social change must be individual, not collective, based on gradual reform, not violent revolution.

Whitman's challenge to such an ideological position could hardly be more radical.[21] For he seeks not simply to blur the line between discourse and action but to obliterate it. And beyond the loss of a distinction between the subject and object of representation, Whitman would also dispense with conventional notions of subjectivity themselves.

His poems of 1855 fuse the notions of representation and incarnation or embodiment. The self they generate or enact is not one distinct from others, but one defined through its absorption of and by a collectivity. And the text is foregrounded as a material object, also the product of a collective social process. From this perspective, Whitman's open aesthetic form becomes a democratizing political act. To use Walter Benjamin's terms, Whitman seeks, as "producer," to "recast" the distinction between author and reader, and to transform the "productive apparatus" through which he works.[22] The space of the text becomes a transformed

America, one spoken into being in the exchange between author and readers.

The kind of politics I have been describing here—that of Hawthorne's romance, the 1855 *Leaves,* and Thoreau's *Walden*—need not be simply a discursive or textual phenomenon. Their work is designed not merely to speak to or incite its readers, but to act upon them, and thus upon their world. Whitman's urban catalogs are continuous with—not distant from—the political discourse and practice of antebellum New York; and Thoreau's text relocates Walden as a stop on the Underground Railroad. Such a politics may have its twentieth-century embodiments as well: in Situationist slogans in the Paris of 1968, or, perhaps, in Prague's Velvet Revolution of 1989, the social and political upheaval that Timothy Garton Ash has called "The Revolution of the Magic Lantern."[23] The latter is a model worth considering for a moment—for it was a transformation through both political action and aesthetic performance, through both charismatic individual leadership and a collective response that filled the public spaces of the Czech capital.

The central figure of the Czechoslovak opposition was, of course, dissident playwright Vaclav Havel, whom Garton Ash describes as "at once director, playwright, stage manager, and leading actor in this, his greatest play" (42). It was not only Havel who blended politics and theater, though: the protests began with students, who were soon joined by actors, meeting in "the Realistic Theater" (42). The opposition coalition, Civic Forum, had its headquarters in "the Magic Lantern" theater, where speakers emerged for press conferences out of a stage set (43). Throughout the country, actors went on strike, closing the theaters for dramatic performances, but opening them as spaces for political activity.[24] Audiences, often primarily working class in composition, responded with applause.[25]

This was not, however, a case of the theatrical displacing or substituting for the political, as in Marx's "Eighteenth Brumaire." As Garton Ash describes it, dramatized representation and direct democracy were at this moment continuous, the former offering both the form and the occasion for the latter. While the Civic Forum may have been a self-selected group, it was at the same time "profoundly, elementally democratic. The *demos* spoke, in demos [demonstrations], and declared the Forum to be its mouthpiece" (44). Crowds did not simply listen to speakers and applaud; they began to "converse with the speakers in rhythmic chant," a dialogic interchange that set the tone of political gatherings (46). Formal drama, the impromptu street theater of political demonstrations, and direct collective action–each helped to generate and propel the others.

In many of his essays of the 1980s, Havel speaks of artistic representation as a mode of political resistance. Narrativization of events is, for him, a vital political act, for "the totalitarian system is in essence (and in principle) directed against [both] the story [and] . . . the feeling of historicity" itself.[26] "The story," Havel argues, "presupposes a plurality of truths, of logics, of agents of decisions," and thus carries a powerful anti-totalitarian charge.[27] Narrative and visual representation did, in fact, become central to the revolution of 1989; access to television was a crucial issue, as the dissidents struggled to ensure that their revolution would be televised (44).

"Stories" may well embody the essential values of what Havel had spoken of in 1984 as a second or "parallel culture." Such a culture "for various reasons will not, cannot, or may not reach out to the public through the media which fall under state control. . . . therefore, [it] can make use only of what is left–typewriters, private studios, apartments, barns, etc."[28] Faced with the uniformity of official culture, participants in this parallel culture are defined, not by their ideological unity, but by "their diversity and their insistence on being just what they are."[29] Such a culture of resistance "represents an important fertile ground, a catalytic agent," Havel says, in a comment that seems almost to prefigure the "dramatic" events of 1989.[30]

Such a broad vision of cultural and political change, as appearing in many forms and from many sources, corresponds in a number of ways to that of the American writers I discuss below. Among them, only Whitman faced any substantial censorship, but each felt himself to be either marginalized or speaking from and for the margins. Each also saw his writing as a way to move into, not away from, the political, a way to alter and reopen its discursive field–to rewrite the terms of American democracy. And thus, I argue, each sought to make his work a force for political change, the kind of change that Havel would help to bring about from backstage at the Magic Lantern.

Hawthorne envisions his "romance" as a "neutral territory," in which literature and history, artistic representation and political action, can meet and interpenetrate. His recurrent image for this "territory" is a space or room rendered new and unfamiliar by moonlight. Many of his works are built around such moonlight scenes,[31] in which he gives expression to dangerous, even violent impulses toward political or psychological change. In doing so, he tests the limits of aesthetic or imaginative dissent—opening up his texts to incorporate and express the forces of social and political change, even to the point where they threaten his own textual control.

At the same time, however, he presents these scenes as self-consciously theatrical moments, as representations of rebellion rather than "real" revolutionary action. I introduce my argument with readings of two short stories, "My Kinsman, Major Molineux" and "Howe's Masquerade," in which Hawthorne's romance offers the possibility of political or historical change but at the same time suggests its own discursive limits.

Chapter 2 focuses on *The House of the Seven Gables,* the work in which Hawthorne's romance most fully achieves its radical potential. Holgrave, both romance writer and political radical, achieves a hypnotic power over his audience, and Hawthorne's narrator mounts a vicious attack on the political and economic status quo in describing the death of Judge Pyncheon. But Hawthorne finally recoils from the full expression of such violent impulses, for they threaten to destabilize the text itself, fragmenting the plot and undermining the interplay between the political and the aesthetic on which the romance depends.

In *The Blithedale Romance,* on the other hand, Hawthorne speaks directly of social and sexual reform, but depicts such projects as *merely* theatrical, insubstantial and unreal. The "aesthetic labor" of his communal farm amounts to little more than a masquerade; here the charisma of a political speaker is no different in kind from the manipulative power of a mesmerizing showman.

Hawthorne thus sees both the liberating potential of art and the essentially conservative demands of conventional representation, and he builds his romance on the tension between them. He offers us an exemplary instance of the way in which an artist may seek to engage the forces of history and politics, but at the same time to maintain a mediating position, creating a space between the realms of imagination and ideology.

The second part of the book turns to Whitman's decidedly more radical poetics. He and Hawthorne may both have called themselves "Locofoco" Democrats, but Whitman's egalitarianism leads him to reject traditional aesthetic forms and hierarchies, attempting instead to create a poetry of inclusion rather than selection or representation. The encyclopedic lists of "Song of Myself" abandon conventional syntax in favor of unranked juxtapositions based on commas and ellipses. The 1855 version of *Leaves of Grass* claims, in fact, to give or show the reader things themselves, things that are already poems. "The United States themselves," Whitman announces, "are essentially the greatest poem"; they do not need the mediating filter of language to make them one.[32]

Beyond this, the poetic "self" created within the 1855 *Leaves* ostensibly incarnates and includes the life of the nation; its multiplicity and inconsistency—even physical permeability—mark a clear and decisive break from the conventions of nineteenth-century liberal individualism. If Whitman aims to overcome the opposition between things and their representations, he would also do away with the distinction between self and other, poet and reader. His goal is ultimately to transcend the mediation that Hawthorne sees as central to the romance; he seeks to dissolve the lines between the imaginary and the actual, the aesthetic and the political, representation and action.

The Whitman I have described here is, however, that of the 1855 *Leaves* alone. As early as the 1856 edition, his visionary conception has given way to a different approach, based on mediation and interconnection. In "Crossing Brooklyn Ferry," a third term stands "between" the poet and his readers—the poem itself. And by the time of the third edition of *Leaves* in 1860, Whitman has in some respects retreated even further, redefining his work as a response to an originary and constitutive absence or loss.

This trajectory – from affirmation to withdrawal and denial – appears in Thoreau's work as an oscillation or split rather than a diachronic development. Thoreau's project begins, in *A Week on the Concord and Merrimack Rivers,* by laying out a set of conflicts: between the fixed inscriptions of official white history and the unrecorded Indian past, and between human history and the slow evolutionary flux of nature. *Walden* seeks to reconcile such oppositions through a reconstructed landscape, historicized but still changing, still bearing the traces of its "Former Inhabitants" – Native Americans, immigrants, slaves, free blacks, and others. Here Thoreau problematizes the relation between center and periphery, taking Walden Pond and not Concord as his geographical, historical, and textual center. He seeks to clear or demarcate a space in which observation, cultivation, writing, and political or cultural resistance may all find a ground. And it is in this setting that he projects a counterhistory, one that may yet culminate in a renewed vision of unalienated labor and community.

Thoreau's abolitionist essays and lectures, on the other hand, seem to reject such a project in its entirety. They are written and delivered during the same period, but they speak of division, not connection, and fall back into a radical individualism in which moral purity is pitted against both history and community. Indeed, discourse itself is rejected as incommensurate with the moral entanglement of slavery: Thoreau ends by turning to John Brown, a figure who offers moral clarity through apocalyptic violence.

My final section is designed to conclude, but also to complicate, the readings that precede it. It is built on two juxtapositions: one between Hawthorne's *Marble Faun* (1859) and Margaret Fuller's European dispatches of a decade before, and the second between Whitman's "When Lilacs Last in the Dooryard Bloom'd" and Louisa May Alcott's story "My Contraband." Hawthorne and Whitman both step back and mark their distance – a distance they feel forced upon them *as writers* – from the possibilities of collective political change. Fuller and Alcott, on the other hand, commit themselves anew amid the crises of revolution and racial conflict, asserting a transgressive authorial freedom that carries them across the lines of both gender and genre.

PART ONE

Hawthorne

ONE

⌒

Hawthorne's
Drama of Revolt

Written in 1828 or 1829, "My Kinsman, Major Molineux" is one of Hawthorne's earliest tales. But even here, two decades before *The Scarlet Letter,* he has begun to develop the conception of romance that he will elaborate and build on in his later novels.

The story's events take place, Hawthorne notes again and again, in moonlight rather than daylight. Here, as throughout his work, Hawthorne associates the romance not with daylight order but with the opposing or subversive force of moonlight.[1] In "The Custom-House," he speaks of romance as "a neutral territory"; but it is also an unsettled, altered space, the kind created by the play of "moonlight, in a familiar room" (1:36, 35). The power of romance, for Hawthorne, comes from its ability to invest its materials "with a quality of strangeness and remoteness," or, as he puts it in "My Kinsman, Major Molineux," "a beautiful strangeness" (1:35, 11:221). His writing thus begins, not in confirmation and continuity, but with a critical defamiliarization and estrangement.

Hawthorne's use of the word "neutral" is, however, more than a little disingenuous. It suggests a place of safety, but this "territory" comes into being through a *dis*placement, as the site of a newly freed (and potentially dangerous) energy. Here "the Actual and the Imaginary may meet, and each imbue itself with the nature of the other. Ghosts might enter here, without affrighting us" (1:36). The romance becomes a place of dissolving boundaries and oppositions—between actual and imaginary, natural and supernatural, past and present. It takes the form of counterhistories, oppositional possibilities that haunt and trouble the present.

Over the years, critics have often discussed the romance in terms of its internal dynamics, emphasizing issues of epistemology and representation. Richard Brodhead, for instance, speaks of Hawthorne's concern with "how the mind envisions and makes sense of experience."[2] And Evan Carton claims that questions about "language's mediation between reality and imagination—questions of its authority, its method, its effectiveness, its morality—constitute . . . the heart of romance."[3] My interest, however, is less on *how* the romance connects to reality than on the fact that it *does* connect, and the difference that connection makes. My emphasis will be on the romance as artistic *performance,* beginning with the moments in which "acting" becomes both "acting out"—representing—and "acting on"—changing or affecting the actual and historical.

"My Kinsman, Major Molineux" is set in prerevolutionary Boston, but its implicit subject is the Revolution itself. It obviously predates the upheavals of 1848, but the late 1820s were themselves a time of political change and uncertainty. As Sacvan Bercovitch describes it, "with the deaths of Jefferson and John Adams, the Revolution passed officially . . . into the possession of a new generation. It was a troubled succession. . . . [B]oth parties [Jacksonians and anti-Jacksonians] agreed that the nation was in a crisis of identity, and both parties, each from its own perspective, proposed the same solution. They sought to stabilize society by rallying their countrymen, once again, to the chronometer of continuing revolution."[4] What Hawthorne's story does, I would suggest, is challenge precisely this notion of revolution as continuity or inheritance; it deliberately reinscribes discontinuities—class conflict and racial violence—into its narrative of revolutionary change.[5] Where Bercovitch links the American Revolution to an American tradition of consensual reform, Hawthorne invokes images of 1789 (surely even more powerful than those of 1848) and locates them *within* the Revolution itself. And where Bercovitch assumes a radical difference between revolutionary action and its representation, Hawthorne's work focuses on their interrelation.

Hawthorne's protagonist, Robin, seems at first to be operating within the ideology Bercovitch describes: he comes to Boston to pass from the protection of one paternal figure to another, as part of the controlled transfer of authority and identity between country and city, older generation and younger, Britain and America. He expects to find a single, integral social order in the city, in which the lines of political, economic, and genealogical power coincide. It does not take long, however, for this to be characterized as an ideologically suspect vision, an "anti-American" or Tory one at heart.

What Robin actually finds are a series of rifts and gaps in social and power relations, culminating in the breakdown of almost all structures of authority. When he enters a tavern, the youth is welcomed by the innkeeper and immediately concludes that " 'The man sees a family likeness! the rogue has guessed that I am related to the Major!' " (11:213). Robin assumes, first, that his kinsman's military and political authority extends throughout the city and across class lines, and second, that social position is primarily a matter of genealogical connection. The landlord, however, sees Robin in purely economic terms; his apparent deference is not personal at all, but only that given to any potential customer.

The course of their conversation confirms this displacement of personal or familial ties by economic ones. When Robin admits that he is poor and that he wishes only to ask directions to the Major's dwelling, the innkeeper's tone changes abruptly: glancing toward a poster offering a reward for a runaway indentured servant, he notes Robin's resemblance to the young man it describes and suggests that he had " 'Better trudge' " (11:214). Robin's acknowledgment of filial dependence is thrown back at him as a criminal breach of contract. His mention of the Major does not reveal a shared allegiance to royal authority; it instead reveals the gulf between citizen and state, rebel and Tory. Hawthorne's description of the inn and its customers thus opens up a series of conflicts – geographical and economic, as well as political – to create a context of "strange hostility" in which Robin's social and economic marginality is sharply thrust upon him (11:214).

Boston at night is thus a place of instability and conflict, in which Robin is left disoriented and unrecognized. He eventually finds himself seated on the steps of a church, alone on an empty street. The door to the church is locked, and Robin can only peer in through a window: "There the moonbeams came trembling in, and fell down upon the deserted pews, and extended along the quiet aisles. A fainter, yet more awful radiance, was hovering round the pulpit, and one solitary ray had dared to rest upon the opened page of the great Bible" (11:222). What the moonlight reveals is not a comforting, authoritative presence, but its absence or inaccessibility: an empty pulpit in a locked and deserted church, a Bible open and illuminated but unread.[6] Robin cannot help wondering, looking at the graves around the church, if "the object of his search," the "kinsman" who will serve as his fatherly guide and protector, may not be "all the time mouldering in his shroud" (11:222).

The boy recoils from this thought, envisioning instead a more reassuring scene, that of "his father's household," assembled beneath "the great old tree" beside their country home (11:222). There, at sunset, "it was his father's custom to perform domestic worship, that the neighbors might come and join with him like brothers of the family . . . he saw the good man in the midst, holding the Scriptures in the golden light that shone from the western clouds" (11:222, 223). This scene combines several different images of paternal power: the father's centrality in both family and community, his possession and display of the Scriptures, and the illumination of patriarch, family tree, and text by the setting sun. It is Robin's place in the family circle, within the structure defined by his father's authority, that has given him his identity. Now, however, he imagines himself spoken of only as "the Absent One," "excluded from" the family home (11:223). He finds himself driven back to the empty anonymity of the sleeping town, where he has already been repeatedly shut out.

What the moonlight shows us, then, is a destabilization or loss of both paternal authority and filial identity. Robin soon finds himself wondering whether the Major—and by extension his authority—even exist: " 'is there really such a person in these parts, or am I dreaming?' " (11:224). Rather than filling this vacuum, however, Hawthorne's tale extends the instability even further—from the psychological into the political, and from the individual into the social.

Robin has been nearly overcome by sleep and feels himself "vibrating between fancy and reality" (11:223). An "uproar" disturbs the neighborhood, the city's "sleep suddenly broken" by a crowd that moves toward Robin on the church steps:

> A single horseman wheeled the corner in the midst of them, and close behind him came a band of fearful wind-instruments, sending forth a fresher discord. . . . Then a redder light disturbed the moonbeams, and a dense multitude of torches shone along the street, concealing by their glare whatever object they illuminated. . . . In [the horseman's] train, were wild figures in the Indian dress, and many fantastic shapes without a model, giving the whole march a visionary air, as if a dream had broken forth from some feverish brain, and were sweeping visibly through the midnight streets. (11:227–28)

The mob appears as a disruptive, disorderly force, the repressed material of nightmare or delirium forcing itself into consciousness. Hawthorne's images suggest not the comic subversion of popular festival but the violent conflict of Indian warfare or the rampant "contagion" of disease (11:230).

The flames of the torches "conceal" rather than "illuminate" the members of the procession, but when the group halts and falls silent in front of Robin, its central object is revealed: "There the torches blazed the brightest, there the moon shone out like day, and there, in tar-and-feathery dignity, sate his kinsman, Major Molineux" (11:227, 228). This is the moment of recognition for which the youth has wished, but the Major appears to him stripped of his daylight dignity and power; the moonlight of romance represents paternal authority only in a way that robs it of economic and political force. The very fact that Robin and the Major recognize each other means the loss of their daylight relation, the estrangement of protégé from potential patron.

The complexity and ambivalence of this scene are worth examining further. On one hand, this is a prerevolutionary crowd triumphing over a symbol of British royal authority; insofar as it prefigures the revolutionary impulse that will bring America into being, it should, according to Bercovitch, suggest a positive transformation that fulfills rather than rejects the past.

But when the rebels clothe themselves in "Indian dress," they perform an ironic historical reversal, disguising themselves as the natives they have themselves violently displaced, whose return remains one of the archetypal colonial terrors. They thus recast themselves as the "natural" owners of the land and characterize the British as colonizing oppressors. Their Indian disguises, however, place this revolutionary "beginning" within a different kind of history, one in which white colonists are victimizers rather than victims.

Hawthorne describes this moment as the fruit of a dark conspiracy and the crowd as a mob of "fiends that throng in mockery round some dead potentate, mighty no more, but majestic still in his agony. On they went, in counterfeited pomp, in senseless uproar, in frenzied merriment, trampling on an old man's heart" (11:230). In these terms, the Major is the honorable, even tragic, victim of a fiendish outburst of antipatriarchal violence. When Robin joins in the chorus of mocking laughter, he, America, and the romance are all for a time identified with such destructive impulses.

This may well be a moment of initiation and transition for Robin, but it is also a nightmare image of the Revolution as parricidal disorder; the way the crowd carries the Major along in "an uncovered cart" suggests not only a Boston popular festival, but also a Parisian mob bringing a victim to the guillotine (11:228). It is most emphatically not Bercovitch's "ritual of revolution," according to which "Revolution meant improvement, not hiatus; obedience, not riot; not a breach of social order, but the fulfillment of God's plan" (*Jeremiad,* 134, 123). Bercovitch quotes from a number of contemporary responses to the "license" of "the European 1848," and many of them could apply to this scene: they speak of " 'radicals' " who wish " 'not merely to lop off diseased branches, but for the sake of getting rid of these to uproot . . . the tree itself'; and 'Red Republicans' who hope to institute 'the principles of the Terrorists' . . . and so to 'overturn the laws of . . . civilization . . . the tribunal of reason, and the voice of the natural conscience' " (*Office,* 75, 76; ellipses—except second set—in original). Hawthorne too associates his rebels with unreason, the violation of ties based on natural feeling, and threats to the family tree. He finds the violent discontinuity and disorder of 1848's "red revolution" on the streets of eighteenth-century Boston—at one of the very points of origination/renewal on which the ideology of pluralism and reform depends.

Hawthorne does far more than simply undermine the myth of the American Revolution as continuity and fulfillment, however. Even as he offers his depiction of revolt, he turns on his own representation, calling into question its subversive force. If the chaos of the Boston mob is frightening, it is also somehow fleeting or insubstantial, somewhere "between fancy and reality." The incident may have a nightmarish intensity, but if the crowd and the wishes it expresses belong to the realm of dream, what, then, is their relation to the daylight world of "real" power and civil authority? That world remains the Major's, not the mob's—or even the romancer's. Does the scene demonstrate a popular power that remains merely latent, not yet fully exercised, or does it simply foreshadow a revolution that such demonstrations cannot themselves bring about?[7]

Hawthorne deliberately emphasizes both the dreamlike nature of the spectacle and the open theatricality of its "counterfeited pomp." Robin certainly responds to it as theater, with the "pity and terror" (11:229) that Aristotelian tragedy should produce. Beyond this, Hawthorne alludes to *A Midsummer Night's Dream* (3.1.60–62) in comparing a watchman to "the Moonshine of Pyramus and Thisbe" (11:218). First of all, this suggests that Robin's experience may also be only the dream of a "summer night" (11:209). Second, it refers not merely to a play, but to *a play within a play,* to an instance of redoubled, foregrounded theatricality. The procession Robin observes thus appears as one (dramatic) performance presented within the context of another (literary) one—Hawthorne's tale.

What we have here, certainly, is not simple conflict—certainly not the straightforward confrontation with cudgels that Robin has longed for (11:215, 219–20). Instead, violence toward an individual (tarring and feathering the Major) is offered as a *representation* of societal rebellion, an *image* of revolutionary excess. And it is offered as such by both the mob and Hawthorne himself: in the first case, street theater is an act of unquestionable political force; what does it amount to in the second, in Hawthorne's story?[8]

Hawthorne offers a vision of radical, revolutionary change, but he embeds that change within a secondary or derivative realm of illusion or dream. This suggests a relation between artistic representation and revolution, but what kind of relation is it?[9] Is the depiction of revolution enabling, a first step in the revolutionary process? Or is it really only a substitute for action, a reduction of the political realm to the level of the "merely" aesthetic?

These are the questions that animate the romance as a whole; it exists as a genre precisely in order to bring into contact the actual and the imaginary, the political and the aesthetic. Hawthorne may wish to preserve a distinction between the two, but he does not, like Bercovitch, assume an opposition between them, with the former as the privileged term and the latter only a type of cultural superstructure. Where Bercovitch sees the aesthetic or theatrical as simply domesticating or co-opting revolutionary action, Hawthorne asks whether the romance may not instead make possible a revolutionary incursion of the imaginary into the actual. In this story, after all, drama is not simply a spectacle for individual aesthetic appreciation; neither is it linked to the mechanisms of parliamentary representation, as in Marx. It is instead a mode of direct popular expression and collective action, in a world characterized by radical and violent disjunctions between different interests and classes, not by consensus.

When Hawthorne speaks directly of the romance as a genre in "The Custom House," he does not offer a true definition—he describes a scene. He *stages* the romance itself, as a performance, rather than grounding it in abstract or theoretical terms. And the quintessentially "romantic" moments in his texts are almost always visual displays or tableaux, scenes of revelation and spectatorship.

For the antebellum American reader, allusions to the theater would have suggested either melodramatic spectacles or star performers appearing in a limited and familiar selection of roles. In both cases, the emphasis would have been on performer and performance, not on realistic representation or thematic content. Stage settings were thoroughly stylized and conventional, with stage effects meant to be appreciated *as effects.*[10]

Hawthorne's references to theater are more than just examples of aesthetic self-consciousness, however. From one perspective, they deliberately open his work to cultural and critical suspicion. But from another, they turn the romance toward a wider cultural and historical world.

Hawthorne's earliest projected volume, a collection to have been called "The Story Teller," framed its tales as oral performances to be delivered alongside or in between melodramas and comic turns. In "Passages from a Relinquished Work," planned as the book's opening section, Hawthorne's storyteller appears on a stage erected in a village tavern, after a performance of "the tragedy of Douglas," and, if the previous night's bill is an indication, before a farce or comic recitation (10:418). The story he tells is one of Hawthorne's, of course, "Mr. Higginbotham's Catastrophe." Hawthorne thus places his work within the realm of popular culture, albeit with some discomfort, perhaps — his narrator is torn between the tavern stage and the schoolhouse nearby, in which the itinerant preacher Eliakim Abbott is addressing a much smaller crowd.[11]

As this juxtaposition of tavern, theater, classroom, and sermon may suggest, nineteenth-century drama was not fully distinct from other forms of popular entertainment and "education." Melodramas were often based on historical events or "American" themes. And circuses and minstrel shows could alternate with "straight" drama in a single theater, with equestrian acts and set pieces incorporated into the plays themselves. A showman like P. T. Barnum might offer a series of successful productions in the "lecture rooms" affiliated with his museums.[12]

The theater was also a politicized realm, in which audiences interacted — sometimes violently — with performers. In a culture based on public oratory, the roles of actor, lecturer, preacher, and politician often blended together — actor Edwin Forrest, for instance, was a successful Democratic stump speaker.[13] Forrest's Bowery audiences could drive unpopular English actors like his rival William Macready off stage, and nationalistic, aesthetic, and class tensions spilled over into the streets in several riots during the 1830s and '40s.[14]

Theater was thus an ambiguous and transitional medium, linked to both high culture and low, history and fantasy. Hawthorne's use of theatrical imagery places his work in the context of a broad public culture,

within a range of popular and collective forms including everything from
Shakespeare to minstrel shows, Barnum's museums to patriotic historical pageants. He thus positions himself within the kind of "circulation of
social energy" that Stephen Greenblatt describes in relation to the Renaissance stage.[15]

Hawthorne examines the interplay between artistic representation and
historical action even more directly in "Howe's Masquerade," first published in 1838. In one sense, at least, this tale is more complex than "My
Kinsman, Major Molineux" in that Hawthorne also opens the question
of *historical,* rather than strictly aesthetic, representation. In this story,
revolutionary theater comes with a commentary, in which one can see
the tradition of Whig historiography (and Bercovitch's jeremiad) coming
into existence.

The tale is set in Boston during the Revolutionary War, at a "masqued
ball" given by Sir William Howe, the last British governor of the city
(9:243). This "spectacle" is part of a deliberate "policy," contrived "to
hide the distress and danger of the period, and the desperate aspect of
the siege, under an ostentation of festivity" (9:243). For both Howe and
Hawthorne, the theatricality of the masquerade does here serve a conservative political function, to disguise the precariousness of British rule.
Beyond this, the masque has a long tradition of use for the display of
royal power—a tradition in direct contrast to the antitheatrical culture
of Puritan Massachusetts. It was, in fact, British troops who mounted
the first theatrical performances ever seen in Boston. And elsewhere in
the colonies, all theaters were closed down during the Revolution. As
Hawthorne's story begins, then, the aesthetic or artistic values of theater
are linked to conservative, antirevolutionary politics.

The figures at the ball "seemed to have stepped from the dark can-
vass of historic portraits, or to have flitted forth from the magic pages
of romance, or at least to have flown hither from one of the London
theatres" (9:243). Their costumes allude only to other representations;
Hawthorne's sequence of descriptions moves away from history toward
romance, and then to open theatricality—away from the actual rather
than into a relation with it. There is only one exception among the Tory

partygoers – a group of men dressed to caricature Washington and his generals, whose troops are on the verge of taking the city.

A surprising presence at the masquerade is that of Colonel Joliffe, an old man known to be a rebel sympathizer: "there, amid all the mirth and buffoonery, stood this stern old figure, the best sustained character in the masquerade, because so well representing the antique spirit of his native land" (9:244). The Colonel is not in costume, but he is nevertheless "in" the masquerade – he "show[s] himself" and "sustains" a "character." Even nonfictional *self*-representation is still representation, not just a form of simple "being." Joliffe is both like and unlike the other masqueraders; his very presence in the theatricalized realm of the masquerade begins to blur the distinction between revolutionary "act" and Tory "representation."

Just before midnight, there occurs "a singular interruption": "A sound of music was heard without the house, as if proceeding from a full band of military instruments stationed in the street, playing not such a festal strain as was suited to the occasion; but a slow, funeral march" (9:245–46). The music appears as a disruptive element – not itself ugly or discordant, as in "My Kinsman, Major Molineux," but a violation of convention or decorum, suggesting a subversive counterorder to that of the masquerade. Its political overtones become clear when the British drum major notes that he has heard the music "but once before, . . . at the funeral of King George II" (9:246).

There now appears a succession of figures, each descending the steps into the governor's hall and heading toward the street: "It was the idea of the beholders, that these figures went to join the mysterious funeral that had halted in front of the Province-House" (9:247). Howe wonders whether they form " 'a procession of the regicide judges of King Charles, the martyr' " (9:247). Once again, the death of kings seems implicit in the performance. This theatrical representation, insofar as it undermines the conventions through which royal power is asserted and displayed, does achieve a profoundly unsettling effect.

After Joliffe identifies the passing figures as representing past governors of the province, one of Howe's comrades comments suspiciously that " 'There may be a plot under this mummery' " (9:248). The "mummery" has, of course, been planned or plotted, but the more important plot may well be *in* rather than under or behind it—for it is the historical narrative of British decline that is being laid out before the present governor.

As the lamp dims, the shapes begin to seem "rather like shadows than persons of fleshly substance" (9:251). At this point, the relation between spectacle and reality, performers and audience, becomes more ambiguous: "A wild and dreary burst of music came through the open door . . . [as if it] were a call to some loiterer to make haste. Many eyes, by an irresistible impulse, were turned upon Sir William Howe, as if it were he whom the dreary music summoned to the funeral of departed power" (9:252). Howe finally steps forward to confront the last figure, whose dress and bearing resemble his own. In so doing, he breaks through the line between performance and reality, becoming a transgressor even in his own house.

The appearance of such a double alongside its "original" necessarily challenges, if it does not directly threaten, the authority of that original. But at the sight of the man's face, Howe recoils and drops his sword: "The martial shape again drew the cloak about his features and passed on; but reaching the threshold, with his back towards the spectators, he was seen to stamp his foot and shake his clenched hands in the air. It was afterwards affirmed that Sir William Howe had repeated that self-same gesture of rage and sorrow, when, for the last time, and as the last royal governor, he passed through the portal of the Province-House" (9:253). The representation has *become* the original, the model for Howe's later, now repetitive, act. As midnight strikes, and the siege draws to a close, the procession gradually becomes history and Howe's tenure as governor, the masquerade. The music dies away, "and its dismal strains were mingled with the knell of midnight from the steeple of the Old South, and with the roar of artillery, which announced that the beleaguering army of Washington had intrenched itself upon a nearer height than before" (9:253).

This subversive theater of rebellion both reflects and generates the emergence of a new historical order. But we are witnessing more than just the victors' ascension to power here. Joliffe's commentary on the pageant begins the writing of a history that will justify their revolt, redefining it according to "whig principles" (9:244), as in fact an assertion of order and continuity. One of Hawthorne's subjects, then, is also the creation of Whig history, the ideological structure Bercovitch will analyze a century and a half later.[16]

Hawthorne casts "Howe's Masquerade" as the first of four "Legends of the Province-House," a sequence whose structure suggests an alternative, losers' version of history, a narrative of dissolution and loss rather than national progress. In Hawthorne's nineteenth-century narrative frame, the old mansion is in decay, and his narrator finds it impossible to "throw a tinge of romance and historic grandeur over the realities of the scene" (9:255). All four "legends" focus on loyalists rather than revolutionaries, and the last is openly Tory in its sympathies.

Such historiographical conflict – Whig vs. Tory – is, in one sense, played out within the boundaries of fiction. But three of the legends – "Howe's Masquerade," "Edward Randolph's Portrait," and "Lady Eleanore's Mantle" – all first appeared in John L. O'Sullivan's *United States Magazine and Democratic Review,* a bastion of Jacksonian liberalism and democratic nationalism. Even as fictions, their publication placed them in a political context, as contributions to an ongoing historical and ideological debate.

The categories of history, politics, and literature have, finally, become inseparable here: the rebels' pageant has little meaning without Joliffe's interpretation of it as historical allegory; and "Howe's Masquerade" – even more directly than "My Kinsman, Major Molineux" – is shaped by its nature as *historical* fiction.[17] Hawthorne closes his tale, in fact, by comparing "the actors in the scene" to "that wild Indian band who scattered the cargoes of the tea ships on the waves, and gained a place in history, yet left no names" (9:254). The Boston Tea Party too was an act of merely symbolic rebellion, carried out in costume.

TWO

Mauling Governor Pyncheon

Hawthorne offers several different definitions of the romance; perhaps the best known are those in his first two novels, *The Scarlet Letter* and *The House of the Seven Gables*. There is, however, at least one key difference between these definitions – a difference that suggests both Hawthorne's own political ambivalence and the flexibility of the romance as a form.

In "The Custom-House," where Hawthorne delineates the "neutral territory" of romance, his image for this territory is "a familiar room," illuminated "distinctly," but differently, by moonlight, which now invests it with "a quality of strangeness and remoteness."[1] The tableau is a domestic interior, an explicit contrast to the exterior daylight world of the Custom House. Lauren Berlant describes the everyday materiality of this scene as part of a counterorder, one that "contests the hegemony of the political public sphere."[2] But this is not a scene of successful artistic creation; it is, Hawthorne later tells us, a moment of imaginative failure, one in which he *cannot* write (1:36). Actual and imaginary may be placed in tension, but the revisionary potential of such contact is blocked or contained rather than released.

There is a comparable scene in *The Scarlet Letter* itself, another moment at which the transforming, defamiliarizing power of moonlight comes into play. In the second of the novel's "scaffold scenes," the light of moon and meteor combine to show "the familiar scene of the street, with the distinctness of mid-day, but also with the awfulness that is always imparted to familiar objects by an unaccustomed light. . . . [Dimmesdale, Hester, and Pearl] stood in the noon of that strange and solemn splendor, as if it were the light that is to reveal all secrets, and the daybreak that shall unite all who belong to one another" (1:154). But this is not the light of Judgment Day, the "'other time'" the minister has spoken of to Pearl (1:153). It is only "as if" the child's paternity could be privately or indirectly revealed in such a fashion. When the moonlight "as if" of romance is invoked in *The Scarlet Letter,* its potentially liberating vision is dismissed as insufficient, only an illusory substitute for the noontide submission demanded by both Puritan law and the text itself.

Hawthorne begins the preface to his next work, *The House of the Seven Gables,* with a gesture of exclusion, a defense of the romance against demands for novelistic "probabilities" and moral lessons.[3] He goes on to speak, not of the conditions under which he writes, but of his romance as an already finished work: "The point of view in which this Tale comes under the Romantic definition," Hawthorne says, "lies in the attempt to connect a by-gone time with the very Present that is flitting away from us" (2:2). Central to the operation of *this* text, he claims, is the way in which history and legend may connect "an actual locality to . . . imaginary events" (2:3). The defamiliarizing effect of the romance is thus more specifically defined here than in "The Custom-House": here it alters the comfortable familiarity of the present by *historicizing* it. In a sense, the historical connections that were only "introductory" to *The Scarlet Letter* become central to *The House of the Seven Gables.* This version of romance confronts and incorporates the actual in a way that its predecessor could not.[4]

What I propose to do in the following pages is to couple the primary elements of Hawthorne's two definitions—moonlight and historical connection—to examine two moments in *The House of the Seven Gables.* In these scenes, I will argue, moonlight and history combine to reveal the radical potential of Hawthorne's romance. The first amounts to a meditation on the revisionary power of romance—on the link between representation and action, and on the problem of re-envisioning, rather than simply reversing, existing structures of power. In the second, past and present intersect in an eruption of psychological and physical violence, in a killing that splits open the book's temporal and narrative structures, creating a gap through which the world of the actual enters the text. Taken together, these two moonlight scenes demonstrate the romance's potential for critical engagement with—and even direct attack upon—the forms of legal and economic power.

In most of Hawthorne's texts, history manifests itself primarily as *family* history or genealogy. But the transmission of patriarchal legality and tradition is almost always troubled by a countertradition that challenges or undermines it. Conflicts over power and authority are thus most often expressed in familial terms: the determining force of Freudian genealogy is pitted against its critical Nietzschean shadow.[5]

In "The Custom-House," the clearest connection offered between seventeenth-century Puritanism and nineteenth-century politics is through the Hawthorne family itself. On one level, Hawthorne suggests, nineteenth-century political and economic authority retains the patriarchal structure of seventeenth-century theocracy. As Surveyor, Hawthorne has "a patriarchal body of veterans under his orders," his "position in reference to them, being paternal and protective" (1:12, 15). He finds himself, on the one hand, a father to fathers. On the other, however, he envisions himself as an "exterminating angel" with the power "to bring every one of those white heads under the axe of the guillotine" (1:14)—a vengeful, even parricidal force.

This political and generational ambivalence has its psychological counterpart in Hawthorne's relation to his own ancestors. He is "haunted" by his family's Puritan past, he says: "I, the present writer, as [his ancestors'] representative, hereby take shame upon myself for their sakes, and pray that any curse incurred by them . . . may be now and henceforth removed" (1:9, 10). But he "represents" them in two different senses: first, as a bearer of the family name; and second, as the writer who describes them.

In this second sense, however, Hawthorne suggests that he fulfills rather than removes the family curse: "[They] would have thought it quite a sufficient retribution for [their] sins, that, after so long a lapse of years, the old trunk of the family tree . . . should have borne, as its topmost bough, an idler like myself. No aim, that I have ever cherished, would they recognize as laudable; no success of mine . . . would they deem otherwise than worthless, if not positively disgraceful" (1:10). The last career they would wish for him would be as a " 'writer of story-books' " (1:10). Ironically, though, it is only *as a writer,* as a rebel against family tradition, that Hawthorne can preserve his family history and declare himself its representative. By identifying himself as "Nathaniel Hawthorne, writer," he simultaneously accepts and rejects the historical continuity of genealogical identity.[6]

Such ambivalence lies behind and structures both historical and literary representation in "The Custom-House" and, arguably, in *The Scarlet Letter* as a whole. But this internal tension splits into a network of open oppositions in *The House of the Seven Gables:* between written law and unwritten tradition, between institutional history and subversive counter-memory, between Pyncheons and Maules. As an artist, Hawthorne declares himself a Hawthorne who is not a Hawthorne after all—or, in his terms, a Pyncheon who is at bottom a Maule.

The resemblance between the Hawthorne and Pyncheon families has been noted by a number of critics.[7] In "The Custom-House," Hawthorne describes his first American ancestor, William Hathorne, as "a soldier, legislator, judge," remembered for his persecution of Quakers (1:9). His son John "inherited the persecuting spirit," and made himself "conspicuous in the martyrdom of the witches" at Salem (1:9). In *The House of the Seven Gables,* these two figures are conflated into the character of Colonel Pyncheon, the Puritan soldier who acted as Matthew Maule's "persecutor" when he was made a "martyr" to the witchcraft scare (2:8).[8] Maule's curse upon the Colonel, " 'God will give him blood to drink!' " (2:8), is, in fact, derived from the dying words of one of the Salem "witches."[9]

Throughout their history, it is the Pyncheon family who are the "soldiers, legislators, and judges," the masters of legal force and textual precedent.[10] They mark the landscape with both the family name and its physical embodiment, the House of the Seven Gables. Their hereditary antagonists, the Maules, are merely artisans or skilled craftsmen, and by the time of the main action of the story, their name has vanished from "town-record, . . . grave-stone, [and] directory" alike (2:25). Their memory may be kept alive in local legend, but Maule's curse is the only point at which such oral tradition intersects with written history. The family's mysterious powers are mentioned in stories "for which it is difficult to conceive any foundation"—in the tale, for instance, that speaks of an old mirror in the House of the Seven Gables and of the Maules' "mesmeric" ability to "make its inner regions all alive with the departed Pyncheons" (2:20, 21).

Hawthorne's text thus occupies an ambiguous position. It may be created in opposition to his Puritan heritage, but its form aligns it, at least initially, with the legal authority and orthodoxy of the Pyncheons' documents. The narrator lacks the Maules' ability to see the ghosts of the old Pyncheon mirror, but he clearly wishes he could: "we would gladly sit down before it," he says, "and transfer its revelations to our page" (2:20). In a sense, it is the goal of the entire book to acquire that power, to bring the subversive force of popular memory and culture into the text.[11] Ultimately, it is through a procession of Pyncheon ghosts, reflected in the mirror of this moonlit room, that Hawthorne will announce the end of the Pyncheon dynasty. Such a redistribution of textual power requires the romance to open itself to a number of conflicts and oppositions—between historical periods, economic classes, and modes of representation—and this it does in its two moonlight scenes.

The current representative of the Maule family, the daguerreotypist Holgrave, is both the book's most potentially subversive presence and its primary artist figure. At age twenty-two, he has been a schoolmaster, the political editor of a newspaper, a peddler, a dentist, and "his present phase, as a Daguerreotypist, was of no more importance in his own view, nor likely to be more permanent, than any of the preceding ones" (2:177).[12] He is an unsettling force, with a "lack of reverence for what was fixed" and an outright contempt for the " 'odious and abominable Past' " (2:177, 184). Holgrave seems an embodiment of social and psychological instability, but Hawthorne insists on the consistency of the young man's "innermost" character (2:177); it will prove a crucial reservation.

Holgrave associates with "reformers, temperance-lecturers, and all manner of cross-looking philanthropists;—community-men and come-outers, as Hepzibah [Pyncheon] believed, who acknowledged no law"

(2:84). She suspects that he practices "animal-magnetism," or even possibly "the Black Art" (2:84). He is a published (though uncanonized) magazine author, but the only reference to his work Hepzibah has seen is to "a speech, full of wild and disorganizing matter, at a meeting of his banditti-like associates" (2:84). Hawthorne, too, presents Holgrave's fiction as an *oral* performance, thus placing it somewhere between convention and lawlessness. He links Holgrave's art to subversive elements from both the seventeenth century – witchcraft – and the nineteenth – political and social radicalism.

Holgrave is forced to confront the question of art and its relation to power in the first of the book's moonlit scenes, in which he tells one of his own tales. He tells Phoebe the story of one of her ancestors, Alice Pyncheon. In so doing, he offers the Maule version of " 'Pyncheon family-history' " – a fusion of oral history or " 'legend' " with publishable written narrative (2:186). In Holgrave's story, carpenter Matthew Maule plays on Gervayse Pyncheon's greed to assert a hypnotic power over his daughter. Maule, grandson of the early settler, "was fabled . . . to have a strange power of getting into people's dreams, and regulating matters there according to his own fancy, pretty much like the stage-manager of a theatre" (2:189). Gervayse Pyncheon is, similarly, the old Colonel's grandson, a wealthy slave owner with a battery of lawyers; the opposition between the two families is repeated in them.

Pyncheon agrees to exchange the House of the Seven Gables for the deed that will assure him possession of the lands the family has long claimed in Maine. Maule insists, however, on using Alice as a "medium," whose "pure and virgin intelligence" he will use to find the document (2:200). The girl consents, feeling herself invulnerable " 'in her father's presence, and under his all-sufficient protection,' " as Maule mockingly puts it (2:202).[13] But Alice cannot withstand the carpenter's hypnotic power, and she falls into a trance from which her father cannot awaken her. " 'She is mine,' " Maule exults (2:206), and even though the trance yields no information for her father, the craftsman retains his psychic control over Alice for the rest of her life.

Both men are willing to use the girl as a "medium," a vehicle through which to continue the family feud, and the result is her humiliation and death. Both are frustrated, Pyncheon in his pursuit of wealth and Maule in his search for revenge. Alice becomes "Maule's slave, in a bondage more humiliating, a thousand-fold, than that which binds its chain around the body" (2:208). But the carpenter's triumph is extinguished at the moment it is made complete—the journey to witness Maule's wedding is what leads to Alice's death. Beyond this, his success does not mean the victory of a power different in kind from the Pyncheons'; Maule has only made himself into another, even more oppressive, slave owner. Reversing the distribution of power is, in the end, merely to reduplicate its illegitimate and oppressive structure. Maule may be able to "stage-manage" the "theatre" of the unconscious, but in the waking world he imitates—and thus implicitly accepts—the terms and forms of the established order.

The sun has gone down during Holgrave's reading, and the moon's "silvery beams were already powerful enough to change the character of the lingering daylight. . . . [The garden's] common-place characteristics— which, at noontide, it seemed to have taken a century of sordid life to accumulate—were now transfigured by a charm of romance" (2:213). Holgrave's tale has been a historical romance as well, and its recital has left him with an unanticipated power: "It was the effect, unquestionably, of the mystic gesticulations, by which he had sought to bring bodily before Phoebe's perception the figure of the mesmerizing carpenter. . . . A veil was beginning to be muffled about her, in which she could behold only him, and live only in his thoughts and emotions" (2:211). If the Maules' mesmeric ability has been heretofore only a matter of hearsay, Holgrave's "mystic gesticulations" have realized this element of his romance. His performance is both representation and action; the power it describes is also the power it creates for him as artist.

Hawthorne here gives us a representation of the act of representation, a literary description of a theatrical performance. The power he ascribes to Holgrave as romancer is one he claims for himself. The problem—for both character and author—is how, or even if, to exercise that power: "His glance, as he fastened it on the young girl, grew involuntarily more concentrated; in his attitude, there was the consciousness of power . . . he could complete his mastery over Phoebe's yet free and virgin spirit; he could establish an influence over this good, pure, and simple child, as dangerous, and perhaps as disastrous, as that which the carpenter of his legend had acquired and exercised over the ill-fated Alice" (2:211, 212). The romance may stand opposed to "a century of sordid life," but at this point neither Hawthorne nor Holgrave sees it as able to transform or escape inherited patterns of conflict. Beyond this, Hawthorne chooses to describe the storyteller's power in terms that are, for him, particularly traumatic – as mesmeric control over another. The mesmerist, like the romancer, blurs the line between representation/performance and action; but his power is exercised over the "virgin spirit" of his subject, in a violation Hawthorne sees as tantamount to rape.[14] Empowerment thus appears only in coercive or self-destructive terms, as a "temptation" Holgrave must resist (2:212).

The daguerreotypist is, in fact, doubly tempted, to both revenge and repetition, to a version of romance that sacrifices precisely its own revisionary potential. Revenge means settling, like the carpenter, for a temporary reversal of existing familial and power relations rather than an escape from them.[15] And vengeance confirms those relations as it mirrors them, annihilating temporal and individual difference as it seeks to repeat the past.

Repetition is, in a way, a Pyncheon family trait, both in their hereditary illness and in the facial resemblance between the Judge and the Colonel. But if Matthew Maule seems to echo his grandfather in his use of "magic" against the Pyncheons, Holgrave has, to this point, appeared as the embodiment of difference or variety itself. There seems, however, no positive way for such difference to manifest itself at this point in Hawthorne's text. Genealogy functions only in the Pyncheons' legalistic and repetitive terms; the possibilities for romance as critical genealogy – embracing difference and discontinuity – appear completely foreclosed.

Hawthorne responds to this dilemma with a decisive shift in terms, in which internal difference or variability is silently redefined as stable and consistent individualism. He contrasts Holgrave's politics, his "scorn for creeds and institutions," with the "integrity" that gives him a "reverence for another's individuality" (2:212) – it is now the *fixity* of Holgrave's commitment to individuality that prevents him from acting. Issues of politics and class are redefined in terms of individual psychology: Holgrave's potential " 'lawless[ness]' " becomes obedience to " 'a law of his own' "

(2:85). The alternatives are thus narrowed to only two extremes – mastery or enslavement[16] – and the only way for Holgrave to preserve his sense of difference from the past is to refuse the terms of the opposition, to relinquish the power conferred by either inheritance or art.

When the daguerreotypist simply awakens Phoebe, he does so in order to break the cycle of genealogical repetition, to keep open the possibilities of difference and revisionary change. But such a renunciation of power leaves only the most mystical (and limited) possibilities for transformation: "Could I keep the feeling that now possesses me, the garden would every day be virgin soil, with the earth's first freshness in the flavor of its beans and squashes; and the house! it would be like a bower in Eden . . . Moonlight, and the sentiment in man's heart, responsive to it, is the greatest of renovators and reformers. And all other reform and renovation, I suppose, will prove to be no better than moonshine!" (2:214). Moonlight is reduced to the most conventionally "romantic" force, whose transformative power offers no threat to the status quo.[17]

Hawthorne thus offers us an instance of the romancer's power, but that power cannot be directly expressed without threatening both the principle of individual agency and its own transformative capacity. Faced with the possible loss of psychological or artistic control, he reinstates the distinction between representation and action, restricting the romance to the former; here the artistic imagination cannot enter the realm of the actual except through a violence and coercion unacceptable to both Holgrave and Hawthorne himself.

The scene in the Pyncheon garden is, of course, an episode *within* the frame of Hawthorne's narrative, a moment at which he considers the possible limits of his larger project. But in the book's second moonlight scene, Hawthorne moves beyond the impasse he has described; he uses the narrative voice itself to align his romance with the oral or folk culture of the dispossessed Maules and thus to claim an openly adversarial role for the genre.

Hawthorne's second scene carries a greater weight than his first, for it resonates on both narrative and metanarrative levels. And, perhaps more important, it is at this juncture that elements of history and the actual – nineteenth-century law, politics, and economics – enter *The House of the Seven Gables* most directly. But the text's acceptance of psychological and class conflict is not without cost: it leads to a splintering of narrative structure, a breakdown in representation that threatens the form of the romance itself.

This crucial scene occupies an entire chapter, the remarkable "Governor Pyncheon." Here the narrator stands before the Maules' haunted mirror in the moonlit interior of the house – and here he seizes, even exults in, the critical power that Holgrave has let slip away. As a romance, *The House of the Seven Gables* is built, Hawthorne says, "of materials long in use for constructing castles in the air" (2:3) – this romance, too, is a mesmerizing tale whose power is, like the stories of Maule magic, only apparently "without foundation."

In "Governor Pyncheon," Hawthorne spends fifteen pages describing, addressing, and finally taunting a corpse. On one hand, this is a narrative tour de force; on the other, it seems clearly excessive, not to say obsessive, in its combination of anxiety and vehemence, trepidation and rage.[18] The corpse is that of Judge Pyncheon, the nineteenth-century embodiment of the Pyncheon family's drive for power and wealth. Not once in the course of the chapter does Hawthorne state the obvious fact of the Judge's death; instead, he spends page after page speculating about the man's reasons for lingering in his "ancestral arm-chair" (2:248). Hawthorne's narrators can certainly be coy at times, but there is more than coyness here. For what Hawthorne has to announce – tentatively, fearfully, but also exultantly – is both the end of the Pyncheons' power and the eventual extinction of the family. His narrative has carried out Holgrave's wish that "once in every half-century, at longest, a family should be merged into the great, obscure mass of humanity" (2:185). And, given the link between the Pyncheon and Hawthorne families, this narrative killing is nearly parricidal in its implications.

As the chapter progresses, the narrator's tone shifts from mock puzzlement to increasingly venomous sarcasm. A political dinner "surely cannot have slipt your memory," he says, before enumerating the delicacies of the table, lingering longest over the "old Madeira," a wine that "would all but revive a dead man! Would you like to sip it now, Judge Pyncheon?"

(2:273–74). Hawthorne need only "whisper" the dinner's purpose, he says—"ambition is a talisman more powerful than witchcraft," and it is this meeting that is to seal the Judge's nomination for governor (2:274). The corpse still fails to rise, however, and darkness descends upon the room, leaving only the "swarthy whiteness" of the Judge's face visible before an "infinite, inscrutable blackness" annihilates the "universe" (2:276). All the Pyncheon ambition has come to nought; it is now the turn of Maule artistry and magic.

When the wind shifts and blows away the clouds, it is not the Judge but the narrator who seems resurrected. When "effectual light" returns, it is that of "moonbeams" falling "aslant" into the room and "play[ing] over the Judge's figure" (2:278). It is midnight.

At this point Hawthorne mentions "the ridiculous legend, that, at midnight, all the dead Pyncheons are bound to assemble in this parlor," and decides to "make a little sport with the idea" (2:279). He runs down the list of Pyncheons, from the old Colonel through his nineteenth-century descendants, to "young Jaffrey Pyncheon," the Judge's only child and heir, and then "a stout, elderly gentleman": "Is it the Judge, or no? How can it be Judge Pyncheon? We discern his figure, as plainly as the flickering moonbeams can show us anything, still seated in the oaken chair!" (2:280–81). This is the way in which Hawthorne conveys the fact that the Judge is dead, by placing him among the Pyncheon ghosts appearing in the moonlight. And by having the Judge's son precede him, Hawthorne lays the groundwork for the end of the Pyncheon family and the reversion of its property to Holgrave and the Maules. The sequence of ghosts thus does more than simply represent the past—it advances the plot of the narrative and shapes its future course and resolution.

Hawthorne quickly dismisses this "fantastic scene," however, as one that "must by no means be considered as forming an actual portion of our story. We were betrayed into this brief extravagance by the quiver of the moonbeams; they dance hand-in-hand with shadows, and are reflected in the looking-glass, which . . . is always a kind of window or door-way into the spiritual world" (2:281). Such authorial protestations notwithstanding, the scene is of course central to the story. Shadows, lit by moonbeams, reflected in the looking glass—Hawthorne's "brief extravagance" is in fact an explicit entrance into the territory of romance. And seeing Pyncheon ghosts in this mirror identifies the romancer not just with the imagination, but also with the Maules and their mesmeric or magic power. Hawthorne could not claim that power at the outset, but, as romancer, he has re-created *himself* as a Maule. He may still be "a representative of" the Hawthorne/Pyncheon family, but insofar as he "represents" them in his fiction, he is an artist and a Maule.[19]

In Hawthorne's plot, it was Clifford Pyncheon, the self-absorbed aes-thete, who had been thought guilty of his uncle's murder, while Jaffrey, the greedy power broker, was the man really capable of such an act. But when Hawthorne connects the realms of politics and art in "Gover-nor Pyncheon," he declares himself an artist capable of murder, a Maule who can kill off the Pyncheon line without parricidal guilt. "Rise up," the narrator cries to the Judge's corpse, "The Avenger is upon thee!" (2:283). In a sense, he is now the "exterminating angel" Hawthorne could only imagine himself becoming in "The Custom-House" (1:14).

The confrontation that takes place here is the one envisioned by Hol-grave when he denounces the repressive force of the past: "'Whatever we seek to do, of our own free motion, a Dead Man's icy hand obstructs us! Turn our eyes to what point we may, a Dead Man's white, immiti-gable face encounters them, and freezes our very heart!'" (2:183).[20] But in "Governor Pyncheon," the narrator looks into the dead father's face without a loss of power; a key feature of the romance, Hawthorne notes, is that the romancer gains the ability to face down such specters: "Ghosts might enter here, without affrighting us" (1:36).

Hawthorne's narrator also embraces the repetition and revenge that Holgrave has sought to resist. Hawthorne makes the contrast quite ex-plicit, describing the Judge's death in the same terms as that of his seven-teenth-century ancestor. The Colonel too was repeatedly summoned— with a "racket" that "might have disturbed the dead"—to a public event, the "consecration" of his house (2:14, 11). And the colony's lieutenant governor also joked about wine, suggesting that the Colonel might have "'taken a sip too much of his Canary'" (14). If the Judge's death repeats an earlier moment in the historical chain, such repetition does not, in this case, mean simple re-enclosure in a circular pattern. The narrative may serve as the fulfillment of Maule's curse, but it does so by destroying the inherited continuity of Pyncheon power—and thus the structure of class and familial opposition in which that power has been grounded.

This second moonlight scene gains its critical or subversive force not simply by invoking oral tradition and popular belief, but by doing so in the wider context of nineteenth-century economic and political change. One of Hawthorne's primary sources, Brook Thomas suggests, is the Joseph White murder trial of 1830, a scandalous and highly politicized case involving families from Salem's economic and social elite. More specifically, according to F. O. Matthiessen, Hawthorne draws from the language of Daniel Webster's prosecutorial summation: "The assassin enters. . . . With noiseless foot he paces the lonely hall, half lighted by the moon; he winds up the ascent of the stairs, and reaches the door of the chamber. . . . The face of the innocent sleeper is turned from the murderer, and the beams of the moon, resting on the grey locks of his aged temple, show him where to strike."[21] Hawthorne does seem to echo Webster's moonlight image in describing the Judge's corpse. But what neither critic has noted is that Hawthorne performs a striking reversal as he does so, adopting what Webster imagines as the *murderer's* perspective.[22] At this key moment, then—one whose interplay of actual and imaginary epitomizes the romance—Hawthorne's narrator moves to align himself *against* legal and political authority, choosing not just an adversarial but a criminal role in relation to Salem's merchant classes.[23]

Not long before writing this passage, Hawthorne had been charged with both improper political activity and criminal malfeasance by Whig party members seeking his removal from the Salem customhouse. When he brings echoes of earlier legal and political history into the text, he thus does more than merely contextualize his fiction; he considers what he calls "a literary crime," expanding what had been a small-scale conflict over political appointments in "The Custom-House" into a wider attack on the state's political and economic establishment (2:1).[24]

"Governor Pyncheon" begins in the morning, and Hawthorne notes the many engagements that Judge Pyncheon is missing as the day goes on: at this point, as the Judge's death plunges the interior of the house into stasis, Hawthorne turns his full attention to the social and economic activity of the world outside the house, bringing it into the aesthetic order of his work.

Hepzibah's cent-shop is often described as a "threshold" (2:36) or middle ground between the house and the life that flows past it in the street. But, as Hawthorne notes several times, hers is only a feeble attempt at individual entrepreneurship, already almost anachronistic in midcentury Massachusetts (2:38–40, 291). The Judge, on the other hand, moves in the world of large-scale financial manipulation and political brokering, of "planning . . . and speculating" (2:270).[25] It is he who, "dropping some deeply designed chance-word," shapes the next day's gossip before moving on to preside at a meeting of bank directors (2:270). His days are a series of speculations and investments—in stocks, real estate, philanthropy, and the "great game" of politics (2:270, 272). In a sense, the Judge stands as an embodiment of the interlocking political, social, and economic elites that dominated antebellum Massachusetts.

It is Judge Pyncheon's "stake" in the coming election that is to lead him to a crucial private dinner, at which "practised politicians," a "little knot of subtle schemers," will gather to "adjust those preliminary measures, which steal from the people, without its knowledge, the power of choosing its own rulers. The popular voice, at the next gubernatorial election, though loud as thunder, will be really but an echo of what these gentlemen shall speak, under their breath. . . . They meet to decide upon their candidate" (2:274). Bay State politics is here a matter of property and power, the theft of popular choice rather than its representation. For all the ostensible "democracy" of antebellum political conventions, political candidates were still selected by a small group of party leaders. As with the Judge's deliberate manipulation of Salem gossip, a mode of ostensibly popular expression is again shown to be the private product of an economic and social elite. If Hawthorne had fallen back on an ideology of psychological individualism in dealing with Holgrave, he now sharply questions the adequacy of a comparable political view.

In his description of this dinner, Hawthorne also alludes to the issue that would come to dominate antebellum politics: when the Judge fails to appear, his friends conclude "that the Free Soilers have him" (2:275).

In late 1850 and early 1851, at the time Hawthorne was writing *The House of the Seven Gables,* a crucial realignment of Massachusetts parties was in fact underway. A group of Free Soilers, defectors from the long dominant Whig establishment, joined Democrats to take control of the Massachusetts legislature and send abolitionist Charles Sumner to the U.S. Senate, filling Webster's old seat.[26] The economic and electoral reforms enacted by this session of the legislature would set off a chain of reaction and counterreaction, leading first to the emergence of Know-Nothingism, and then to the end of Whiggery itself.[27]

In this second moonlight scene, then, the romance historicizes the familial and psychological crisis of the Judge's death, situating it at a key moment in the demise of the Whig oligarchy and the political emergence of antislavery. What on one level may be part of a repetitive genealogy of family history becomes, on another, a critical depiction of political discontinuity and rupture.

Hawthorne had mentioned slavery in his first moonlight scene—in Holgrave's story of Alice Pyncheon (2:192, 208)—and he invokes it here as well, as a matter unassimilable into the structures of party politics and forcibly excluded from conventional political discourse. Both Whigs and Democrats strove to keep the slavery issue out of Massachusetts politics, using intimidation and even mob violence to silence abolitionist speakers.[28] Only a year after writing *The House of the Seven Gables,* Hawthorne himself would take part in this process, in his campaign biography of Franklin Pierce, where he describes slavery as a matter requiring providential rather than political intervention.[29] His romance, however, simply points toward abolition as the issue that would first fragment and then reshape the norms of both political and fictional representation.

If the Judge's death coincides with a breakdown in both historical and fictional structures, it also sets off an entropic spiral of spatial and geographical dispersion. After discovering the body, Clifford rushes his sister Hepzibah out of the house, whirling her away from Salem aboard the railroad until they reach a point of emotional and physical exhaustion. Hawthorne's narrative follows, leaving the House of the Seven Gables for the first and only time. In terms of textual sequence, this movement actually precedes—displaces and defers—the "Governor Pyncheon" chapter. But its "flight" from genealogy and death leads to an encounter with the text's primary symbol of technological modernity—the railroad (2:256). Again, it is at this point—over the Judge's dead body, as it were—that the romance confronts nineteenth-century actuality, in the form of what Leo Marx has termed "*the* revolutionary machine of the age."[30]

Clifford and Hepzibah have earlier tried, and failed, to join in different forms of human community, either religious (2:168–69) or political (2:165–66). But aboard the train, they are "drawn into the great current of human life, . . . swept away with it, as by the suction of fate itself" (2:256). History, nature, and technology all come together here, as Hawthorne takes the mechanical movement of the railroad as his image for both nineteenth-century life and the history of which it is a part. Indeed, the railway station seems at once a large, enclosing public structure, whose "arched entrance" opens onto "a spacious breadth, and an airy height from floor to roof," and also a world in itself, in which smoke and steam rise to form "a mimic cloud-region" over the passengers' heads" (2:255, 256).

The railroad, less than a generation old in Massachusetts, changed the experience of travel in a number of ways. The train compartment brings together "fifty human beings in close relation," but they remain a mass of isolatoes, separate individuals or groups united only by their position as consumers (2:257). They seldom acknowledge each other's presence, but they nevertheless exist as a single market for the boys selling goods on the station platforms. Hepzibah is reminded of the items in her own shop, but in this case, salesmen, customers, and commodities are all in motion across the landscape of the marketplace. Indeed, a nineteenth-century image of passengers as "living parcels" lumps them together with the train's freight items as commodities to be delivered.[31]

Once the train is in motion, none of the passengers seems to pay any attention to the world outside the compartment. As Wolfgang Schivelbusch points out, one of the effects of rail travel was to do away with the "travel space" between points, reducing journeys to points of departure and destination.[32] It is only Clifford and Hepzibah who look out, and Hawthorne describes their sense of visual disorientation: "they could see the world racing past them. At one moment, they were rattling through a solitude;–the next, a village had grown up around them;–a few breaths more, and it had vanished, as if swallowed by an earthquake. The spires of meeting-houses seemed set adrift from their foundations. . . . Everything was unfixed from its age-long rest, and moving at whirlwind speed in a direction opposite to their own" (2:256). Beyond the obvious illusion that the landscape is moving and the traveler standing still, physical movement and temporal change have become confused here, as a village "grows up" and is then "swallowed" by an unseen earthquake. The world itself, both man-made and natural, seems "unfixed," as if Holgrave's vision of reform has come to pass.

Indeed, when Clifford speaks of the railroad as a liberating improvement, " 'destined to do away with those stale ideas of home and fireside,' " he sounds much like the young radical: " 'There is no such unwholesome atmosphere as that of an old home, rendered poisonous by one's defunct forefathers and relatives!' " (2:259, 261). For both men, freedom from family and from the past is a freedom from place.

But Clifford's tendency throughout is toward a transcendental view of technological progress as a spiritualizing upward curve, what Leo Marx calls "the rhetoric of the technological sublime."[33] He sees the telegraph, for instance, as an " 'almost spiritual medium' " that has turned the globe into " 'a vast head, a brain, instinct with intelligence' " (2:264).

Clifford's fantasy is not, however, the period's conventional fusion of technological and national progress, which saw the railroad as breaking down both regional and social barriers to produce a newly unified and egalitarian country.[34] For Hawthorne, both railroad and telegraph are part of the rather different, and very material, world described by one of their fellow passengers, who fears that " 'the speculators in cotton and politics [will] get possession of' " the telegraph–for this man, its primary value lies in " 'the detection of bank-robbers and murderers' " (2:264). Here, too, we are on Judge Pyncheon's turf, for railway and telegraph building were primary engines of nineteenth-century economic development, investment, and speculation. Railways became a matter of increasing political debate in Massachusetts, as both the legislature and local governments were asked to subsidize construction.[35] Once again, the romance has opened up into a network of economic and political speculation, corruption and crime.

From this perspective, Clifford does begin to find the technological change threatening. He sympathizes with the fleeing criminal, who finds that word of his crime precedes him, carried by the telegraph, to deprive him of a " 'city of refuge' " (2:265). Here the technological compression of time and space is a trap rather than a liberation.[36] It is at this point that brother and sister hurriedly disembark, onto an empty platform amid a ruined landscape. Hawthorne too seems to find himself disoriented, unable to return his narrative to Salem from this point – he simply abandons his "two owls," leaving their return journey undescribed. Just as the railroad profoundly altered the teleology of the journey for nineteenth-century travelers, so its appearance in *The House of the Seven Gables* seems to undermine or threaten the book's narrative form and coherence.

In a sense, the narrative rage of "Governor Pyncheon" seems almost as directionless as the Pyncheons' railway journey, finally exhausting itself as Clifford has done; the narrator too speaks of simply escaping from the House of the Seven Gables at the end (2:283). The chapter's very intensity, the excess of its verbal and physical violence, its nearly apocalyptic rhetoric – these throw the romance into disequilibrium, seeming to overwhelm the process of representation itself.

Hawthorne's own process of composition reached an impasse at this point; he broke off reading the manuscript to his wife and spent ten days rewriting the final chapters before continuing.[37] He wrote his publisher, James T. Fields, that the book " 'darkens damnably towards the close' " and that he felt pressed to " 'pour some setting sunshine over it.' "[38]

The dark and murderous energy of the romance has led to a death that it cannot directly represent – Clifford has alluded to it earlier (2:261, 265), but neither Holgrave nor the narrator can speak of the Judge's corpse *as a corpse*. Confronted with this problem, both Holgrave and Hawthorne forsake the language of romance for the visual evidence of the daguerreotype, turning from moonlight to " 'pictures [made] out of sunshine' " (2:91). In response to her repeated demand that he " 'tell me what has happened,' " Holgrave instead offers Phoebe a pair of images, from which she must infer the fact of the Judge's death: " 'This is death!' shuddered Phoebe . . . 'Judge Pyncheon dead' " (2:301, 302). It is only after this fragmented half-acknowledgment that Holgrave (and, through him, the text) can put the fact into words.

Such problems in representation do have consequences; they are not just self-reflexive gestures pulling the text away from history and the actual. The photograph is, after all, a nineteenth-century technological challenge to verbal narratives like the romance: " 'The sun . . . tells quite another story," Holgrave says (2:92). It is at once rooted in the daylight of actuality and linked to Holgrave's political and economic radicalism. As a potentially democratic form, it promised to alter the relation between the visual artist and his audience; and, beyond this, its claims for "truth" were based on a notion of mechanical objectivity that eliminated the photographer/artist as an active participant in the creative process.[39] In turning to the daguerreotype, Hawthorne reformulates issues of representation in terms of art as an economic and technological process, in which the artist "works" by tending a machine. By the end of the book, in fact, the balance between oral, written, and visual authority has been dramatically unsettled—Holgrave's revelation of the old Indian deed behind the Colonel's portrait is also a revelation of its worthlessness, of the impotence of both texts and legends against the force of historical change.

The romance has, however, succeeded in bringing into contact different modes of knowledge and representation—the "actual" force of technology and the law, for instance, and the "imaginative" power of oral tradition. Magic and mesmerism are no longer clearly opposed to legal and historical truth: "Many persons affirmed, that the history and elucidation of the facts [of the Judge's earlier 'crime'] had been obtained by the Daguerreotypist from one of those mesmerical seers" (2:311). These "facts" are, of course, the ones now presented as part of an ostensibly omniscient narration. Modes that earlier seemed incompatible—Maule magic and Pyncheon legalism, popular belief and written history—coexist within the narrative voice at the close of *The House of the Seven Gables*.[40] The interpenetration of these realms has a powerful destabilizing impact, but again, it is here that Hawthornian romance finds its limit. It may offer a sharp critique of the existing order, but it can provide no clear ground – political, economic, or aesthetic – for an alternative.

Much has been made of the supposed conservatism of the novel's ending, but its intermingling of actual and imaginary effectively prevents a simple return to the status quo ante.[41] Its most problematic aspect may be the characters' move to the Judge's "country-seat," despite the elements of crime and guilt on which it has been built (2:314). On the surface, this seems a cyclical return to a deterministic version of genealogy and inheritance, albeit with the terms reversed and a Maule in possession. But Holgrave acquires his "inheritance" through a decidedly complex and indirect route: first, it requires the deaths of a series of childless heirs – the Judge's son, Clifford, Hepzibah – and then his marriage to Phoebe, "the last and youngest" of the Pyncheons (2:24). As the novel opens, her class and family position seems almost as marginal as that of Holgrave and the Maules: she is "the daughter of another of the Judge's cousins, who had married a young woman of no family or property, and died early, and in poor circumstances. His widow had recently taken another husband" (2:24). By the end, family identity seems tenuous rather than oppressive, as Phoebe can " 'assume the name of Maule' " as easily as Holgrave had adopted his (2:316).

Holgrave now calls himself " 'a conservative,' " but there is a key difference between his position and that of the Pyncheons (2:315). Both Holgrave and the novel maintain their opposition to the old Pyncheon desire to " 'plant and endow a family' " (2:185), to establish and preserve a "house" in both senses of the term. The Pyncheons had sought to veil their claims to property in the language of natural right or possession, which placed the House of the Seven Gables in the same category as the Pyncheon elm. A primary thrust of the entire romance, however, has been to demystify the notions of "family" and "inheritance" as "natural" grounds for the defense of property rights and class position.

Phoebe and Holgrave inherit the House of the Seven Gables as well, of course, but they abandon that family mansion in favor of one only recently constructed. For what Holgrave seeks in a house is not permanence, but the " '*impression of* permanence' " around a changeable interior (2:314–15, emphasis added). If the former is an illusion meant to escape both history and the market economy, the latter is no more than a matter of appearance, a marketable value or attribute.

Hawthorne thus resists a fully conservative, repetitive closure. But this does not mean that his romance offers a commitment to, or even a basis for, any thoroughgoing or radical change. It gives expression to numerous conflicts within American political culture – over technology, slavery, and class – but it can do no more, finally, than bring them out into the open. The social, political, and geographical instabilities that it anticipates simply cannot be recontained or given form within the text.

Hawthorne's preface makes no claim for the romance's ability to reconcile or preclude conflict: it is an "attempt to connect" past and present, actual and imaginary – but "historical connection" is not synthesis (2:2, 3).[42] Michael Davitt Bell describes a "conservative" form of romance that tries to connect historical fact with fiction, but in *The House of the Seven Gables,* linking past and present only throws into sharper relief the disjunctions and conflicts within that present.[43]

This romance, at any rate, does not enforce or ratify a consensus so much as it describes, and enacts, the breakdown of consensus and the shift of established values into the play of the marketplace. Its last words belong to two workingmen, who comment wryly on the contradiction between Hepzibah's sudden inheritance and her economic failure as shopkeeper. Whether it be " 'luck' " or " 'Providence,' " – random or determined – it all comes down to " 'Pretty good business' " in the end (2:318, 319). The last notes heard from Alice Pyncheon's harpsichord are decidedly uncertain ones of economic disparity and potential discord.

THREE

Moonshine
and Masquerade

"'Moonlight, and the sentiment in man's heart, responsive to it, is the greatest of renovators and reformers,'" Holgrave remarks, "'And all other reform and renovation, I suppose, will prove to be no better than moonshine!'" (2:214). The daguerreotypist's distinction is a crucial one for Hawthorne's romance—that between the real reforming power of "moonlight" and the pleasant illusion of mere "moonshine." In *The Blithedale Romance,* published only a year after *The House of the Seven Gables,* Hawthorne's view has darkened considerably; here reform is just illusion, moonlight and moonshine one and the same.

The House of the Seven Gables offers only a qualified belief in romance's power to link the economic and the aesthetic, but its exploration of the possibility does suggest a continuing desire for such a liberating connection. *The Blithedale Romance,* on the other hand, sees only the bleakest of consequences for artistic effort. Its pessimism is both double edged and thorough: on one hand, aesthetic production is vitiated by either self-referentiality or self-interest; and, on the other, the process of socioeconomic reform is reduced to the level of aesthetic play or self-delusion.

This shift is visible even in Hawthorne's preface to *Blithedale,* in which he describes his model, the Brook Farm community, as itself already a romance. His stay there, he says, was "the most romantic episode of his own life—essentially a day-dream, and yet a fact—and thus offering an available foothold between fiction and reality."[1] Hawthorne is, in a way, only echoing George Ripley, the community's founder, who saw the farm as "a model of life which shall combine the enchantment of poetry with the facts of daily experience."[2] But where Ripley would combine "poetry" and "experience," Hawthorne places the community between "day-dream" and "fact"—not so much in "neutral territory" as in no-man's-land. For him, the politics of such utopian reform do not belong to the actual; the interplay between actual and imaginary, politics and art, thus can never quite take place, for the political appears only as a representation, already aestheticized. In one sense, then, *The Blithedale Romance* is an attempt to construct a romance of an already existing romance, and the result is a text doubly aestheticized, doubly removed from the real.

In Hawthorne's earlier work, theatrical performance often serves as a neutral ground for aesthetic engagement with the actual, but now, in *Blithedale,* such performances are characterized, in Sacvan Bercovitch's terms, as an evasion or diminution of the political. Throughout the book, the sign of this aestheticization and distance is the veil. As a theatrical prop, it marks the boundary between performance and action; as a curtain, it structures a spectatorial relation between observer and observed. In contrast to the revolutionary theater of "My Kinsman, Major Molineux" or "Howe's Masquerade," these performers exhibit themselves (or are exhibited) before a passively observing audience; they do not seek to act upon that audience politically, nor do the viewers interact with or participate in the drama.[3]

In a different sense, Hawthorne's use of a characterized first-person narrator, Miles Coverdale, also amounts to a kind of veiling. Where Hawthorne deliberately implicates himself in the plot of *The House of the Seven Gables* by drawing on his own family history, he moves in the opposite direction in *Blithedale,* distancing himself from a narrator whose experience is based even more directly on his own.

By thus foregrounding the process of narration, Hawthorne further problematizes the position of the artist, offering an implicit critique of Coverdale's text as a failed romance. One of *Blithedale*'s primary themes becomes, in fact, the undoing or impossibility of romance as Hawthorne has earlier conceived it.

If any figure in the novel has the potential to integrate the artistic with the economic and political, it would seem to be Zenobia. In her, Hawthorne connects feminism and political radicalism quite specifically to theatrical performance.[4] Although Zenobia is known only by her pen name – and thus as a writer – Coverdale sees her " 'public name' " as " 'a sort of mask in which she comes before the world . . . a contrivance, in short, like the white drapery of the Veiled Lady, only a little more transparent' " (3:8). He turns a verbal construction, the pseudonym, into a physical object, a mask or veil, because, he says, Zenobia is by nature a speaker or performer rather than a writer – "She was made (among a thousand other things that she might have been) for a stump-oratress. . . . The stage would have been her proper sphere" – a judgment in which the mesmerist Westervelt concurs (3:44, 240).

Coverdale calls Zenobia " 'an enchantress . . . a sister of the Veiled Lady' " (3:45), the latter being a clairvoyant exhibited in highly theatrical fashion by the evil and manipulative "Professor" Westervelt. The Lady is perhaps the paradigmatic instance of theatricality in *Blithedale,* but, both in performance and in life, she is striking in her passivity and subjection. Theatrical performance is not, in this case, enabling for a woman – the Veiled Lady seems enchanted rather than enchanting, as she is "exhibited" by one man to others, to an audience that includes Coverdale himself (3:5). Similarly, Coverdale sees it as Zenobia's "duty . . . to sit endlessly to painters and sculptors," to have her "image" reproduced and multiplied for circulation among male viewers (3:44).

It is in this problematic context that Zenobia offers her "legend" of "The Silvery Veil," *Blithedale*'s closest equivalent to Holgrave's retelling of the story of Alice Pyncheon. The legend stands as a separate unit in the text, framed by a title rather than quotation marks, although still contained within chapter 13. But while Holgrave reads from a published work, Zenobia's storytelling is an impromptu oral and dramatic performance. And where Holgrave's reading ends with his ability to literally mesmerize Phoebe, Zenobia's storytelling imbues her with a more ambiguous—but also more ominous—power.

"[F]ragmentary bits of theatrical performance" are common at Blithedale, but as an alternative to, not an aesthetic extension of, the community's "laborious life" (3:106). On this particular evening, the group has been creating *tableaux vivants,* costuming themselves and posing in imitation of various works of art. Zenobia expresses some impatience with this activity, but not because it is too artificial, too firmly grounded in the imaginary. Her complaint is that it contains too much of the actual: " 'We have so much familiarity with one another's realities, that we cannot remove ourselves, at pleasure, into an imaginary sphere' " (3:107).

Zenobia introduces her "wild, spectral legend" with an image of mirroring or specularity: the Veiled Lady's life, she says, "seemed to have no more reality than the candlelight image of one's self, which peeps at us outside of a dark window-pane" (3:107, 108). The window is not a magic mirror like that in the House of the Seven Gables or one that intermingles reality and imagination like the one in Hawthorne's moonlit room. Instead, it suggests reflexivity and insubstantiality, self-alienation rather than transformation or empowerment. This is, after all, a performance with a performer as its subject.

Nevertheless, Zenobia's legend does contain many of the ingredients for a feminist critique of patriarchal theater and display. It depicts the Veiled Lady as the object of male observation and discourse, as a group of young men seeks to establish her identity in conventional patriarchal terms—through a father's name or a brother's protection. The Lady calls herself a " 'prisoner' " behind her veil (3:112), either virgin or wife, at the whim of her male pursuer. But, in keeping with her earlier remark, Zenobia does not widen the tale into the political; instead, she redirects it toward the personal.

She has been using a "piece of gauze" as a prop, a representation of the "magic veil" of her story. "Arriving at the catastrophe," Coverdale says,

> she flung the gauze over Priscilla's head; and, for an instant her auditors held their breath, half expecting, I verily believe, that the Magician would start up through the floor, and carry off our poor little friend, before our eyes.

As for Priscilla, she stood droopingly, in the midst of us, making no attempt to remove the veil. (3:116)

Zenobia has no new physical power over the girl; she has merely represented the assertion of such power. Her gesture does reach across the line between performer and audience, but its primary force is as a communication between the two women. It tells Priscilla that Zenobia knows her to have been the "real" Veiled Lady and implicitly threatens her with a return to Westervelt's control. For all intents and purposes, power and its representation are identical here.

But such theatricality is not here presented as a mode of transformation or a way of moving beyond the level of the personal. Zenobia and the Veiled Lady are "sisters" in several senses: as women, as theatrical performers (in Coverdale's eyes, at least), and as biological half-sisters as well. But on this continuum between the political, aesthetic, and personal, *Blithedale* moves, here and always, toward the last, the personal and psychological. Because Coverdale has conflated Zenobia's writing and her feminist activism with her theatrical self-presentation, her political or reforming force is sharply undercut by this scene. He emphasizes Zenobia's charismatic appeal throughout, but the narrative context undermines and reduces her power, revealing it as based in purely private feeling—in this case, sexual jealousy. In fact, Coverdale believes her entire public "character of eccentricity and defiance"—her feminist commitment, in other words—to have begun when her "passionate womanhood" was disappointed in love (3:103).

In *Blithedale,* the realization of aesthetic power is only reifying and destructive; where Holgrave resists the temptation offered by his power over Phoebe, Zenobia eventually does return Priscilla to Westervelt. Her theatrical presentation is thus continuous with and complicit in the coercive exploitation—both economic and, potentially, sexual—of Westervelt's mesmerism.

If such private theatricals are suspect in the novel, so too is public performance—and popular culture in general. This is made clear in "A Village-Hall," in which Westervelt and the Veiled Lady appear at a small-town

lyceum. The Lady has been mentioned or discussed on a number of occasions, but this is the first and only time that one of her performances is
to be directly described. The hall serves interchangeably as a site for lec-
turers and ventriloquists, choirs and historical dioramas, wax museums
and "strolling players"—high culture and low, from "legitimate drama"
to mesmerism (3:196). Handbills advertising the production appear
throughout the village, "in the bar-room and on the sign-post of the hotel, and on the meeting-house porch" (3:196), but this is not the vibrant
country setting of the earlier "Passages from a Relinquished Work." The
Veiled Lady, like the lyceum's other attractions, has no apparent link to
any local or popular culture; she is just another of a series of commodities
traveling on a circuit of commercial entertainment. The viewers seem to
regard themselves as consumers, to be furnished with theatrical spectacle
as a purchased commodity; they soon become impatient, "signif[ying]
their desire for the entertainment to commence, by thump of sticks and
stamp of boot-heels" (3:199).[5]

Professor Westervelt's performance begins as a lecture, a compound
of the discourses of science, education, and transcendental fantasy, but
he hardly seeks to explain what he has advertised as a "celebrated and
hitherto inexplicable phenomenon" (3:200, 197). His presentation of the
Veiled Lady emphasizes her separation from the audience, not her connection to them; here and elsewhere, she is said to "appear" or to be
"exhibited," displayed as a product for visual consumption alone (3:5,
108, 200). And the veil, of course, allows her body to be both displayed
and withheld from sight at the same time.

In this case, the handbills have promised "an interview" with the Lady,
but the veil that puts her "in communion with the spiritual world" makes
her see the actual world as insubstantial and unreal (3:197, 201). She may
cross the line between the two realms, but they remain distinct, with no
narrative or discursive link between them. If anything, the dividing line
is now more firmly established, physically delineated by the veil.

Westervelt may describe the Lady as spiritually empowered by the veil,
but she is also physically isolated and socially disempowered by it at the
same time. Her clairvoyance requires both her dependence and passivity
before the Professor and her inaccessibility to the audience, whom West-

ervelt encourages to shout or stomp on the floor in unsuccessful attempts to break her trance. When Hollingsworth simply steps forward and calls to her, Priscilla's response means not an enlargement of the theatrical but its collapse, in a sudden fall out of character and into the real.

Before the performance, the talk among the audience had concerned spiritualism and hypnosis, but the result is no more than a handful of outlandish stories – tales offering only parodic echoes of the powers attributed to Matthew Maule and his descendants. Westervelt's exhibition seems, in fact, to be another version of Alice Pyncheon's enslavement, not just reported in narrative, but acted out on a nightly basis. This version of the aesthetic is hardly a form of liberation, or even a means of connection; it is just another mode of subjugation, now commodified as spectacle.[6]

The other side of aesthetic production or performance is spectatorship or interpretation. For Coverdale, the key is to watch "unrecognized, unseen" as if the characters are figures in his own "private theatre" (3:207, 70). This combination of theatricality and voyeurism appears both at Blithedale, where Coverdale overlooks the farm from the hidden vantage point of his treetop "hermitage" (3:98–100), and in town, where he watches the windows of a boarding house opposite his hotel. There he sees Zenobia "like a full-length picture, in the space between the heavy festoons of the window-curtains" – in other words, as a framed representation of herself (3:155). When she ends the scene (and Coverdale's chapter as well) by drawing the curtain, "[i]t fell like the drop-curtain of a theatre, in the interval between the acts" (3:159). Coverdale's use of theatrical images marks an aesthetic observation that reifies its objects, precluding the observer from acting on or engaging with them.[7]

Hollingsworth has accused him of being interested in Blithedale only as " 'a theme for poetry,' " and Zenobia has charged him with intending to " 'turn the affair into a ballad' " (3:131, 33). Coverdale himself admits that he " 'cares for' " Priscilla not " 'for her realities . . . but for the fancy-work with which I have idly decked her out' " (3:100). He busies himself in speculation about Zenobia's marital status and sexual experience, imagining her as a statue, "because the cold decorum of the marble would consist with the utmost scantiness of drapery" (44). Even when Coverdale does become more than an eavesdropper or audience, his intervention is only another reductive objectification, performed by the imagined gaze of the sexual connoisseur.

Coverdale's self-description suggests, on one hand, the darkest possibilities of the artist's role, those which Holgrave has renounced because of his feeling for Phoebe, those which Westervelt–and, through him, Zenobia–has exercised over Priscilla. On the other, his merely speculative interest in the lives of others relegates the aesthetic to a clearly secondary position, no more than parasitic upon the real.

Hawthorne's larger critique of social reform begins with his recurrent image for both Brook Farm and Blithedale as masquerade or pageant–a theatrical escape from reality rather than an engagement with it (3:1). Movement to the level of the aesthetic here implies a reduction, a diminution of both power and seriousness of intent, as well as a disengagement or flight from the actual–the representation or image of change functions only as a substitute for change itself.

If Coverdale sees Zenobia's political oratory in terms of theater, Westervelt characterizes Blithedale and its " 'Æsthetic . . . laborers' " through a reference to *As You Like It:* " 'This is your forest of Arden; and you [Coverdale] are either the banished Duke, in person, or one of the chief nobles in his train. The melancholy Jacques, perhaps?' " (3:91). The farm, from the perspective of the power-hungry magician, stands as only a temporary refuge from the intrigues and power plays of urban politics. Its "labor" takes place entirely *within* the realm of the aesthetic, not *between* the aesthetic and the actual; for Westervelt, the reformers have merely " 'planted themselves,' " posing as farmers rather than doing any actual planting (3:91). Whatever transformations do take place at Blithedale will be no more than temporary illusions, mere representations of change with no effect on the realities of city life.[8]

When Coverdale comes back to Blithedale after a period in the city, it is two days after his encounter with Westervelt and the Lady. The members of the commune now appear to him, too, as "masqueraders" (3:204).

As he approaches the farm through the woods, he first hears the sound of voices: "The wood . . . seemed as full of jollity as if Comus and his crew were holding their revels" (3:209). There is indeed a masquerade taking place, with all the reformers in costume; their choices are a combination of mythic and domestic: Diana, Arcadian shepherds, "allegoric figures from the Faerie Queen," as well as an Indian, a Shaker, and Puritans and revolutionary officers (3:209).

Hawthorne bases this scene on a notebook passage written at Brook Farm—but the entry describes a child's birthday party, and the group contains children as well as adults.[9] In *Blithedale,* on the other hand, this becomes an example of purely adult theatricality. Hawthorne also eliminates the presence of historical figures such as Emerson and Margaret Fuller and substitutes Coverdale's hidden observation for his own direct participation. Where the actual Brook Farm scene does bring uncostumed historical figures into contact with a world of imagination and play, *Blithedale*'s is one in which theatricality simply displaces the real.

Hawthorne's own flight from the political may be clearest in his treatment of Fuller, a figure whose political and social radicalism troubled him even years after her death.[10] She is, strangely enough, the only one of Hawthorne's contemporaries to be named directly in the book, when Coverdale receives a letter from her (3:52).[11] But Hawthorne brings her into the text precisely in order to exclude her from it, by referring to her as a figure from the world outside the book. Naming Fuller also serves to differentiate her from Zenobia and thus to deny her importance as a source or model. Once again, the romance does reach out to the historical, but only in order to distance itself from it.

Myth and history, literature and politics, are still blended in the array of costumes Coverdale describes. But these characters resemble the ones in British General Howe's masquerade rather than those of Colonel Joliffe's revolutionary antimasque. Beyond this, Coverdale's allusion to Milton's *Comus* links this spectacle quite directly to the masque of the seventeenth-century English court, a form detested by the Puritans both because of its depravity as theater and because of its association with and service to political conservatism.[12] The masque is indeed a form in which the aesthetic and the political may interact, but here the effect is to reassert the difference between theatrical play and political action, and thus to reaffirm the social and political status quo.[13]

Westervelt's earlier sneer at the idea of "Æsthetic labor" opens up another of the novel's major issues, the relation between aesthetics and economics, art and labor. One of Ripley's main objectives at Brook Farm was "to insure a more natural union between intellectual and manual labor than now exists; to combine the thinker and the worker, as far as possible, in the same individual."[14] In thus challenging the opposition between mental and manual labor, Ripley was confronting "the paradigm that structured virtually all antebellum thinking about work," according to Nicholas Bromell.[15] Beyond this, he saw shared labor and working conditions as the first and most important step in overcoming class and other differences.[16]

In *The House of the Seven Gables,* Hawthorne's romance also sought a middle ground between these categories: as storyteller and photographer, Holgrave could be both artist and artisan, both a creative performer and a participant in a partly mechanized process. Coverdale, too, had hoped that "between theory and practice, a true and available mode of living might be struck out" (3:63). But, like Hawthorne in his own days at Brook Farm, he finds himself unable to connect the roles of poet and worker: "The clods of earth, which we so constantly belabored and turned over and over, were never etherealized into thought. Our thoughts, on the contrary, were fast becoming cloddish. Our labor symbolized nothing, and left us mentally sluggish in the dusk of the evening. Intellectual activity is incompatible with any large amount of bodily exercise. The yeoman and the scholar . . . are two distinct individuals, and can never be melted or welded into one substance" (3:66).[17] For him, Blithedale's transcendental pretensions are no more than that. The gulf between intellectual and worker cannot be overcome, no matter what "costume" (3:63) the former may adopt.

From one perspective, Hollingsworth's reform project might seem another way to bridge this gap, by joining the philosophical to the physical.

He offers Coverdale a vision of brotherhood and labor in the service of a shared purpose. But the power of his plan derives from neither its objectives nor its reasoning; it is based instead on Hollingsworth's "magnetism" (3:134). The term is a damning one: first, its homoerotic charge returns the enterprise to the level of the personal; and, second, it links Hollingsworth and Westervelt, reformer and performer–both coercive egotists who "labor" only to produce illusions.

What may, in the end, be most striking about Coverdale's description of Blithedale is the apparent lack of any actual production there. Ripley's goal may have been to "unite" and "combine" thought and labor, but Coverdale seeks only to "etherealize" and "symbolize," to abstract from the physical without ever working with or in it. The closest he comes to a description of the actual work of farming is a summary of the neighbors' misconceptions about the reformers' incompetence; he devotes almost as much space to the effects of labor on his and his companions' bodies (3:64–65). The real Brook Farm, on the other hand, proved quite successful as both a farm and a school–in economic terms and in joining the agricultural and the intellectual.[18] But if the Veiled Lady cannot seem to reach outside the circuit of commercial display to link the spiritual with the actual, Coverdale's performance as farmer fails for the opposite reason–because his aesthetic self-absorption never makes contact with the actual processes of production or the market.[19]

The gap between aesthetic and other forms of labor has, in fact, already been touched on, in an exchange between Coverdale and Zenobia. When Coverdale first meets Priscilla, he assumes she is an admirer or devotee of Zenobia's. Zenobia, however, sees this as a decidedly " 'poetical' " view, one worthy only of a ballad (3:33). Her explanation is cast in terms of social and economic class: Priscilla is " 'a seamstress from the city, and she has probably no more transcendental purpose than to do my miscellaneous sewing' " (3:33).

Zenobia is the more precise observer–she notes " 'the needle marks on the tip of [Priscilla's] forefinger . . . her paleness, her nervousness, and her wretched fragility' " (3:34). The seamstress's work is hardly aestheticized; it is nowhere described as self-expression or artistry (as Hester's needlework is on several occasions in *The Scarlet Letter*). Zenobia sees the exploitation that is its essence, something of which Coverdale is completely unaware: he even owns one of Priscilla's purses.

Both explanations for the girl's presence are correct, however; Priscilla is a seamstress, but she is also Zenobia's half-sister, who has fled to Blithedale for protection from Westervelt. This is a moment at which Hawthorne's romance does juxtapose, even if it does not combine, the economic and the aesthetic, the social and the personal. A fusion of theatrical and economic exploitation is, however, precisely what Priscilla is fleeing, and she turns to Blithedale not as a political alternative, but as the site of a personal connection. Coverdale's aesthetic distance is, finally, an inadequate and reductive response, but Zenobia's economic analysis is also a reactionary one, for it assumes and reasserts her class superiority over her sister. Both end in elitism and detachment, having reinscribed the categories of class and sexual difference on the ostensibly egalitarian community.

In *Blithedale,* moonlight illuminates not the power of romance but its failure. This is foreshadowed early in the book, as Coverdale wakens from a dream to see the moon "shining on the snowy landscape, which looked like a lifeless copy of the world in marble. From the bank of the distant river, which was shimmering in the moonlight, came the black shadow of the only cloud in heaven" (3:38).[20] As in *The House of the Seven Gables,* the book's culminating moment reveals a corpse, but here it is a scene that closes off the narrative rather than projecting it outward toward the actual.

In Zenobia's last conversation with Coverdale, she tells him that "her face will [soon] be behind the black-veil" (3:227–28). So when he finds her handkerchief near the river, he fears she has committed suicide; but it takes Silas Foster's blunt remark that " 'you think she's drowned herself,' " to bring out "the hideous idea in its full terror, as if he were removing the napkin from the face of a corpse" (3:230). The combined images of veil, handkerchief, and napkin make death at once a mystery and the occasion for a dark theatrical revelation.

At midnight, Coverdale, along with Hollingsworth and Foster, begin dragging the river for Zenobia's body: "The moon, that night, though past the full, was still large and oval, and . . . now shone aslantwise over the river, throwing the high, opposite bank, with its woods, into deep shadow, but lighting up the hither shore pretty effectually. Not a ray appeared to fall on the river itself. It lapsed imperceptibly away, a broad, black, inscrutable depth, keeping its own secrets from the eye of man" (3:232). The river's potentially reflecting surface remains "black, inscrutable" in the moonlight. This mirror has no ghosts within it or texts behind it, only death. A "Black River of Death," Coverdale calls it (3:234).

The body is found when Hollingsworth strikes it with the pole he has been plunging into the water, and the iron tip leaves a wound near Zenobia's heart. Coverdale is shocked by her corpse's terrible inflexibility: "she was the marble image of a death-agony" (3:235). It is a nightmarish fulfillment of his own earlier wish to see Zenobia's body represented in marble. But he goes on to take the twisted, rigid shape of the corpse as his text for a moralizing commentary: "Being the woman that she was," he says, "could Zenobia have foreseen all these ugly circumstances of death, how ill it would become her . . . she would no more have committed the dreadful act, than have exhibited herself to a public assembly in a badly-fitting garment!" (3:236). The comparison turns suicide into yet another public exhibition, but Coverdale denies his own urge to objectify and fix Zenobia's body; he suggests instead that she has attempted to pose her own corpse in a "lithe and graceful" attitude (3:326).[21]

It is, I think, worth comparing this scene with the passage from the *American Notebooks* from which it derives. In an entry from July 1845, Hawthorne describes the terrible rigidity and distortion of a drowned girl's body: "If she could have foreseen, while she stood, at 5 o'clock that morning, on the bank of the river, how her maiden corpse would have looked . . . it surely would have saved her from this deed," he concludes.[22] His original horrified gasp becomes, in Coverdale's narration, a misogynistic sneer. The end result is a double critique–of Zenobia's theatricality and self-consciousness, but also of Coverdale's antifeminism and his own spectatorial impulse.

In another sense, however, this scene also reflects upon the romance as a whole. For it is not just Coverdale's narration, but Hawthorne's plot

structure as well, that builds toward the recovery and unveiling of Zenobia's corpse. *The Blithedale Romance,* like Westervelt's stage performance,
culminates in the exhibition of a passive female body. In this respect, it
too is implicated in the economic and sexual exploitation it describes.

Months earlier, Coverdale had remarked that it would take a death to
make Blithedale "a real, practical, as well as poetical, system" (3:130) – in
other words, to bring it from the realm of fancy onto the plane of romance. Now it is Zenobia's death that moves the community forward,
into history, in a combination of "progress" and repetition: "She was
buried very much as other people have been, for hundreds of years gone
by" (3:238). The ceremony is not the newly drafted "symbolic expression of our spiritual faith and eternal hopes" that the reformers had discussed; instead, they decide "to content ourselves with the old fashion,
taking away what we could, but interpolating no novelties" (3:238–39).
Historical progress, such as it is, is a matter only of deletion and loss.

Hawthorne's conclusion amounts, obviously, to a rejection of both
Zenobia's feminism and the collective reform project of Blithedale. In
a way, his use of Brook Farm as ground or referent for the romance has
been problematic from the start. Hawthorne's "concern with the Socialist Community," according to the preface, is merely as a place in which
"to establish a theatre, a little removed from the highway of ordinary
travel, where the creatures of his brain may play their phantasmagorical
antics. . . . His whole treatment of the affair is altogether incidental to
the main purpose of the Romance" (3:1). Where *The House of the Seven
Gables* moves outward from the family conflict between the Pyncheons
and the Maules into larger issues of politics and class, *The Blithedale Romance* travels in the opposite direction, from a politicized setting back
toward a focus on familial and psychological matters. In the former, it is
the business of romance to connect the seventeenth-century past with the
mid-nineteenth-century present; in the latter, the romance seems instead
designed to disavow the impact of even the recent political past.

Coverdale sees the radical possibilities – both imaginative and political – of reform, but for him they are a disorienting nightmare: "I was
beginning to lose the sense of what kind of a world it was, among in-

numerable schemes of what it might or ought to be. It was impossible, situated as we were, not to imbibe the idea that everything in nature and human existence was fluid, or fast becoming so; that the crust of the Earth, in many places, was broken, and its whole surface portentously upheaving; that it was a day of crisis, and that we ourselves were in the critical vortex" (3:140). Such a prospect would have invigorated Holgrave in *The House of the Seven Gables,* but it sends Coverdale, as both observer and artist, scurrying back to "the settled system of things" (3:141). If destabilization and fluidity offered creative openings for Hawthorne's earlier romances, they are anathema to Coverdale's version of the form, and he pulls himself and *Blithedale* back quite abruptly from the brink.

Hawthorne has, in a way, undercut his own project from the start, in the very language of his preface. If writing *Blithedale* has been like "establishing a theatre," then all of Hawthorne's reservations about theater must be read as reflections on the romance as well. If both Hawthorne and Coverdale are simply engaged in theatricalizing reality, then the romance—and the entire realm of the aesthetic—has been drained of its revisionary power and direction.

PART TWO

Whitman

⌁

FOUR

Whitman
in 1855:
Against
Representation

Of the twelve poems in the first edition of *Leaves of Grass,* only one had previously appeared in print. An early version of "Europe: The 72d and 73d Years of These States," entitled "Resurgemus," had been published in the June 21, 1850, edition of the *New York Tribune.* Whitman's choice of this particular poem to revise and reprint is significant, for it is one of his more openly political ones—a response to the failed European revolts of 1848 and 1849. Beyond this, his choice of a final title both reinforces the poem's historical reference and places it in a specifically revolutionary time frame, seventy-two years after 1776.[1] Given the chance to connect *Leaves of Grass* with his earlier work, Whitman makes the link an explicitly historical and political one.

One of the striking things about Whitman's writing in the 1840s and '50s—both his poetry and prose—is the continuity of its political rhetoric. In a March 15, 1847, book review in the Brooklyn *Eagle,* he clearly antici-pates the conflict of 1848: "we would rather at this moment over ev-ery kingdom on the continent of Europe, that the *people* should rise and enact the same prodigious destruction as those of the French Revo-lution, could they thus root out the kingcraft and priestcraft which are annually dwindling down humanity there. . . . only some great retching of the social and political structure can achieve the blessed consummation."[2] Whitman's conception of social change through revolutionary, even apocalyptic upheaval reemerges three years later in "Resurgemus," which speaks of the failure of the uprisings he had called for:

> Not a disembodied spirit
> Can the weapon of tyrants let loose,
> But it shall stalk invisibly over the earth,
> Whispering, counseling, cautioning.
>
> Liberty, let others despair of thee,
> But I will never despair of thee:
> Is the house shut? Is the master away?
> Nevertheless, be ready, be not weary of watching,
> He will surely return; his messengers come anon.[3]

These lines appear almost unchanged in content in *Leaves of Grass;* it is the changes in form that are crucial:

> Not a disembodied spirit can the weapons of tyrants let loose,
> But it stalks invisibly over the earth . . . whispering counseling cautioning.
>
> Liberty let others despair of you . . . . I never despair of you.
>
> Is the house shut? Is the master away?
> Nevertheless be ready . . . . be not weary of watching,
> He will soon return . . . . his messengers come anon.[4]

By 1855, Whitman has abandoned the conventional poetic line and its normal internal punctuation, turning to long lines held together largely by ellipses. He has, by this point, left conventional party politics behind as well, but his new and radical poetic form does more than simply correspond to his political positions; it extends them further, reconceiving aesthetic creation as itself a revolutionary act. *Leaves of Grass* enacts in language—and impels its reader toward—a democratic reconstruction of America itself.

My argument intersects with two primary themes in Whitman criticism: the relation between poetic form and political content, and the nature and role of the Whitmanian "self." The New Critical tendency has always been to separate Whitman's revolution in poetic form from its political context and contents, and such a view still persists in judgments such as David Reynolds's: "Although his sympathies generally stood with the radical side on such issues, [Whitman] continued to explore the imaginative rather than the political possibilities of reform rhetoric, so that popular reform was chiefly important as a training ground in zestful, defiant writing."[5] Here Reynolds is speaking of Whitman's early reform fiction and journalism, but the shift from politics to style ("zestful, defiant writing") is characteristic of his approach to the poetry as well.

In *Whitman the Political Poet,* Betsy Erkkila responds to such readings by attempting to rehistoricize both poet and work, to relocate Whitman in a tradition of artisanal republicanism and revolutionary individualism.[6] The result is a refocused reading that now emphasizes Whitman's political content but understates his formal radicalism; Erkkila never takes full account of Whitman's attack on representation itself or of his attempt to implicate both himself and his readers in the ongoing democratic process of the poem.[7]

My objective, in contrast, is not simply to readjust the balance between aesthetics and politics, but to try to move beyond such oppositions—for this, it seems to me, is Whitman's aim in the 1855 *Leaves of Grass.* He writes in what Jay Cantor calls "the revolutionary moment": "Revolutionary words," Cantor says, "do not bring things to us: they are bodies, that is to say, speaking them makes us, or changes us. . . . The word has become a kind of deed."[8] As Whitman puts it in his preface, the poet "can make every word he speaks draw blood" (8). These poems do not just contain or express political ideas; they work to demonstrate and enact them. Their fluid and unstructured form is the democratic practice their words proclaim.[9]

The 1855 *Leaves* thus offers a number of different challenges to conventional reading. If Hawthorne's romance seeks a mediating realm between the imaginary and the actual, Whitman's work begins by claiming to annihilate such differences, and with them the very need for mediation. And if poetic representation is ultimately based on structures of difference, then he will abandon ordinary representation as well.

The volume opens, in fact, with an attack on the kind of poetic privilege that would distinguish between the aesthetic and the factual or historical. In its format, the book offers the reader an apparently anonymous product, in which poetry and prose appear together under a single repeated title.

Within the text, Whitman abandons symbolic or metaphoric representation, in which one thing stands for another, in favor of antihierarchical, inclusive catalogs punctuated only by ellipses and commas.[10] As Wai Chee Dimock puts it,

> The objects of Whitman's attention are admitted as strict equals, guaranteed equals, by virtue of both the minimal universal "Me" they have in common, and of a poetic syntax which greets each of them in the same way, as a grammatical unit. . . . "Song of Myself" is thus a poetry of sequence without sedimentation, a poetry that sallies forth, its syntactic possibilities unmarked and undiminished by what it has been through. . . . The operative process here is something like the transposition of seriality into simultaneity – the constitution of memory as a field of spatial latitude rather than temporal extension.[11]

Dimock offers a superb description of the syntactic and formal features of Whitman's poem; but she has deep reservations about the "Me" to which she refers. Her critique of Whitman's form – what she sees as a flattening of memory and a loss of particularity in the elements of his poetic catalogs – spring from her view of a universalizing impulse in Whitman, a desire to abstract a noncontingent self out of the contingent particulars of ordinary experience.

This notion of a dominant or transcendent "self" is another core element of the critical tradition.[12] At one extreme, Quentin Anderson speaks of Whitman's "imperial self" as almost totalitarian in its inability to entertain the possibility of other existences.[13] And even a more sympathetic reader, such as Roy Harvey Pearce, sees "a Whitman sufficiently conscious of his own commitment to isolated, egocentric creativity to manifest it even as he tries to transcend it."[14]

I differ from both critics in taking Whitman's goal to be a poetry based on a fluid and permeable poetic "self" rather than a more conventional representative individualism. Whitman does not extract an enlarged and coercive authorial self from the particulars of his catalogs; rather, he disperses and dissolves the poetic (or philosophical) self into these particulars, into the space of the text and the collectivity of its readership. The initial radicalism of *Leaves of Grass* thus goes far beyond the level of literary form; its ultimate goal is the visionary reconstruction of national, gender, and individual identity as well – all within a poetic space filled not by words but by the direct and overwhelming presence of America itself. [15]

In making this argument for Whitman's radicalism, I am, I should note, speaking solely of the 1855 *Leaves of Grass*. Even as early as the second edition (1856), Whitman has begun to move toward more conventional modes of representation and mediation between author and reader, a shift that continues through the edition of 1860–61, and to which I will turn in the following chapter. I would not claim, as Malcolm Cowley does, that the first *Leaves* is its "best" or "purest" form, but I do see Whitman's later poems as qualitatively different, in their poetic form and practice, from those of 1855. [16] My approach to Whitman's work is thus diachronic rather than synchronic, treating the poems as they first appear in *Leaves of Grass* rather than in their final form in the 1892 Deathbed edition.

My discussion in this chapter alternates in focus between Whitman's poetry and prose. It begins at the edge of *Leaves of Grass* by considering the format of the first edition and the role of the preface. These "marginal" elements in fact help to shape and situate the text, connecting Whitman's poems to his earlier notebooks and journalism. My second section treats "The Sleepers," which describes the fluid and transforming self that serves as ground for Whitman's poetic vision. My third turns to some of Whitman's newspaper sketches of 1856, which engage with political issues most powerfully at the moments that most resemble his poetry. And I conclude with a longer examination of "Song of Myself," which both elaborates and performs the fusion of psychological and political that "The Sleepers" has announced. [17]

Opening Whitman's Leaves

In its opening pages, the format of the 1855 *Leaves* unsettles the reader's assumptions about both the boundaries and contents of literary texts. A title page normally individualizes a text by giving it a name and then claims it as the property and product of an individual author. But instead of simply placing his own name under the title, Whitman opens this text with a visual image: a facing-page engraving of a carefully posed but unidentified male figure. Rather than a name as a point of origin for the book, we are given a second, visual text for interpretation. But the figure's deliberately casual pose also seems improper and disruptive; its working-class attire, where one would expect to find more formal dress, seems also to demand rather than close off interpretation.

The author's proper name usually serves as a link between the poetic voice inside the text and the individual owner/author outside it. But Whitman's name is given only on the verso, as that of the copyright owner. His name will not appear in the body of the text until more than twenty pages later, in section 24 of "Song of Myself." And there he is "Walt Whitman," not the "Walter Whitman" of the copyright page.[18]

In *Leaves,* then, the relationships between the author, the copyright owner, the subject of the portrait, and the subject of the poem are never directly established.[19] Whitman sets out, in fact, to enter the nineteenth-century debate over copyright and texts as property by deliberately undercutting assumptions about naming, reference, and ownership. In an earlier decade, anonymous self-publication would have been the preserve of "gentleman authors" such as Irving and Cooper, but in this case it moves Whitman's work in the opposite direction—away from the elitist realm of individualized art works and artists, and closer to the journalistic world of anonymous or pseudonymous publication—the world in which he worked throughout the 1840s.[20] Both "Resurgemus" and Whitman's other political poems of 1850 were, after all, published (some pseudonymously) in daily newspapers, William Cullen Bryant's *New York Evening Post* and Horace Greeley's *New York Tribune.*[21] Just as the engraving constructs a deliberately chosen image for the poet, so the text aims to create a poetic voice and persona that cannot, finally, be reduced to the expression or reflection of a singular author/owner.

Whitman's title, *Leaves of Grass,* refers to the pages of the book as a physical object rather than to its verbal contents. Just as Whitman rejects a straightforward identification of work with author, so he also undermines conventional generic distinctions—the book actually opens with prose, with an extended ten-page preface.[22] A standard preface would provide a frame or border for the poems that follow, separating them from the world outside the text. Whitman, however, sets out to attack the idea of the poem as aesthetic object, as something distinct from and superior to other forms of discourse. His preface bridges the gap between inside and outside—not just in what it claims for the book, but in what it performs. Its two-column, newspaper-style format, for instance, along with the large size of the book (11 by 8¼ inches), links Whitman's work to the tabloids and magazines of popular journalism—in effect, blurring the distinction between the literary and the nonliterary.[23] And its style—long sentences, often connected by ellipses—anticipates that of the poems to follow.

If one takes a step back from the published text, into Whitman's notebooks of the period, one finds no hierarchical divisions between poetry and prose, "protoliterary" material and casual notes. The manuscripts move continually back and forth between forms; Whitman often speaks of all writing as a single activity: "*Rule in all addresses—and poems and other writings, etc.*—Do not undertake to say any thing however plain to you, unless you are positive are [*sic*] making it plain to those who hear or read."[24]

In the notebook entitled "Memorials," for instance, which includes some drafts of material used in the 1855 *Leaves,* two pages are taken up by a list of names—nicknames of omnibus drivers, according to the editors. The second of these pages reads as follows:

> Dry Dock John Raggedy Jack Smith's Monkey Emigrant Wild Man of Borneo Steamboat Elephant Buffalo Santa Anna Blind Sam Rosy Baltimore Charley Long Boston Short Boston Manneyunk Pretty Ike Jersey Mountaineer. (*Notebooks,* 1:146)

This is immediately followed, however, by an attempt at an aesthetic and political manifesto:

> It is not a labor of clothing or putting on or describing—it is a labor of clearing away and reducing—for every thing is beautiful in itself and perfect—and

the office of the poet is to remove what stands in the way of our perceiving
the beauty and perfection /

My final aim

To concentrate around me the leaders of all *reforms* – transcendentalist,
spiritualists, free soilers (*Notebooks,* 1:147)

The following pages in the notebook contain early versions of sections 7
and 8 of "I Sing the Body Electric." The result is a continuum between
poetry, prose, and the "raw material" of simple "facts."[25] Such an alternation between the collection of details and the announcement of general
claims will be characteristic of *Leaves* as well; in a sense, these notebook
entries are themselves examples of Whitman's aesthetics. If the poet's
job is to "clear away" obstacles and blockages rather than to "describe,"
then a list of nicknames may indeed be a kind of poetry. Whitman's description also emphasizes writing as a physical activity, a labor of clearing
and removal that is to some extent analogous to the work of drivers and
others.

Beyond this, the juxtaposition of such disparate materials also accords
with Whitman's "final aim," which is to bring together elements of high
culture ("transcendentalist"), popular culture ("spiritualists"), and radical
politics ("free soilers"). On one side of this passage stands the street slang
of nicknames; on the other are drafts of passages from "I Sing the Body
Electric" that focus on slavery:

A Man at Auction

How much for the man
He is of ? value
For him the earth lay preparing billions of years without one animal or plant
For him the things of the air, the earth and the sea
He is not only himself
He is the father of other men who shall be fathers in their turn.

(*Notebooks,* 1:147)

If, as I have suggested, the preface can be linked to the notebooks
that precede it, it is also continuous with the poetry that follows, both in
pagination (although the preface is numbered with roman numerals and

the poetry with arabic numerals) and in style. The sentences of Whitman's prose move like the lines of his poems; they too feature catalogs, often punctuated with only dashes or ellipses (the characteristic punctuation mark of the 1855 edition): "On him rise solid growths that offset the growths of pine and cedar and hemlock and liveoak and locust and chestnut and cypress and hickory and limetree and cottonwood and tuliptree and cactus and wildvine and tamarind and persimmon . . . and tangles as tangled as any canebrake or swamp . . . and forests coated with transparent ice and icicles hanging from the boughs and crackling in the wind . . . and sides and peaks of mountains . . ." (7; ellipses in original). Here, too, Whitman sometimes structures his paragraphs through repetition: "Here at last . . . Here is not merely a nation . . . Here is action . . . Here is the hospitality . . . Here are the roughs . . . Here the performance . . ." (5). Given these formal continuities between poetry and prose, it is easy to see how Whitman could have turned portions of the preface into poetry in the 1856 edition (in "By Blue Ontario's Shore," "Song of Prudence," and "Song of the Answerer").

Such shifts in form have been characteristic of the *Notebooks* as well. In the "albot Wilson" notebook, an early version of a piece of "Song of Myself" appears in prose: "But I will open the shutters and the sash, and hook my left arm around your waist till I point you to the road along which are the cities of all living philosophy and pleasure.–Not I–not God–can travel this road for you" (*Notebooks,* 1:66). Four pages later in the manuscript, another passage from the same poem is presented as poetry:

> I am the poet of slaves and of the masters of slaves
> I am the poet of the body
> And I am. (*Notebooks,* 1:67)

Just as there is no ranking or selection of different forms in the *Notebooks,* so the boundaries between forms seem permeable and fluid, as ideas and phrases move back and forth across them. Even before the reader comes to the poems, then, the frame and format of Whitman's text have begun a process of breaking down oppositions–between literary and extraliterary forms and materials, poetry and prose, and, potentially, those between self and not self, words and things.

The argument of Whitman's preface makes the radicalism of his project quite explicit, when it announces that "The United States themselves are essentially the greatest poem" (5). He does not say that the United States are material for poetry, objects to be made into poems, or that they are "poetic"—the nation itself, its things and persons, are already "unrhymed poetry" (6).[26] In one sweeping gesture, Whitman thus discards the distinction between objects and their representations, things and words.

In the paragraphs to follow, Whitman uses a number of different terms to describe the poet's activity, but "represent" and "representation" are not among them: "The American poets are *to enclose* old and new for America is the race of races. Of them a bard *is to be commensurate with* a people. To him the other continents arrive as contributions . . . he *gives them reception* for their sake and his own sake. *His spirit responds to his country's* spirit . . . he *incarnates* its geography and natural life and rivers and lakes" (6–7; emphases added, ellipses in original). If the notion of representation implies a loss of or substitution for an original no longer present, Whitman's verbs—"enclose," "reception," "responds," "incarnates"—insist on that physical presence. Even "to be commensurate with" suggests a simultaneous presence, a measurement against something. So too does "tally," a term that appears two sentences later in the paragraph (and often throughout Whitman's later work).

Facts, according to Whitman, "emit themselves . . . Each precise object or condition or combination or process exhibits a beauty . . ." (17; ellipses in original). Objects exhibit or present themselves independently, apart from any action by the writer. The poet's speech is to have the same independent existence, as a natural act in itself, "with the perfect rectitude and insouciance of the movements of animals and the unimpeachableness of the sentiment of trees in the woods and grass by the roadside" (12). He is to judge "not as the judge judges but as the sun falling around a helpless thing" (9). Poetry is not a second-order activity, a response to a preexisting fact or event. Verbal expression is like the "fall" of sunlight, an event in and of itself, but one that is also an illumination.[27]

If poetry is not superior to things, neither are things superior to poetry as mere "representation." The poem's function is to "give all subjects their articulations," in an interactive process that "gives" them the expressions that seem already to belong to them somehow (12).

In political terms, the consequence of Whitman's claims is direct democracy: "Other states indicate themselves in their deputies . . . but the genius of the United States is not best or most in its executives or legislatures, not in its ambassadors or authors or colleges or parlors, nor even in its newspapers or inventors . . . but always most in the common people" (5–6; ellipses in original). Whitman's list brings together various forms of "representation," both political and cultural or linguistic. But just as things "exhibit" themselves, so the common people "indicate" themselves without mediation by either political or intellectual elites.

Whitman speaks of "crowds and groupings," the action of "vast masses"—of a collective grounding rather than an individual or elitist one (5). "The great master," he says, "sees health for himself in being one of the mass . . . he sees the hiatus in singular eminence" (15; ellipsis in original). Paradoxically, mastery lies not in "singular eminence," but in membership in the crowd or mass. "The proof of a poet is that his country absorbs him as affectionately as he has absorbed it" (24). The poet does not stand apart from, and thus represent his country; neither does the nation acknowledge that representation at a distance. The process is instead one of mutual "absorption" and "affection."

For Whitman, the American language is "the dialect of common sense," a "language of [popular] resistance" rather than a discourse of authority (23). Political liberty is central to the language of the street, the notebook, and the preface and poems. When he declares that "The American bard shall delineate no class of persons nor one or two out of the strata of interests," it is a statement of both aesthetic and political principle (14). The rejection of symbolic hierarchy and selection in the poems is, for Whitman, a democratic and egalitarian political act as well.

"The Sleepers"

One way to approach the poetry of the 1855 *Leaves* may be through one of its less radical poems, later titled "The Sleepers," but here still headed "Leaves of Grass." I call it less radical not because of its content, but because its visionary claims are mediated through (and in a sense contained by) the literary convention of the dream vision.[28] Hawthorne invokes the world of dream in "My Kinsman, Major Molineux" we should recall, in order to further problematize the status of Robin's vision: a dream may alter our perception of the world for a time, but it cannot in itself transform that world. Whitman both employs, and seeks to move beyond, such limits.

"I wander all night in my vision," the poem begins (line 1). But some crucial ambiguities are thrust upon us here: does the speaker have a vision of himself wandering, or is he wandering, following or possessed by the vision itself? Is it a vision of the real world, or of an altered or alternative one? Such problems of agency and identity reappear almost immediately, as the speaker moves on,

> Stepping with light feet . . . . swiftly and noiselessly stepping and stopping,
> Bending with open eyes over the shut eyes of sleepers;
> Wandering and confused . . . . lost to myself . . . . ill-assorted . . . .
>   contradictory,
> Pausing and gazing and bending and stopping. (lines 2–5; ellipses in original)

If his movement is directionless and seemingly unmotivated, so too is the movement of the poem. If he describes himself as fragmented – "lost to myself . . . ill-assorted" – so too is the poem broken up by its ellipses. All in all, this visionary state brings with it a dissolution of fixed categories, both poetic and psychological.

This opening stanza is structured by its parallel verb forms, the repeated present participle conveying the continuing movement of the speaker. The second stanza arrests that movement, however; its two lines break the flow, through both visual brevity and alliterative force:

> How solemn they look there, stretched and still;
> How quiet they breathe, the little children in their cradles. (lines 6–7)

Now the objects of vision, not the viewer/dreamer, become the poem's focus—faces, bodies: "The night pervades them and enfolds them" (line 11). It is not the speaker's voice or vision, but night as a universal condition that "pervades and enfolds" the poem and its objects. The verb "sleep" becomes the repeated link between the next dozen lines, eventually coming to enclose the speaker as well:

> I go from bedside to bedside . . . . I sleep close with the other sleepers, each
>   in turn;
> I dream in my dream all the dreams of the other dreamers,
> And I become the other dreamers. (lines 29–31)

We move here from a sequence of incidents—"from bedside to bedside," "each in turn"—to a fusion. First there is an interfusing of dreams, and then of dreamers. Whitman does not just imaginatively identify with others here; when he says, in the next line, "I am a dance," he deliberately leaves behind the distinction between dancer and dance, between the subject and its transforming movement.

The notion of the self as a fixed and stabilizing point has gone by the board:

> I am the actor and the actress . . . . the voter . . the politician,
> The emigrant and the exile . . the criminal that stood in the box,
> He who has been famous, and he who shall be famous after today,
> The stammerer . . . . the wellformed . . the wasted or feeble person.
>   (lines 42–45; ellipses in original)

This cannot be described as simply a series of metaphors for the self. If that were the case, the vehicles (both here and in many of Whitman's catalogs) would clearly overwhelm and jeopardize their tenor. The implicit hierarchy between vehicle and tenor is, in fact, what is sacrificed here—the "I," no longer privileged, becomes the site of a circulation of different roles and identities.

Especially liberating, perhaps, is the fluidity of gender identity, as gender oppositions (actor/actress) disappear; the male speaker is now

> . . . she who adorned herself and folded her hair expectantly,
> My truant lover has come and it is dark.

Double yourself and receive me darkness,
Receive me and my lover too . . . . he will not let me go without him.

I roll myself upon you as a bed . . . . I resign myself to the dusk.
                                        (lines 46–50; ellipses in original)

The shifting pronouns – from "He who has been famous" to "she who adorned herself" – leave the first person's gender unclear. As a result, the desire expressed may be either homo- or heterosexual; there is, at this point, no differentiation between them.

Beyond this, the passage is full of images of physical folding, doubling, and turning: just as the woman has "folded her hair," so she calls on the night to "double" itself (either fold over or multiply) to receive and enclose the lovers. Physical shapes and boundaries seem to break down in the metaphorical fusion of the lovers and in the speaker's rolling him- or herself upon the darkness as if it were a tangible physical object. He or she then "resign[s] myself to the dusk," a surrender of identity that occurs in a half-lit, marginal time and space, before, finally, some lines later, "fad[ing] away" (line 59).

What the poem offers us, then, is a movement from detached, individual movement ("I wander all night") to an inclusive, participatory fusion with the things and people encountered. Such a flux of continual identification and reidentification means the disintegration of a stable or bounded observing self. There is no longer a poet/observer who can stand aside from the object to represent it. Seeing and becoming are one and the same, as the barrier between subject and object disappears, and consciousness even seems to surpass its own limits:

A shroud I see – and I am the shroud . . . . I wrap a body and lie in the coffin;
It is dark here underground . . . . it is not evil or pain here . . . . it is blank
   here, for reasons. (lines 77–78; ellipses in original)

In its final sections, the poem moves outward from the individual and away from the first person, toward the political and social in a series of flowing, enfolding catalogs:

Elements merge in the night . . . . ships make tacks in the dreams . . . . the
   sailor sails . . . . the exile returns home,

> The fugitive returns unharmed . . . . the immigrant is back beyond months
> and years. (lines 142–43; ellipses in original)

Merging is here a reunification, a homecoming or return to the communal. And foremost among the elements brought together are the figures
mentioned earlier, as the poem turns back to re-enclose its own elements:

> The actor and actress . . those through with their parts and those waiting to
> commence,
> The affectionate boy, the husband and wife, the voter, the nominee that is
> chosen and the nominee that has failed,
> The great already known, and the great anytime after today,
> The stammerer, the sick, the perfectformed, the homely,
> The criminal that stood in the box, the judge that sat and sentenced him, the
> fluent lawyers, the jury, the audience. (lines 152–56; ellipsis in original)

The catalog ranges across categories – political, familial, legal – equalizing
power relations in each:

> . . . they are averaged now . . . . one is no better than the other,
> The night and sleep have likened them and restored them.
>   (lines 160–61; ellipsis in original)

The inclusive activity of the poet, the "averaging" and "likening" performed by the poem, is profoundly restorative:

> The breath of the boy goes with the breath of the man . . . . friend is inarmed
> by friend,
> The scholar kisses the teacher and the teacher kisses the scholar . . . . the
> wronged is made right,
> The call of the slave is one with the master's call . . . . and the master salutes
> the slave,
> The felon steps forth from the prison . . . . the insane becomes sane . . . . the
> suffering of sick persons is relieved. (lines 186–89; ellipses in original)

The list sweeps away distinctions of status and power, those between
teacher and scholar, jailor and felon, master and slave. In this segment
of *Leaves of Grass,* then, the innovation of Whitman's poetic form corresponds to a radical or visionary political content. Whitman's democratic
vision emerges from a fusion that replaces representation and redefines

the self as the site of a process or movement rather than a fixed point of origin.

As I have said, however, the poem's structure as dream vision does in some ways limit its claims for democratic and redemptive force. The darkness of Whitman's poem goes beyond Hawthorne's moonlight in that it radically transforms and fuses objects rather than just altering them. But this, like the street theater of "My Kinsman, Major Molineux," is a nighttime phenomenon only. It describes a new discourse between master and slave, but leaves unclear what will become of that discourse, or the power relations it expresses, in the light of day. The poem remains at the level of abstract proclamation, without embodying its claims in particular actions or historical moments. And it ends with the idea of a cyclical return rather than an advance into a transformed or revolutionary future.

"New York Dissected"

There would seem to be two ways to break out of such literary constraints, to move beyond cyclical closure into a more direct engagement with the political. The first would be for Whitman to return to journalistic prose, and the second, to adopt a more open, even more revolutionary poetic stance. In a sense, Whitman pursues both routes, and a look at his journalism of the period may help to highlight the more thoroughgoing radicalism of the poetry.

In July and August 1856, between the first and second editions of *Leaves,* he wrote a series of pieces for *Life Illustrated* under the title "New York Dissected." His topics included the city's July Fourth celebration, the need for improved middle- and working-class housing, life on the city streets, and a visit to an impounded slave ship.

In these prose pieces, as in the poems and notebooks, Whitman's descriptions habitually move toward lists and catalogs. In "Broadway," he surveys the changing composition of the crowd as the day progresses, beginning with day laborers going to work at 5:00 A.M., followed by shop girls, then clerks, and, finally, their employers. Both laborers and clerks are described through lists of objects; the laborers are "uniformed in brick-dusty shirts and overalls, battered hats, and shoes white or burnt with lime, armed with pick, spade, trowel, or hod, and with a complex tin pail that holds drink, dinner and dessert in safe but separate neighborhood."[29] The "downtown clerks," on the other hand, are a "jaunty crew": "a slender and round-shouldered generation, of minute leg, chalky face, and hollow chest—but trig and prim in great glow of shiny boots, clean shirts—sometimes, just now, of extraordinary patterns, as if overrun with bugs!—tight pantaloons, straps, which seem coming a little into fashion again, startling cravats, and hair all soaked and 'slickery' with sickening oils" (120). The formal features of these descriptions may be those of his poetic catalogs, but the underlying objective seems quite different. The observer maintains a fixed position, apart from all these groups. And the primary goal is to distinguish types and categories from each other, not to connect or fuse them.

This is even more obvious in "Street Yarn," published a week later, which moves from types to individuals, one of whom is Whitman himself. In terms of appearance, he places himself among the laborers, as a "[t]all, large, rough-looking man, in a journeyman carpenter's uniform": "Coarse, sanguine complexion; strong, bristly, grizzled beard; singular eyes, of a semi-transparent, indistinct light blue, and with that sleepy look that comes when the lid rests half way down over the pupil; careless, lounging gait. Walt Whitman, the sturdy, self-conscious microscosmic, prose-poetical author of that incongruous hash of mud and gold—'Leaves of Grass'" (130). This is, obviously, a pose like that of the engraving that opens the "prose-poetical" *Leaves*. In one sense, Whitman is including himself in the crowd, but he does so by reemphasizing himself as an individual and author. Given that *Life Illustrated* was published by Fowler and Wells, in whose shop *Leaves of Grass* could be purchased, it is also a bit of shameless (and all too characteristic) commercial puffery.[30]

Interestingly enough, it is in the most openly political of these pieces that Whitman adopts the technique of identification with and involvement in the scene he describes. "The Slave Trade" begins with an explanation of how ships are purchased and outfitted in New York for carrying slaves from Africa to the Caribbean. Its most powerful section, however, is the closing one, in which Whitman visits an impounded slaver in the

Brooklyn Navy Yard. He descends into the "narrow den" of the hold, in which

> the black wretches [would] have been stowed, laid together "spoon-fashion," half lying, half sideways, and close in one another's laps, in ranges across the deck—to smother, groan, and perhaps to perish, in the hot pestilential atmosphere, during the passage across the Atlantic.
>
> We look about and imagine that we hear the barbarous gibberish of the miserable chattels, lamenting their savage homes, and wondering to each other whither their white captors are carrying them. Perhaps in desperation they attempt to rise upon the crew. They are quieted either by promiscuous musket volleys fired down the hatchway, or by a few pounds of tacks plentifully dispersed among them, so that the motion of a limb in the dense crowd inflicts smarting punctured wounds. We gladly drive away the horrid vision, and glance once more about the empty hold, the spars, the watery-looking weeds, sprouting in the dirt, close to the kelson, about the narrow, littered deck, and leave the crime-stained craft. (114)

The passage begins at a distance from the "black wretches" whose speech is just a "barbarous gibberish," but by the end it is vividly imagining the pain of physical constraint and torture, with both observer and slave inhabiting the same present tense. And it is no coincidence that the shift is one from representational difference and failure ("gibberish") to a powerful and immediate identification with physical sensation and suffering.

If the editorial "we" is a gesture of rhetorical authority in relation to the reader, it also moves both narrator and reader toward a collective identification with a communal or group experience. This seems, in a way, less a "vision" than a keen imagining of physical experience. Again and again in Whitman's work, and especially in "Song of Myself," bodily presence and touch simply overwhelms both sight and speech.

The key point here is that this is a strikingly unusual moment in "New York Dissected," whose sketches are based on a carefully established observational and narrative distance from their subjects. Fusion or identification with them is, on the other hand, essential to the poetry, to both "The Sleepers" and, in even more extreme form, "Song of Myself." Whitman the journalist and Whitman the poet work in the same social setting and marketplace, and both forms of discourse are economically and so-cially grounded. But Whitman claims a far greater formal and representa-tional freedom for himself as a poet, and the result is a far different—and far more subversive—response to that context. That subversive or oppo-sitional force is hinted at in "The Sleepers" and worked out more fully and explicitly in the poem that will become "Song of Myself."

"Song of Myself"

"What I experience or portray shall go from my composition without a shred of my composition," Whitman insists in his preface to *Leaves of Grass* (13). In other words, the poet leaves no trace of himself (his bodily or psychological composition) in his work and no sign of his own creative effort (his act of composition). But the first poem in the 1855 *Leaves* (later "Song of Myself") seems to announce the very opposite:

> I celebrate myself,
> And what I assume you shall assume,
> For every atom belonging to me as good belongs to you. (lines 1–3)

Not only is the poet's work foregrounded from the very start ("cele-brate"), but he also functions as the poem's "subject"—in not one but two different senses: its language emerges from his subjectivity, and he also serves as the poem's topic. This grandiose and contradictory self-assertion is only an opening gambit, however; the speaker's double po-sition as "subject" contains the elements of its own dissolution. If "I" and "myself" are not the same, and, as line 4 suggests ("I loafe and invite my soul"), "my soul" is yet another entity, then the self to be "celebrated" is hardly a stable or integral one.

The second line seems to move from self-assertion to rhetorical coer-cion ("you shall assume"), but it is, after all, a position of equality that is being thrust upon the reader. And the different possible meanings of "assume" make it a rather complex process: "to assume" can mean "to take for granted," "to take or put on [an identity]," or "to appropri-ate or accept [a debt]." Knowledge, identity, and property or possession are all put into question here: if "you" can assume the same identity or obligations as "I" can, then the two can no longer be so easily distinguished.[31]

This instability is only heightened by the claim of line 3: "every atom belonging to me as good belongs to you." This may be just hyperbole, no more than an offer to share possessions. But if we take it at face value, Whitman is seen to be raising two crucial and related issues, one of selfhood and the other of "belonging" or possession. What is it that can be said to "belong" to me? Is it just my "property," or is it all those things or qualities that can be described as "proper to" me? Whitman's choice of the words "every atom" rather than "every thing" suggests that he means the latter. But how can "every atom" of my being also belong to someone else? Here Whitman's qualifying words "as good belongs" come into play, opening the possibility of a different, nonexclusive form of possession or identity, in which there would be no clear line between things and less tangible "properties," and no fixed barrier between "I" and "you."

What the opening stanza does, in a way, is analyze the fluid, permeable self that we have already seen in "The Sleepers." But "Song of Myself" goes further, for it undermines the rhetorical hierarchy—and, in fact, even the very difference—between writer and reader. By the second stanza, the celebratory "I" of the opening has modulated into a comparatively passive one: "I lean and loafe at my ease . . . . observing a spear of summer grass" (line 5; ellipsis in original). This, perhaps, is the pose depicted on the frontispiece—that of an observer or reader rather than a writer. Whitman's reader is himself perusing "leaves of grass" at this moment, of course; speaker and reader are thus linked rather than opposed, joined in a shared act of observation.

The poem and, in a sense, the volume as a whole, begins with this destabilized and fluid subject position, one that can be occupied by both poet and reader.[32] The opposition between writing and reading no longer serves a necessary mediating function, for the neutral territory of the poem includes writer and reader. The booming, assertive voice of the poem's opening has not claimed the authority to "represent" reality for the reader; instead, it has announced a surrender of poetic privilege, to be replaced by the egalitarian and democratic poetics of the catalog.

As the title page had suggested, the "voice" of the poem cannot be assumed to be self-identical and exclusive, claiming the poem as its singular product or property. Both "self" and poem act instead as neutral sites or spaces, points of fusion and transformation:

> Through me many long dumb voices,
> Voices of the interminable generations of slaves,
> Voices of prostitutes and of deformed persons,
> Voices of the diseased and despairing, and of thieves and dwarfs,
> . . . .
> Through me forbidden voices,
> Voices of sexes and lusts . . . . voices veiled, and I remove the veil,
> Voices indecent by me clarified and transfigured.
>
> > (lines 509–12, 518–20; ellipsis in original)

Here, the self seems to exist solely as vessel or transmitter, but the transmission is not a merely passive process. Removing veils may "clarify" what is spoken behind them, and allowing "long dumb voices" to speak (or allowing passage to that speech) also "transfigures" them.

Reality is thus articulated through the self, but it is defined as something that exists before and beyond representation or reproduction: "The atmosphere is not a perfume . . . it has no taste of the distillation . . . . it is odorless" (line 9; ellipses in original). It is not something outside the self, an object of perception, but a state in which the self participates. "The atmosphere" becomes one with "The smoke of my own breath," and then with "My respiration and inspiration . . . . the beating of my heart . . . . the passing of blood and air through my lungs," integral to the body itself (lines 13, 15; ellipses in original). Finally, in "The sound of the belched words of my voice . . . . words loosed to the eddies of the wind," the poem, too, is recast as a natural object, not restrained or ordered but "loosed" (line 17; ellipsis in original).

As Whitman's language insists throughout this passage, this "self" is not an abstract entity but an utterly physical one. The poem is not described as a written text, after all, but as a song, an ongoing act of speech. Voices pass through the poem, their words dependent upon the immediate presence of their speakers.[33]

Whitman's demand for immediate contact—between writer and reader, subjects and objects—also appears in his emphasis on the physical, on the speaker's bodily presence:

> Encompass worlds but never try to encompass me,
> I crowd your noisiest talk by looking toward you.
>
> Writing and talk do not prove me,
> I carry the plenum of proof and every thing else in my face,
> With the hush of my lips I confound the topmost skeptic. (lines 579–83)

His look alone establishes a physical, spatial dominance, "crowding" speech. "The plenum of proof" is physical, embodied in the silent face and untouchable by "writing and talk."

This version of identity—fluid and permeable but at the same time defiantly embodied and physical—is hardly the product of pastoral solitude and reflection. Rather, I would suggest, it springs from a specifically urban consciousness. The pace and density of the antebellum city (what M. Wynn Thomas calls the "urgent presentness" of its "jostling coexistence of things and lives") would have generated just such an awareness of both the physical self and the "crowding" of its surrounding space.[34] Whitman's New York was a center for both commerce and immigration, a space of continual circulation and contact for goods and persons alike. In the crush of activity on its streets, the observer would be simultaneously aware of both the physical presence of others as individuals and of the mass of the crowd as a continually moving, changing collectivity.[35] Beyond this, what Mary Ryan calls "[t]he kaleidoscopic stage of antebellum street life" made possible precisely the kind of destabilized interplay of identities and voices that Whitman envisions here.[36]

Whitman's insistence on the physical has a political content as well, I would argue: it seeks to counter the economic drive toward quantification and abstraction, the reduction of both individuals and the living presence of the crowd to mere labor power. The members of his crowd are, paradoxically, at once identical and incommensurable, resistant to the process of commodification and exchange.

Whitman's poetry, based on a comparable flow of objects through the space of the text and into immediate contact with the reader, requires a new way of reading. It, like the crowd, cannot be "reckoned" (line 22) or measured in distinct and separate units; the length of its lines is determined not by conventions of meter or rhythm, but by the movement of the voice itself. "Have you practised so long to learn to read?" Whitman asks, "Have you felt so proud to get at the meaning of poems?" (lines 23–24). The "meaning" of this poem is not an interior point or object to be neatly quantified and possessed.

Whitman's plans for the reader are much different:

> Do you guess I have some intricate purpose?
> Well I have . . . . for the April rain has, and the mica on the side of a rock has.
>
> Do you take it I would astonish?
> Does the daylight astonish? or the early redstart twittering though the woods?
> Do I astonish more than they? (lines 381–85; ellipsis in original)

The poem is to exist as a natural object does, in and for itself, prior to any system of exchange or representation – not as the rhetorical product of a specific authorial intent. The reader is not asked to read, but simply to remain "in" the poem, and thus "with," in the presence of, the poet: "Stop this day and night with me and you shall possess the origin of all poems" (line 25). The result will not be the transmission of an object from writer to reader, but the latter's renewed "possession" of the poetic principle itself, the generative or creative force already within him.[37]

This is, then, a poetry that aspires to a condition of complete and natural transparency:

> You shall no longer take things at second or third hand . . . . nor look through
>   the eyes of the dead . . . . nor feed on the spectres in books,
> You shall not look through my eyes either, nor take things from me,
> You shall listen to all sides and filter them from yourself.
>
> (lines 27–29; ellipses in original)

The mediating function of both poem and poet are to be transcended, with speaker and reader equally "present" and "in possession of" its receptive and generative space.

Here we have the essential Whitmanian gesture, the opening of the poem to the reader and to the world, in the movement of democratic inclusion promised by his preface. Inclusion without selection or ranking—this will be the principle behind the catalogs to come. Lawrence Buell describes "catalogue rhetoric" as an "inherently 'democratic' technique," whose "prosodic equalitarianism" means that "each line or image is of equal weight in the ensemble; each is a unit unto itself"; in Whitman, he suggests, "catalogue poetry" appears as a kind of "political action."[38] And the inclusiveness of Whitman's catalogs will in turn generate a sense of collective or communal identity, giving the poet access to an ongoing tradition of popular opposition and revolt.

The process begins with language itself:

> The blab of the pave . . . . the tires of carts and sluff of bootsoles and talk of
>   the promenaders,
> The heavy omnibus, the driver with his interrogating thumb, the clank of the
>   shod horses on the granite floor,
> The carnival of sleighs, the clinking and shouted jokes and pelts of snowballs;
> The hurrahs for popular favorites . . . . the fury of roused mobs.
>
> (lines 146–49; ellipses in original)

Here are the speech, sounds, and labor of the urban crowd, ranging from jokes to oaths and blows, from individual exclamations to the collective expressions of "hurrahs." "What living and buried speech is always vibrating here," Whitman exclaims (line 157). The words of the poem emerge, not from a domestic interior, or even from a single individualized scene, but from the mass, as words "of the modern," words "en masse," as he later calls them (line 484).

The city of Whitman's poem is lower Manhattan and its working-class and commercial districts, not the midtown of middle- and upper-class residences whose development began in the 1840s and '50s.[39] The congestion and disorder of street scenes like this one would have been a source of particular anxiety for New Yorkers of the period. Imposing order on dirty, crime-ridden streets was a major campaign theme for both reform and nativist politicians.[40] But Whitman turns his back on the enclosed and ordered space of bourgeois domesticity, a realm detached both psychologically and geographically from the world of work. His city is defiantly public and communal in both its work and recreation. And by taking the noise and latent violence of the crowd as a point of origin for his poem, Whitman positions it within a public and contested space, aligning it with both immigrant and working classes.

As the passage continues, it moves beyond just an immersion in the mass, toward the criminalized and rejected, those "long dumb voices,"

> . . . howls restrained by decorum,
> Arrests of criminals, slights, adulterous offers made, acceptances, rejections
> with convex lips. (lines 157–58)

Whitman later puts forward such inclusiveness as his explicit intent:

> I will not have a single person slighted or left away,
> The keptwoman and sponger and thief are hereby invited . . . .
> the heavy-lipped slave is invited . . . . the venerealee is invited,
> There shall be no difference between them and the rest.
> (lines 374–76; ellipses in original)

The poem absorbs individuals in order to annihilate the differences between them in a process of democratic leveling and fusion that turns margin into poetic center.[41] In a sense, Whitman's poem takes on the attributes of the street itself, as a space through which all classes, genders, and races pass in turn.

It is in this context that the reader encounters the poem's first extended catalog, in section 15. It begins with an explicit link between artist and worker:

> The pure contralto sings in the organloft,
> The carpenter dresses his plank . . . . the tongue of his foreplane whistles its
> wild ascending lisp. (lines 257–58)

The connection here is not between two products—the song and the plank—but between two physical acts, each of which generates a sound.

The "whistle" of the foreplane's "tongue" as it moves across the wood makes physical labor expressive in the same way as high art.

Eight lines later, Whitman makes his refusal to privilege his own work even more explicit, when he includes an image of a graying printer not unlike himself:

> The lunatic is carried at last to the asylum a confirmed case,
> He will never sleep any more as he did in the cot in his mother's bedroom;
> The jour printer with gray head and gaunt jaws works at his case,
> He turns his quid of tobacco, his eyes get blurred with the manuscript;
> The malformed limbs are tied to the anatomist's table,
> What is removed drops horribly in a pail;
> The quadroon girl is sold at the stand . . . . the drunkard nods by the barroom
>   stove. (lines 266–72; ellipsis in original)

The pair of lines used to describe the printer link him to the lunatic, as does the repetition of "case." And the manipulation of letters as physical objects in the printer's case then connects to the amputation of parts of the body, a body that is even more fully objectified as the auctioned slave body in line 272.

The printer's work fuses the mechanical and the artistic–as a poet printing his own work, Whitman can be, in a sense, both contralto and carpenter.[42] Hawthorne's photographer Holgrave may occupy a comparable middle ground, but *The House of the Seven Gables* does not reject such categories as directly and explicitly as Whitman does here. Whitman places himself as writer/printer among an array of individual laborers in an effort to bring the bodily reality of manual labor–free or slave–into a discourse that had systematically excluded and devalued it.[43]

In a way, this juxtaposition also registers the precarious position of the independent artisan in an era of rapid mechanization and industrial transformation. By the 1850s, the shift from a system of artisanal production to commodified wage labor had been underway for half a century.[44] American publishing, in particular, had been transformed by the introduction of steam and cylinder presses, which led to a new era of cheap, mass-produced books and pamphlets.[45] Whitman's focus, however, is on the individual printer setting manuscript into type, not on the finished book as either aesthetic object or commodity. The printer is given no special mediating or central role here, but Whitman's listing of occupations, workers, and slaves does represent a gesture of resistance to the alienating and impersonal forces of the capitalist marketplace.

All of the actions within this catalog occur in the present, presumably simultaneously, and all are placed in a single, forty-line sentence.[46] None is given primacy, either temporal or syntactic. Early in the poem, Whitman's speaker had described himself as "Apart from the pulling and hauling," "Both in and out of the game" (lines 66, 60). But now, the individualized and detached observer of "New York Dissected" has been replaced by the printer, "one of an average unending procession" (line 964).

No one of these figures is set apart as the bearer of special symbolic value, neither "The cleanhaired Yankee girl" nor "The opium eater," "the President" nor the "fare-collector" (lines 290, 301, 305, 309):

> . . . one and all tend inward to me, and I tend outward to them,
> And such as it is to be of these more or less I am. (lines 324–25)

None of these individuals occupies a fixed position; all are in flux, "tending toward" the speaker or each other.[47] Both speaker and poem are "of them"–both equal to them rather than superior, and also composed or made of them.

This is what it means for "Walt Whitman" to call himself "an American, one of the roughs, a kosmos" (line 499). What he claims for himself is participation in a fluctuating collective experience and identity. The fluctuation or circulation of subjectivity is what enables Whitman to claim an immediate presence for the objects and persons in the poem, rather than settling for a nominally representative (but inescapably privileged) individual selfhood. And it is, in turn, this democratic and collective voice that gives the poetry access to a collective social and historical experience.

The move from present-tense catalog into history begins in section 33. The importance of this section is implied by its echoes of earlier moments in the poem, allusions suggesting that it marks an advance on them: "Now

I know it is true what I guessed at; / What I guessed when I loafed on the grass" (lines 709–10). What the speaker now "knows," and the direction in which the poem now moves, is historical and political.

"I am afoot with my vision," Whitman proclaims, as he opens a stanza that sweeps across the nation in a single, eighty-line sentence (line 714). It moves, not just through the night, as in "The Sleepers," but through day and night indiscriminately. These three pages are structured almost solely by the repeated words or phrases with which Whitman begins his lines, most often, "where," "over," or "pleased with." Commas, semicolons, and ellipses seem to be used interchangeably–to signal pauses rather than to establish syntactical order. Insofar as this is a single sentence, it does not build by modifying an initial statement; nor does it lead up to a periodic close.

The first-person emerges only once in this catalog, appearing in a single subordinate clause (line 753), before the sentence core finally emerges in the stanza's closing line, "I tread day and night such roads" (line 796). Indeed, the first person has no apparent unifying or organizing function here; "I" seems to be little more than a neutral place marker or device.

A page later, the implications of such neutrality become apparent, as "I" first take the bridegroom's place and then the wife's:

I turn the bridegroom out of bed and stay with the bride myself,
And tighten her all night to my thighs and lips.

My voice is the wife's voice, the screech by the rail of the stairs,
They fetch my man's body up dripping and drowned. (lines 814–17)

These shifts in gender set up a crucial ambiguity in line 817: "my man's body" may be the body of the man who belongs to his wife; or it may be the speaker's own, now male, body. In the latter case, the speaker has passed beyond, and now looks back on, his own death.

Three lines after this transition, the past tense appears, as the speaker claims to "understand" "How the skipper saw the crowded and rudderless wreck of the steamship, and death chasing it up and down the storm" (lines 818, 820). "All this I swallow and it tastes good," the speaker says:

> . . . . I like it well, and it becomes mine,
> I am the man . . . . I suffered . . . . I was there.
>   (lines 826–27; ellipses in original)

This is the next step after the abolition of distinctions between writer and reader, subject and object. Whitman's speaker does not simply identify with different figures as objects of representation; he becomes them, making them immediately present in the text. "I do not ask the wounded person how he feels . . . . I myself become the wounded person" (line 841; ellipsis in original).

It is, significantly, a series of "martyrs" (line 828) or victims that now enters the poem:

> I am the hounded slave . . . . I wince at the bite of the dogs,
> Hell and despair are upon me . . . . crack and again crack the marksmen,
> I clutch the rails of the fence . . . . my gore dribs thinned with the ooze of my
>   skin. (lines 833–36; ellipses in original)

As in "New York Dissected," physical suffering is the ground for identification, rather than a more abstract conception of enslavement. The fugitive slave is succeeded by "the mashed fireman with breastbone broken" (line 843) and then by the victims of a military bombardment.

We have traveled, then, across the American landscape of the 1850s and into a direct experience of the violence of slavery; and that experience of suffering carries the poem back in time, toward the American revolutionary past. Slaves, injured workers, and revolutionary soldiers are integrated into a single tradition.

Section 34 describes an incident from Texas's 1836 war for independence from Mexico—the execution of Colonel James Fannin and his troops after their surrender at Goliad. It is a carefully chosen example, one that combines revolution with victimization rather than aggression.[48] Whitman emphasizes a particular aspect of the conflict—the suffering of the mass of ordinary soldiers:

> Large, turbulent, brave, handsome, generous, proud and affectionate,
> Bearded, sunburnt, dressed in the free costume of hunters,
> Not a single one over thirty years of age. (lines 874–76)

This is not a story of heroic individual acts, but of the ordinary men of Whitman's catalogs. Fannin is only described once, as "Their colonel" (line 870).[49]

But Whitman has not yet fully connected his poetic present with the historical past. The incident is given a formal storytelling frame: "Hear now the tale of a jetblack sunrise" (line 866). The speaker cannot tell the story of the Alamo, he says, because no one survived—he thus acknowledges his historical distance and dependence on other accounts for access to events.

When he moves back further, to the Revolution, although he continues to use the past tense, his narrative becomes a first-person one, an oral performance specifically contrasted with written accounts:

> Did you read in the seabooks of the oldfashioned frigate-fight?
> Did you learn who won by the light of the moon and stars?
>
> Our foe was no skulk in his ship, I tell you. (lines 890–92)

"I" tell of my own experience here, but the first-person plural of "our foe" also generalizes that experience, for the British are, in a sense, the foes of all American readers. More than just heirs to a revolutionary tradition, we become participants in it.

Whitman's extended example is the battle between the Bonhomme Richard and Serapis, in which both ships were crippled.[50] The climax, in section 36, does at last move into the present tense, but it leaves John Paul Jones behind, describing instead a scene of utter devastation and ruin, ranging from "Formless stacks of bodies and bodies by themselves . . . . dabs of flesh upon the masts and spars," to

> Delicate sniffs of the seabreeze . . . . smells of sedgy grass and fields by the
>   shore . . . . death-messages given in charge to survivors,
> The hiss of the surgeon's knife and the gnawing teeth of his saw,
> The wheeze, the cluck, the swash of falling blood . . . . the short wild scream,
>   the long dull tapering groan,
> These so . . . . these irretrievable. (lines 926, 929–32; ellipses in original)

The point of greatest immediacy, in grammatical person and in tense, coincides with the most physically immediate of descriptions. Once again, experience is rendered most forcefully in terms of the body, the past made present in bodily suffering that exceeds even language itself. Just as the body disintegrates in line 931, so Whitman's description breaks down in line 932 ("These so . . . ."). The ineradicable distance between past and present is thrust sharply back upon both poet and reader—in the irretrievability of the lost leg, the unrecoverability of the once whole body.

This is the poem's most extreme immersion in the American past, its physical intensity overwhelming any temporal or narrative progression: "Oh Christ!" Whitman exclaims, "My fit is mastering me!" (line 933). Both poet and poem have been seized, "mastered," by the force of that collective historical experience.

The poem moves away from revolutionary narrative, back toward the present, through the speech of figures from earlier eras ("What the rebel said . . . / What the savage at the stump . . ." [lines 933, 934]), as Whitman joins them to the feelings of nineteenth-century observers:

> What stills the traveler come to the vault at Mount Vernon,
> What sobers the Brooklyn boy as he looks down the shores of the Wallabout
>   and remembers the prison ships,
>
> .   .   .   .
>
> I become any presence or truth of humanity here. (lines 936–37, 941)

Past acts are linked to present responses, all forming part of an "average unending procession" (line 964) that includes both poet and, as we shall see, reader as well. It is a progression that begins in the prison and hospital and carries within it beggars and risen corpses, "numberless gangs," as it flows across the American landscape (line 970). If the poem's emphasis, one hundred lines earlier, had been on surpassing or overcoming temporal limits, now its focus is on geographical and physical barriers in the present:

> We walk the roads of Ohio and Massachusetts and Virginia and Wisconsin
>   and New York and New Orleans and Texas and Montreal and San
>   Francisco and Charleston and Savannah and Mexico,
> Inland and by the seacoast and boundary lines . . . . and we pass the boundary
>   lines. (lines 965–66; ellipsis in original)

The catalog overfills line 965, leaping across the ellipsis of line 966 as it overwhelms both physical and poetic borders.

In line 1050, the poet hears

> . . . . A call in the midst of the crowd,
>   My own voice, orotund sweeping and final.
>   (lines 1050–51; ellipsis in original)

The voice is identified as his, but only after being heard as another's, or, perhaps, being appropriated from the crowd itself. The crowd may be its point of origin, or the context on which it depends for its existence, but the individual and the collective are not to be separated here.[51]

Both poet and "performer" (line 1054) stand among their audiences, not apart from them; they emanate or emerge from the mass, as in Whitman's preface (15). David Reynolds has described antebellum American culture as profoundly "participatory," with both theatrical and political crowds responding vociferously (and sometimes violently) to speeches on the stage or on the stump.[52] Sean Wilentz notes that scripts for minstrel shows at the working-class Bowery Theater were kept deliberately loose to anticipate and include such audience responses.[53] Theaters and lecture halls, like the streets, became spaces of interchange and improvisational response, as both speakers and audiences joined in the production of a democratic and communal culture.

So too are Whitman's readers to participate in the creation of the poem: "Song of Myself" circles back on itself, returning to the relation between poet and reader – in order to refashion it anew. The tables have been turned; it is not the reader who will "possess" Whitman or the text, but vice versa:

> I am not to be denied . . . . I compel . . . . I have stores plenty and to spare,
> And any thing I have I bestow.
>
> I do not ask who you are . . . . that is not important to me,
> You can do nothing but what I will infold you.
>
> I have embraced you, and henceforth possess you to myself,
> And when you rise in the morning you will find what I tell you is so.
>   (lines 995–98, 1013–14; ellipses in original)

Bestowing, enfolding, embracing, possessing – giving and taking cannot be clearly distinguished here, and neither can poet and reader. Their "possessions" and roles are no longer distinct or mutually exclusive: "[M]y steps drag behind yours yet go before them" (line 972).

By this point,

> It is you talking just as much as myself . . . . I act as the tongue of you,
> It was tied in your mouth . . . . in mine it begins to be loosened.
> > (lines 1244–45; ellipses in original)

Whitman has even begun to relinquish poetic authority itself:

> You are also asking me questions, and I hear you;
> I answer that I cannot answer . . . . you must find out for yourself.
> > (lines 1220–21; ellipsis in original)

Finally, he prepares to surrender the role of speaker: "Listener up there! Here you . . . . what have you to confide to me?" (line 1311; ellipsis in original).

Just as the poem has been carried upon the speaker's breath, it has become part of the atmosphere, and Whitman can "depart as air" (line 1327). With his diffusion into and throughout nature, the "I" with which the poem began has been replaced by the searching, voyaging "you" of the reader.

"Song of Myself" thus breaks down pronominal distinctions, with the first person "I" reduced to its linguistic essence as "shifter," or indicator of the position of speaker. And that position is not apart from, but rather a part of the endless circulation that is the poem's form and content. The point at which the text breaks off is that at which the poem is given over to the voices and possession of its collective readership.

What "Song of Myself" enacts, then, is a democratic dispersion of poetic authority, until that authority is coextensive with, vested in – and indistinguishable from – the poem's subject, "the United States them-selves." In refashioning the "self" as the site and product of continuous interchange, Whitman projects a vision of democratic collectivity and community as well.

⌐

FIVE

1856

and After

In the 1856 edition of *Leaves of Grass,* Whitman gives its longest poem ("Song of Myself") the title "Poem of Walt Whitman, an American."[1] The phrasing still preserves a duality: "Walt Whitman" is both the poem's source and subject. But it is now classed as a poem, a linguistic artifact that comes between Whitman and the reader. So, too, where America was declared to be itself a poem in 1855, now "an American" and a "poem" seem to be quite different things. From the very outset of this edition – in the table of contents – poetic language is already granted less power than before, for it is now distinguished from its referents, confined to a separate category of the linguistic.

If the poetry of 1855 simultaneously asserts and enacts the fusion of reader, poet, and world, the poems of 1856 seek only to connect them. Rather than simply revealing a democratic collectivity as sheer unmediated presence, these poems must construct that collectivity in words.[2] But such notions of connection and construction require the preservation – indeed, the acceptance – of difference and mediation.[3] In this sense, at least, the volume marks a significant retreat from, or even a critique of, Whitman's position of a year before.

Many critics have described a shift toward darkness or conservatism in Whitman's work, beginning in either the 1860–61 version of *Leaves* or his wartime and postwar poems.[4] The movement I am suggesting, however, is a more gradual one, a trend that starts in 1856 and deepens in a more continuous fashion through the later work. As American cultural and political discourse broke apart in the later 1850s, Whitman's poetry lost both its unifying force and visionary confidence. By 1865 and "Memories of President Lincoln," his work had been almost entirely reconceived, as a poetry now dependent upon absence and loss, whose politics imply the acceptance of hierarchy and difference as preconditions for the poet's role as representative national figure.

The differences between the first two editions are perhaps clearest in Whitman's prose addendum to the second edition, his "reply" to a congratulatory letter from Ralph Waldo Emerson. Whitman's "letter" is in some ways analogous to the 1855 preface, but it is now detached from the poetry and displaced into a separate section, headed "Correspondence," at the end of the book. Just as the poems are given separate titles in this edition, conspicuously labeled as "Poem of . . . ," so too are prose—and politics—explicitly separated from poetry.[5]

Whitman no longer sees his poems as radical acts in themselves; he draws a contrast between representation and revolution, but locates both America and *Leaves of Grass* within the realm of the former. "Just so long," he says, "as no revolutionists advance, and are backed by the people, sweeping off the swarms of routine representatives, officers in power, book-makers, teachers, ecclesiastics, politicians, just so long, I perceive, do they who are in power fairly represent that country, and remain of use."[6] Linguistic and political representation are once again grouped together as targets of the revolutionary enterprise. But although Whitman calls for representation to be "superseded," the task is now consigned to some future moment (736).

It is not so much that Whitman is disillusioned with writing, but that he sees it in far more limited terms: "I much enjoy making poems. Other work I have set for myself to do, to meet people and The States face to face, to confront them with an American rude tongue; but the work of my life is making poems" (732–33). "Making poems" is "work," the crafting of objects. But to "meet people . . . face to face" is a different kind of work, a verbal confrontation based on the "rude tongue" rather than the written text. A year earlier, these two activities had been fused in the notion of poetry as song, something as natural, effortless, and, perhaps, as necessary as breathing.

"Expressions do not yet serve," Whitman admits, "but that is getting ready, beyond what the earth has hitherto known, to take home the expression when they come, and to identify them with the populace of The States" (734). The visionary project of the 1855 *Leaves* is here restated, but clearly deferred, poetic practice reduced to prophetic promise.

1856: Expansion and Retrenchment

Such a retrenchment or reduction in Whitman's poetic aims is visible in the first of the new poems added to the 1856 *Leaves*, "Poem of Salutation" (later "Salut au Monde"). It is not, according to the title, an act of salutation in itself, but rather a poem of salutation – an altered and aestheticized version of such an act. It opens, not with a greeting to the reader or the world outside the text, but with a call to "Walt Whitman" (1:161). This initial voice, however, appears only in order to interpellate and briefly interrogate the poet; it soon vanishes, leaving "Walt" as the poem's sole speaker. Its final question – "Who are they you salute, and that one after another salute you?" (1:164) – is itself the final "salutation" that the poet will receive.

"Walt Whitman's" relation to things and persons outside himself is thus not through dialogue or interchange; it is almost exclusively through perception, through what "I hear" and "I see." The split between perceiver and object of perception is not overcome; it becomes, in fact, a primary structural element of the poem's central sections:

> I see the tracks of the rail-roads of the earth,
> I see them welding state to state, county to county, city to city, through North
> America,
> I see them in Great Britain, I see them in Europe,
> I see them in Asia and in Africa.
>
> I see the electric telegraphs of the earth,
> I see the filaments of the news of the wars, deaths, losses, gains, passions, of
> my race. (1:167)

The subject of these lines may be connection, but the first person does not simply initiate a flow of objects through the poem, as in the catalogs of 1855. Rather, its repetitive insertion breaks that flow into discrete and singular units, as in the prose descriptions of "New York Dissected," with each item "specified" (1:173)–detached from each other and from the poet.

Such distinctions and distances have their political implications also. The poet "hear[s] the wheeze of the slave-coffle, as the slaves march on," but he does not identify or merge with them, as in 1855 (1:164). He places "You dim-descended, black, divine-souled African on equal terms with me," but the insistent second person, even in the act of salutation, enacts a rhetorical and grammatical separation (1:172).

The closest the speaker comes to identification or merger is with places:

> I see the cities of the earth, and make myself at random a part of them,
> I am a real Londoner, Parisian, Viennese,
> I am a habitan of St. Petersburgh,
> I am of Adelaide, Sidney, Melbourne. (1:170)

But the section ends with renewed detachment: "I descend upon all those cities, and rise from them again" (1:171).

All in all, "Poem of Salutation" is still profoundly inclusive in both rhetoric and performance. But it addresses the individuals and groups it includes without ever giving them voice as well. Whitman has begun to move toward a claim of poetic privilege–of a place between his reader and the world, from which he "represents" and thus connects them to each other. It is from this point that he can "salute you," as he puts it, "for myself and for America" (1:173).

Such poetic connection–with both its visionary strengths and its limitations–is most fully thematized and performed by "Sun-Down Poem," later called "Crossing Brooklyn Ferry." The purpose of the ferry is, of course, physical linkage or connection, as it carries commuters between Manhattan and Brooklyn. In doing so, however, it moves across rather than with the flow of the East River—its connections and the poem's, unlike those of 1855, are made rather than given.

The poem's first section opens with the distinction between "I" and "you," as the speaker addresses the natural objects before him:

> Flood-tide of the river, flow on! I watch you, face to face!
> Clouds of the west! sun there half an hour high! I see you also face to face.
> (1:217)

The poet may begin by speaking to his own reflection, but this would seem unlikely in the moving water around an operating ferry. Rather, water and sun are given "faces" through the exercise of prosopopoeia or projection—a key term throughout the 1856 version of the poem.

When Whitman speaks of the "simple, compact, well-joined scheme—myself disintegrated, every one disintegrated, yet part of the scheme," this seems to suggest the fluid selfhood based in diffusion and unity that was characteristic of the 1855 *Leaves* (1:218). But there remain discrete units within this "scheme" ("every one") that are "joined" in "similitude" rather than fused in identity.

Indeed, it is simile that becomes the poem's dominant trope:

> I project myself, also I return—I am with you, and know how it is.
> Just as you feel when you look on the river and sky, so I felt,
> Just as any one of you is one of a living crowd, I was one of a crowd. (1:218)

The poet "projects himself" across time, but the distance traversed is continually reinscribed in the difference of tense, present vs. future or past vs. present. Whitman may be "with" his readers, but he does not claim to "become one with" them. The closest he can come is the parallelism and repetition of "just as."

"What is it, then, between us?" Whitman asks (1:220). The question has two answers, one positive and the other negative: time comes between writer and reader to separate them, but words—the poem itself—make a connection between them. The poem begins with Whitman in the "present" of 1856 ("I watch you") and its reader in the future ("you that shall cross . . . years hence"). But by the third section, that temporal relation has been revised; now the generations to come are given the present tense, and Whitman the past: "Just as you feel when you look on the river and sky, so I felt." The links between past, present, and future are created linguistically, in the poem's grammatical slippage between tenses. If the mediating function of language was denied in the poems of 1855, here it is obviously central.

To risk belaboring the obvious, such linkages still depend on the acceptance of temporal difference. The contrast with "Song of Myself" may, perhaps, be clearest in the catalog that takes up most of section 3 of "Crossing Brooklyn Ferry." It begins at sunset, as "the glistening yellow lit up" the bodies of the seagulls, and moves across the harbor, which is "growing dimmer and dimmer," until it reaches:

> On the neighboring shore the fires from the foundry chimneys burning high
>   and glaringly into the night,
> Casting their flicker of black, contrasted with wild red and yellow light, over
>   the tops of houses. (1:219, 220)

On one hand, the list is geographically limited in its scope; on the other, objects are not perceived and fused in a single present moment. They are, rather, individualized and listed—as the members of the Broadway crowd had been in "New York Dissected." The perception and cataloging of objects here takes time; the time of observation—here rendered as a series of discrete moments—parallels the temporality of both writing and reading.

If Whitman had asserted his identity with the reader in 1855, now he remains only a speculative, disembodied presence, hovering somewhere over the reader's world: "Who knows, but I am as good as looking at you now, for all you cannot see me?" (1:222). The qualifications are piled on thickly: "Who knows . . . as good as . . . for all you cannot see me."

Physical presence is still Whitman's touchstone, but it is now a qualitatively different experience than that conveyed by the poem:

> Curious what gods can exceed these that clasp me by the hand, and with
>   voices I love call me promptly and loudly by my nighest name as I
>   approach,
> Curious what is more subtle than this which ties me to the woman or man
>   that looks in my face,
> Which fuses me into you now, and pours my meaning into you. (1:223)

Whitman opens questions rather than resolves them here (these lines will take the form of questions in later editions of *Leaves*). There may be gods superior to these that Whitman can grasp directly, but is there a link more subtle than a look? Is the language of the poem that finer connection? Or is Whitman performing another act of projection, giving the poem a "face"? In his letter to Emerson, Whitman distinguishes between meeting people "face to face" and "making poems"; here, too, the shift from physical to textual, like that between past and present tense, ends by confirming the distinction between them.

The poem, finally, is the essential mechanism that does the "fusing" and "pouring," in an operation to which Whitman can only allude in a series of questions:

> We understand, then, do we not?
> What I promised without mentioning it, have you not accepted?
> What the study could not teach—what the preaching could not accomplish is
>   accomplished, is it not? (1:223)

In the 1856 and 1860 versions of the poem, the next line reads, "What the push of reading could not start is started by me personally, is it not?" (1:223). Whitman's 1867 deletion of the line makes sense, I think, because its words assert the opposite of what the poem actually does. Perhaps the central feature of "Crossing Brooklyn Ferry" is its replacement of the immediacy of the "personal" by the mediation of language and "reading."

If "Crossing Brooklyn Ferry" does finally move toward transcendence, that transcendence remains a mediated and essentially grammatical one. In section 9, Whitman returns to section 3's catalog description of the harbor, recasting its past tense in the imperative mood: "Burn high your fires, foundry chimneys! cast black shadows at night-fall! cast red and yellow light over the tops of the houses!" (1:224). The effect is to release the poem's elements from the temporal categories of past, present, and future, but this is done in such a way as to make the linguistic basis of that transcendence even clearer.

In a similar fashion, the "I" and "you" of sections 1 through 8 become "we" at the poem's close: "We realize the soul only by you, you faithful solids and fluids" (1:225). Poet and readers are grammatically fused in the first person, but both they and the poem are defined only in opposition to "you faithful solids and fluids," the things of this world. Significantly absent from the poem is any description of labor, the physical interaction between persons and things that has brought the crowd together in the first place. And if "I" and "you" do connect in and through the language of Whitman's poem, neither is transformed by that new relation, by the poem's "work"; nor are the elements of his descriptive passages altered or purified by their inclusion.

"Crossing Brooklyn Ferry" is, perhaps, a poem whose energy is contained by the act of reading; it registers the elements of the real world, but no longer seeks to act upon or in it. The link between different generations is not so much an engagement with history as an attempt to escape it. And reading itself is also limited here—if readers are like ferry passengers, then their relation to the poem is a largely passive one, as they are carried along instead of sharing in the process of connection.

Echoes of the ambitions of 1855 do remain in the second *Leaves,* most notably in the book's penultimate poem, "Poem of the Sayers of the Words of the Earth" ("A Song of the Rolling Earth"). Here Whitman seems to reassert an identity between things and words:

Earth, round, rolling, compact—suns, moons, animals—all these are words,
Watery, vegetable, sauroid advances—beings, premonitions, lispings of the
    future—these are vast words.

Were you thinking that those were the words—those upright lines? those
    curves, angles, dots?
No, those are not the words—the substantial words are in the ground and sea,
They are in the air—they are in you. (1:265–66)

"Substantial words" are in the body and in the physical world, but not, however, on the printed page, and not in spoken language ("those delicious sounds out of your friends' mouths") either (1:266). Whitman has broadened his conception of "words" to include natural objects and things, but in doing so he has torn such "words" loose from the poem itself. It is, ultimately, only the earth itself that possesses the "words that never fail," but "The best of the earth cannot be told" (1:267, 271). The poet is left "dumb," cut off from the living process of true expression that belongs to earth and nature.

"Crossing Brooklyn Ferry" is finally, I would suggest, most representative of the 1856 *Leaves* in its acceptance of spatial and temporal distance and difference. But why should Whitman's second volume be so different from his first in its poetic strategies? There is, of course, the obvious answer—that the first *Leaves* did not effect the visionary transformations of world and reader that Whitman had announced, and that poetry had become, for him, a matter of strategy rather than transcendence. A sense of incompletion or insufficiency is implicit, I think, in his inclusion of Emerson's letter in the second edition. And the devastating, almost nihilistic rage of "Poem of the Propositions of Nakedness" ("Respondez") may well have been prompted by the very lack of response to Whitman's "salutation."[7]

On another level, the first *Leaves* both draws from and seeks to transform a civic culture that was beginning to break apart by the mid-1850s. According to Mary Ryan, antebellum urban democracy had simultaneously accommodated and allowed expression to class and ethnic differences—a limited, political version of the poetic task Whitman set for himself in 1855. But that cultural cohesion was splintering: the New York mayoral elections of 1854 and 1856 were marked by a new level of violence, and, a year later, there was guerrilla warfare in the streets of lower Manhattan.[8] M. Jimmie Killingsworth points to a comparable breakdown in national politics; he notes that May 1856 saw both Preston Brooks's attack on Charles Sumner on the floor of the U.S. Senate and John Brown's Pottawatomie Massacre in Kansas.[9] Whitman's notebooks of 1856 show his awareness of these changes: alongside an early draft of "Crossing Brooklyn Ferry" there are notes toward an antinativist lecture and fierce attacks on slavery.[10]

At the same time that such conflicts were breaching the limits of the political and exploding into violence, nativists were employing an abstract rhetoric of universality ("the People's Party," "the American Party") to mask their actual goals of division and exclusion.[11] The result was a gap between, on the one hand, differences no longer containable in discourse and, on the other, a political language that created rhetorical unity by denying difference altogether. To some extent, Whitman's new poems of 1856 also register this split–they contain fewer catalogs, and poems like "Poem of Salutation" and "Crossing Brooklyn Ferry" rely more on types and undifferentiated groups. It is as if the space of the poem, like that of the city itself, can no longer both include the rich specificity of difference and fuse it into a larger whole.

1860: A Poetry of Loss

The 1860–61 edition of *Leaves of Grass* moves even more sharply in this direction, with its new poems grounded not in a sense of communal fullness and life but in the experience of isolation and loss. In many ways, the keynote is struck in "A Word Out of The Sea," later renamed "Out of the Cradle Endlessly Rocking." The poem is set against what seems the defining landscape of this edition–not the New York streets, but the Long Island shoreline; not a shared or crowded space, but an empty natural backdrop. This is also the setting for "Leaves of Grass. I." ("As I Ebb'd with the Ocean of Life"), as well as later versions of the book's new opening poem, "Protoleaf" ("Starting from Paumanok").

In "A Word Out of The Sea," the temporal progression of "Crossing Brooklyn Ferry" becomes a narrative–not a story told within a single, unifying voice, but one that culminates in the interplay of different voices: those of mockingbird, maternal sea, and listening boy. It moves, like the earlier poem, from the inscription of temporal difference toward a kind of transcendence, but not by trying to build connections between time periods–here, Whitman seeks a suspension of temporality, a collapse into a single timeless condition or state.[12] That state, however, is one of perpetual loss, of the awakened but unsatisfiable desire that he now presents as the origin of poetry itself.

The opening stanza condenses the narrative to follow into a single extended moment, compressing past and present in a string of present participles:

A man—yet by these tears a little boy again,
Throwing myself on the sand, confronting the waves,
I, chanter of pains and joys, uniter of here and hereafter,
Taking all hints to use them—but swiftly leaping beyond them,
A reminiscence sing. [13]

The last line brings syntactic closure, but it also reestablishes temporal distinctions, separating past from present with the label "reminis-
cence." [14] The stanza does, however, initiate a pattern—of temporal conflation through participial verb forms—that will return at several crucial
moments.

The primary force behind the remembered scene is deflected or projected male desire: the boy places himself in the position of the she-bird
as audience (and, presumably, object of desire) for the male. In doing
so, however, he removes himself from any social or human context; the
bird becomes "my brother" (2:346). The boy then listens, "translating the
notes" of a song that sees desire as permeating nature itself:

Low hangs the moon—it rose late,
It is lagging—O it is heavy with love.

O madly the sea pushes upon the land,
With love—with love. (2:346)

The bird's "aria" is, as the boy conceives it, sung in response to the loss of
his mate, but the words are, of course, not translated from but projected
onto it by the listener (2:349).

The bird's loss of his mate is further intensified by an internal frag-
mentation: *"O throat! O trembling throat!"* he sings, *"Sound clearer through
the atmosphere!"* (2:347). The consciousness attributed to the bird, its song,
and the body that produces sound are all distinct here. By implication,
the process of poetic creation may involve a comparable self-alienation.
In the poems of 1860–61, it is not just the poetic voice that is fragmented,
but the poetic self.

This is the aria that has awakened the heretofore "sleeping" tongue of
the child (2:349):

O you demon, singing by yourself–projecting me,
O solitary me, listening–never more shall I cease imitating, perpetuating
   you,
Never more shall I escape,
Never more shall the cries of unsatisfied love be absent from me. (2:349–50)

Poetry begins as "cries of unsatisfied love," as the expression of unsatisfiable desire–unsatisfiable because its object is located in the sea, the
maternal sea whose word is "death" (2:351). It is language that is given to
bird and poet in place of the lost object– *"Carols of lonesome love! Death's
carols!"*–the language of an originary and creative absence (2:347).

If the bird is "projecting me" into poetic existence, so, too, "The sea
whispered me" (2:351), at once whispering the word "death" to the boy
and simultaneously speaking "me" into being. The series of present participles ("singing," "projecting," "listening," "imitating") culminates in
"perpetuating," which leads both poet and poem into a seemingly permanent and inescapable condition–one of "unknown want, the destiny
of me" (2:350). It is a destiny, however, that isolates rather than binds
the poet to others: the "meanings" "poured forth" in the bird's song are
ones "which I, of all men, know" (2:346).

The "Calamus" poems have often been described as the visionary center
of the 1860–61 volume. These poems are, on the surface, utopian in their
vision of homoerotic union, but here too the possibility of alienation and
loss is an underlying and constitutive element.[15] The opening poem of the
sequence, later titled "In Paths Untrodden," is predicated upon a movement "away from the clank of the world," toward "the margins," in an
escape "from the life that exhibits itself" (2:365, 364). This is a position
diametrically opposed to that of 1855–it is based on withholding and
seclusion, its source in "the life that does *not* exhibit itself," in a nature
outside the realm of the "published" (2:365; emphasis added). Whitman
"no longer envisions himself as part of a democratic commonality at the
center of American culture," Betsy Erkkila says (*Whitman*, 159); "the public and the private were beginning to unravel in [his] poetry," according
to Ezra Greenspan.[16] His goal is "To tell the secret of my nights and days, /
To celebrate the need of comrades" (2:365). But the "secret" that is told

and "celebrated," finally, is not that of "manly attachment"; it is that of homoerotic desire, "the need of comrades."

In Calamus 20 ("I Saw in Louisiana a Live-Oak Growing"), the tree's "look, rude, unbending, lusty, made me think of myself" (2:390). But while the oak may "utter joyous leaves" "without any companion" near it, the poet's utterance depends upon the presence of "a friend, a lover" (2:390). The solitary poet thus remains incomplete and silent, dependent on relation to another for his access to language. As Allen Grossman puts it, "This 'companion' figure is in the position of the discursive other, by reference to whom (and as a consequence of whose death) the self becomes real."[17] Dependence on the presence of another inevitably involves the structural possibility of that other's absence or death; here, too, as in "A Word Out of The Sea," poetry is born of desire and potential—if not actual—loss.

In Calamus 3 ("Whoever You are Holding Me Now in Hand"), Whitman speaks not so much of immediate contact with his reader as of the possibility of rhetorical and poetic frustration and failure. On the one hand, holding *Leaves* can become a physical gesture of comradeship, but on the other, Whitman begins by giving his reader "fair warning" that "I am not what you supposed, but far different" (2:368). The poet and/in his text may be kissed or placed

> . . . beneath your clothing,
> Where I may feel the throbs of your heart or rest upon your hip,
> . . . .
> But these leaves conning, you con at peril,
> For these leaves, and me, you will not understand,
> They will elude you at first, and still more afterward—I will certainly elude
>   you,
> Even while you should think you had unquestionably caught me, behold!
> Already you see I have escaped from you. (2:369)

Holding or being held, possessing or being possessed, are here opposed to reading or understanding. In "Crossing Brooklyn Ferry," Whitman had relied upon the poem itself to perform what he "promised without mentioning," but here he shows no such certainty:

> . . . all is useless without that which you may guess at many times and not
>   hit—that which I hinted at,
> Therefore release me, and depart on your way. (2:369)

Comradeship must preexist the poem, for reading itself seems to make such a relation impossible.

If, as Grossman has suggested, Whitman is attempting here to escape the limits of representation, he is doing so through an explicit exclusion—and through an exclusion of the reader in particular.[18] Calamus 18 ("City of Orgies") proceeds by thrusting away the public life of the city ("Not the pageants of you—not your shifting tableaux"), in order to affirm a private relation between "lovers" (2:388). When an egalitarian order of masculine comradeship does appear in "Calamus," it emerges in "glimpses"—marginalized, unpublished, even secret (2:397).

The utopian politics of the 1860 edition are defined from the start as belonging to a realm outside or beyond the text. Calamus 5 does proclaim a visionary transformation:

> It shall be customary in all directions, in the houses and streets, to see manly
>   affection,
> The departing brother or friend shall salute the remaining brother or friend
>   with a kiss. (2:372)

But while the repetition of "shall" and "will" holds much of the poem together, that very insistence also projects such change into the future, until a time when

> Affection shall solve every one of the problems of freedom,
> Those who love each other shall be invincible,
> They shall finally make America completely victorious, in my name. (2:372)

Such rhetoric both claims more and performs less than that of the 1855 *Leaves*. If Whitman earlier sought to realize a democratic order in the particulars of his poetic catalogs (the very material excluded from Calamus 18), now he only projects it, in highly abstract terms, into the future.

The rhetoric Whitman would use to join the personal, sexual, and political finally only reconfirms the differences between them. In Calamus 24 ("I Hear it was Charged Against Me"), he proclaims himself "neither for nor against institutions," instead proposing to

> . . . establish in the Mannahatta and in every city of these States inland and
> seaboard,
> And in the fields and woods, and above every keel little or large that dents
> the water,
> Without edifices or rules or trustees or any argument,
> The institution of the dear love of comrades. (2:394)

Sociopolitical conflict is to be transcended, as are all social, physical, or textual structures ("edifices or rules or trustees or any argument"). But the force that is to replace them — "the dear love of comrades" — does not arise in spontaneous or organic fashion. Whitman's language "establishes" it as another "institution." The paradox of the phrase cannot escape the impasse that Whitman's work has reached: the gulf between desire — sexual and political — and the limits of poetic language.

Just as relations between lovers and comrades are vulnerable to alienation and loss, so too is the volume as a whole also marked by an absence — the loss of the integrating, inclusive vision that animates the original *Leaves* and still echoes through the 1856 version. Whitman does recover a version of that unifying authority in the 1867 edition, but when he does so, in "Memories of President Lincoln," it is at an all too obvious cost — the sacrifice of Lincoln himself as comrade and captain. The shift between these two books is registered in Whitman's revisions of Calamus 39; in 1860–61 it reads:

> Sometimes with one I love, I fill myself with rage, for fear I effuse unreturned
> love;
> But now I think there is no unreturned love — the pay is certain, one way or
> another,
> Doubtless I could not have perceived the universe, or written one of my
> poems, if I had not freely given myself to comrades, to love. (2:403–4)

This first version expresses an anxious dependence on the other, as in "I Saw in Louisiana a Live-Oak Growing," as well as a furious mixture of emotions — love, rage, fear. But in 1867, Whitman replaces the last line with a rather different pair:

(I loved another person ardently and my love was not return'd,
Yet out of that, I have written these songs.) (2:404)

Now the poetry springs, not from the gift of himself to others, but from the rejection of that gift, the loss of relation. Just as the sea's word, "death," replaces the mockingbird's lost mate, so here "these songs" take the place of the poet's unreturned love.

The finest poem added to the 1867 *Leaves* is, of course, "When Lilacs Last in the Dooryard Bloom'd," which I discuss in my concluding chapter. When Whitman seeks once again to recover or restore national unity, he will do so not as revolutionary poet, but specifically in response to death, as elegist.

PART THREE

Thoreau

SIX

To Reconcile
the People
and the Stones

In the preceding chapters, I have traced the shifts in Hawthorne's and Whitman's views of literary representation by discussing their works in chronological sequence. The former, I have suggested, abandons the image of romance as dramatic middle ground after *The House of the Seven Gables,* while the latter falls back into a version of poetry as mediation in "Crossing Brooklyn Ferry," after having earlier sought to supersede representation altogether.

Henry David Thoreau shows an even deeper ambivalence about the status of writing, one that leads him to both assert and deny the efficacy of literary mediation—in works of the same period. One of the pieces of "private business" he goes to Walden to "transact" is the writing of *A Week on the Concord and Merrimack Rivers.*[1] But at the same time that Thoreau is composing that manuscript, he is also compiling the journal entries that will lead to *Walden.*[2] And during the writing of *Walden,* he is drafting abolitionist and other essays, several of which, along with materials from his Walden manuscript, he will deliver as lyceum lectures.

Walden, I will argue, takes as its primary task that of fashioning connections—between language and nature, the civilized and the wild, the present and the past—connections that may form the ground for social action. But the abolitionist essays, written and delivered during these same years, emphatically deny the legitimacy of political representation and, by implication, linguistic representation as well. It is as if Whitman were drafting "Crossing Brooklyn Ferry" and his first version of "Song of Myself" at the same time. Read against each other in this fashion, Thoreau's texts reveal a set of internal oppositions and contradictions–problems that become, I would suggest, central features of his work.

On the River

If Hawthorne takes as his starting point an opposition between the actual and the imaginary, Thoreau begins with one between human history and the natural world. His focus is on the intersection between them, on man's presence in and marking of the landscape. Is that marking only violent despoliation and rupture? Or can it be a generative interaction, yielding progressive consciousness and social reform? *Walden* asks whether human labor can become such a natural process, linking the wild and the cultivated–in the farmer's field and on the writer's page. If such links are possible, then they may be used to unearth or build alternative histories and models for social change.

To some extent, *A Week on the Concord and Merrimack Rivers* poses the problems that *Walden* attempts to solve. Thoreau opens his first book by drawing a contrast between natural time and recorded human history– between the ancient origins of the "Musketaquid, or Grass-ground River," and its more recent entry into "civilized history" as the Concord, after a 1635 renaming by English settlers.[3] Since then, Thoreau notes, "the dam, and afterward the canal at Billerica, and the factories at Lowell" have sharply reduced the number of fish in the river, but "Perchance, after a few thousands of years, if the fishes will be patient, and pass their summers elsewhere, meanwhile, nature will have levelled the Billerica dam, and the Lowell factories, and the Grass-ground River run clear again" (33, 34). Human time and natural time seem almost incommensurable here. Nature is a long continuity, punctuated only briefly by the events of human history: first agricultural, then commercial and industrial development. Such manmade changes are characterized not only by their speed, but also by their ephemerality when compared to the slow, inexorable pace of ecological change – "in the lapse of ages," Thoreau says, "nature will recover and indemnify herself" (62).

These different forms and levels of history can be juxtaposed in a single stretch of landscape. In one section of the river, for instance, the voyagers pass "the artificial falls where the canals of the Manchester Manufacturing Company discharge themselves into the Merrimack" (245). Manchester was then "a village of about two thousand inhabitants," Thoreau says, but workers were already "laying the foundation of another Lowell" there, and by the time of writing, its population had risen to fourteen thousand (245). The speed of industrialization and population growth overtakes the processes of memory and composition here, almost exceeding the power of Thoreau's text to absorb or represent them.

In contrast, a mile downstream are the natural Amoskeag Falls, an old Indian fishing place, at which, "[t]radition says," the natives hid provisions in cavities in the rocks (246). The Indians regard these holes as made for them by God, while the Royal Society calls them " 'artificial' " (246). Thoreau, on the other hand, finds an obvious geological origin for the holes, as the water swirled small stones against the surface of the rock. He concludes, however, that "[t]he periods of Hindoo and Chinese history, though they reach back to the time when the race of mortals is confounded with the race of gods, are as nothing compared with the periods which these stones have inscribed" (248). White history and science, native tradition, and geological transformation all come together in this passage, but it is the last and deepest level of history that Thoreau will finally privilege: "The murmur of unchronicled nations has died away along these shores, and once more Lowell and Manchester are on the trail of the Indian" (249). White settlers and industrialists have displaced the Indian, but neither may be more than a flitting shadow on the face of nature. "Most revolutions in society have not power to interest, still less alarm us," Thoreau declares elsewhere, "but tell me that our rivers are drying up, or the genus pine dying out in the country, and I might attend" (129).

Thoreau's impulse is, on one hand, toward transcendence and timelessness – in those "demi-experiences" of life in nature that are "in time, veritably future, or rather outside to time" (8). But these are only moments amid time's continuing flow; he is equally concerned to reassert and reconnect with the slow or deep time of geological and evolutionary change.[4] Recorded or official history is not the only kind; Thoreau's search is less for an alternative to history than for alternative versions of it.

Natural history resists human ordering in two entirely different ways, for it can manifest itself as both stability and continual flux. Long-term natural change may be slow, but in the shorter term it can be multi-leveled and constant: "history fluctuates as the face of the landscape from morning to evening," Thoreau says (154). And in this perpetually shifting present, "the living fact commemorates itself," with the passage of time marked by the shadows of the trees (154, 319).

Thoreau's interest is not in history as a fixed memorial, but in things living and immemorial, things that cannot be lost (135). What he values is not time's "*then,* but its *now,*" he says: "Critical acumen is exerted in vain to uncover the past; the *past* cannot be *presented*" (154, 155). While living, "natural facts" are timeless "*perennials,*" "the *annals* of the country," on the other hand, show only dates and losses (219). No historical text can dam or regulate the onward flow of time, and so bring past and present into contact once again.

"Fame itself is but an epitaph," Thoreau remarks; for him, such a memorializing history is epitomized by the graveyard, whose stones are direct and lasting marks upon the landscape (170, 169). Tombstones represent the exact opposite of the playful, shadowy timekeeping of the trees, which make temporality legible without fixing or inscribing it (319–20). Graves are more than just a break in the continuity of the earth's surface; their inscriptions seek to break the continuity of natural time as well: "Why should the monument be so much more enduring than the fame which it is designed to commemorate," Thoreau asks (170). Such history leaves all men "partially buried in the grave of custom" (132).

Both gravestones and biographies insist on the significance of individual lives, but from the wider perspective of nature, individuals must be subsumed within a larger whole: it is, Thoreau, observes, "As if our birth had at first sundered things, and we had been thrust up through into nature like a wedge, and not till the wound heals and the scar disappears, do we begin to discover where we are, and that nature is one and continuous every where" (349). For the sake of that continuity, the farmer should "leave his body to Nature to be plowed in, and in some measure restore its fertility. We should not retard but forward her economies" (171).

This is a difficult, even traumatic subject in the *Week,* for, to some extent, the book is itself a memorial–to Thoreau's late brother John, his unnamed companion on the river. Henry does recognize this aspect of his work: as he describes the gravestones, "upright and emphatic, like exclamation points!" he uses an exclamation point himself (169).[5] Rather than name his brother, Henry incorporates him into the text through the first person plural (see 118, 289, for example, and elsewhere); the shifting pronoun is, perhaps, his way of resisting the impulse to inscribe and fix–his way of both remembering and releasing his brother at the same time.

Unlike the gravedigger and stonemason, the farmer participates in the natural cycle, and thus perhaps may serve as a better model for the writer. Here and elsewhere in the *Week,* farming is indeed juxtaposed with or likened to inscription: "A sentence should read as if its author, had he held a plow instead of a pen, could have drawn a furrow deep and straight to the end" (107). But this writing too may be a kind of violence. If the headstone is a surface cut out of the earth to be cut once again in the act of inscription, farming and writing involve cutting and destruction as well, as farmers go "clearing, and burning, and scratching, and harrowing, and plowing . . . again and again, erasing what they had already written" (8).

Thoreau is reaching toward a vision of writing as a kind of labor within nature, "a part of the industry of nature" (217)–as a participatory rather than disruptive practice. This, however, is an idea to be realized in *Walden* rather than the *Week.* In the end, the *Week* will privilege not the farmer but the marginalized and problematic figure of the Indian. Thoreau describes the farmer as engaged in a kind of ecological conquest or imperialism: "the white man came, built him a house, and made a clearing here, letting in the sun, dried up a farm, piled up the old gray stones in fences, cut down the pines around his dwelling, planted orchard seeds brought from the old country. . . . The white man's mullein soon reigned in Indian corn-fields, and sweet scented English grasses clothed the new soil. Where, then, could the Red Man set his foot?" (52–53). This process of enclosure and exclusion stands in opposition to the free movement of both Indian and traveler, and the contrast soon becomes a violent one, symbolized by the honey bee, which "stung the Red child's hand, forerunner of that industrious tribe that was to come and pluck the wild flower of his race up by the root" (53).

The "annals" Thoreau consults as he moves through the landscape are often tales of conflict between natives and settlers, and he treats the stories of Lovewell's Fight and Hannah Dustan's captivity at considerable length (119–22, 320–24).[6] But there are no records of the Indians' fates, he laments (122). Unlike the settlers, they have left no monuments to their war dead (254). Their graves are visible, but only as "scars" on the earth, marks of natural healing and regeneration that will in time "disappear" once again, like the marks of birth (237, 349).

Such a contrast with the violent inscription of white history and biography suggests a different relation to the landscape. It is, paradoxically, the "wary independence and aloofness of [the Indian's] dim forest life" that give him admission "from time to time to a rare and peculiar society with Nature" (55): "The Indian's intercourse with Nature is at least such as admits of the greatest independence of each. If he is somewhat of a stranger in her midst, the gardener is too much of a familiar. There is something vulgar and foul in the latter's closeness to his mistress, something noble and cleanly in the former's distance" (56). The Indian passes through the forest and over the landscape, "setting his foot" without leaving a mark and fouling them. In so doing, he is like the river, which itself "steals . . . unobserved through the town . . . with the moccasined tread of an Indian warrior" (11). Here, in fact, Thoreau makes the Indian's tread the primary term in his comparison, the antecedent to which the natural is compared.

The native presence is thus registered indirectly, in the landscape and the way it is perceived; it is not cut into or marked upon the land in destructive or unnatural fashion. This seems like a process close to nature's own mode of self-representation—figured most often for Thoreau in the reflecting surface of the water (48). He prides himself on "not following any beaten path, but the windings of the river," leaving nothing behind him but a momentary wake and some reflections of his own (110). Traveling on the river puts Thoreau in the place of the Indian: he compares his boat to an earlier Indian canoe and says that he sees the country "in its primitive state, and as if the Indian still inhabited it" (221, 194).

Thoreau speaks disparagingly of literature that is artificially "cultivat-ed" (97), preferring "sentences which spring like the sward in its native pasture, where its roots were never disturbed" (100). "What have I to do with plows?" he asks, declaring his affinity for a "wildness" that predates the agricultural (54).[7] He finally describes "[t]he talent of composition" as "very dangerous,—the striking out the heart of life at a blow, as the Indian takes off a scalp" (329). In doing so, Thoreau is not just describing his writing as violent; he is at once aligning it with the natural and placing its force outside the dominant white culture—even, perhaps, directing it against that culture.

His text would form part of a history very different from that of the local annals; it begins, after all, by "floating past" the Concord battle-ground (17). But if the *Week* is a revisionary history, it is also a flawed and conflicted one.[8] Thoreau's opposition between white farmer and In-dian hunter is, of course, an oversimplification, as the arrowheads in his Walden bean field will show (*Walden,* 156). As Robert F. Sayre has ar-gued, Thoreau's early work still depicts the Native American through the romanticized and condescending stereotypes of nineteenth-century "savagism."[9]

On some level, though, Thoreau does realize his implication in the official history of conquest and expropriation. If he would in some sense identify with the Indians, he also knows that he follows Hannah Dus-tan, who had traveled the same river "one hundred and forty-two years before"—fleeing from her captors with "the still bleeding scalps of ten . . . aborigines" in the bottom of her canoe (320–21). She takes the scalps as proof of her story, according to Thoreau; the act thus amounts to the be-ginning of a historical record (322). But Dustan also receives a bounty for those scalps; the opposition between victim and victimizer is confounded at the very moment of its entry into history. And Thoreau's narration only extends this entanglement—he shifts tenses quite disconcertingly, placing both Dustan's flight and the brothers' homeward journey in the same present tense (322–23).

In the end, Thoreau's must be a fallen history rather than a "natural" one, for it derives also from the murder of Dustan's child, its "brains dashed out against an apple-tree" (321). Planting such trees has been part of the process of settling and "civilizing" New England: even gone wild, their shade "impart[s] a half-civilized and twilight aspect to the otherwise barbarian land" (233).[10] Thoreau and his readers thus inherit violence and death from both sides: "there have been many who in later years have lived to say that they had eaten of the fruit of that apple-tree" (324).

Thoreau's first book sets different versions and levels of history against each other: conventional white historical narrative against the unrecorded Indian past, the fixity of historical inscription against the living and fluctuating landscape, and the pace of commercial development against the slower cycles of ecological change. Exactly where he and his text stand in relation to these "histories" remains ambiguous. Thoreau and his brother have followed the river as it moves, Indian-style, through the landscape. And there is a history recorded in the living landscape, its presence implicit in the "wild apple tree" to which Henry ties his boat on the last page of the *Week* (393). The stem of that tree still bears "the mark which [the boat's] chain had worn in the chafing of the spring freshets"–the simple presence of the boat, through changes in the seasons and the water level of the river, has inscribed itself upon the bark (393). And it is, of course, an apple tree, a closing image chosen precisely for its troubling moral and historical echoes.

At the Pond

A Week on the Concord and Merrimack Rivers thus suggests the conflicts and difficulties in man's relation to the natural. *Walden,* on the other hand, sets out to fuse or mediate between the *Week*'s contrasting figures– farmer, writer, and Indian–and to link them to the social realm. Central to this process is the idea of labor–both Walden and *Walden,* bean field and journal, are work sites for Thoreau, and for the heroic reader he requires. But meaningful bodily labor, unalienated and potentially shared effort, has been driven to the margins of rapidly industrializing nineteenth-century Massachusetts.

In focusing on the mediating force of labor, I am taking a very different approach from a critic like Michael Gilmore, who casts Thoreau's project in much more negative terms. He characterizes *Walden* as a flight from exchange relations and the marketplace, an ahistorical and mystifying withdrawal from the social world. My reading, on the other hand, points toward a more positive response, an effort to rehistoricize and reconstitute both social and exchange relations that is also visible in Thoreau's text.[11]

One key point of reconnection and renewal is Thoreau's bean field. He goes to Walden, he says, "to live a primitive and frontier life," one between the natural and the civilized (11), firmly anchored in what Leo Marx calls the "middle landscape."[12] In the 1840s, Massachusetts was in the midst of an agricultural revolution, as farmers moved from self-sufficiency to more intensive production for urban markets; Thoreau's field, however, is to remain "the connecting link between wild and cultivated fields . . . a half-cultivated field" (158). It is, in fact, the site at which such distinctions break down or blur: "They were beans cheerfully returning to their wild and primitive state that I cultivated," Thoreau claims (158). In this case, "cultivated" and "primitive" are no longer opposed, as in the *Week;* the former is no longer simply "progress," nor the latter a regression. "The sun," he says, "looks on our cultivated fields and on the prairies and forests without distinction" (166).

Such a combination of cultivation and wildness comes to the farmer as well, as he "labors" to "cultivate" an "acquaintance" with his beans (155, 161). The beans, Thoreau says, "attached me to the earth" (155). His aim is to "[make] the yellow soil express its summer thought in bean leaves and blossoms rather than in wormwood and piper and millet grass, making the earth say beans instead of grass" (157). Farming is not here a form of human writing on the earth – a cutting or incision, as in the *Week* – but instead the "work" of connecting with the soil and coaxing a form of self-expression from it.[13]

If such work is to yield a kind of natural speech, it will also ground Thoreau's own language in physical labor and in the soil: "[S]ome," he says, "must work in fields if only for the sake of tropes and expression" (162). Indeed, the bodily activity of farming generates its textual counterpart: "Consider the intimate and curious acquaintance one makes with various kinds of weeds,—it will bear some iteration in the account, for there was no little iteration in the labor,—disturbing their delicate organization so ruthlessly, and making such invidious distinctions with his hoe, levelling whole ranks of one species, and sedulously cultivating another" (161). Thoreau's writing is to suggest the iterative rhythm of his work, he says. But it is primarily in his choice of words that he brings together the physical, intellectual, and textual. The movements of his hoe are described in terms usually applied to rhetoric or argumentation ("invidious distinctions"). The language of physical warfare also appears ("levelling whole ranks"), but the cutting force of the hoe is diminished into a metaphorical, purely verbal violence, a ruthless disturbance of delicacy. These, perhaps, are the "truly *labored* sentences" that Thoreau had called for in the *Week* (107), as writing and action intermingle, with each described in terms of the other.

The result is designed as an alternative to official texts—his is "one field not in Mr. Colman's report," Thoreau notes (158). In response to Colman's descriptions of "the expensive experiments of gentlemen farmers," Thoreau does render his accounts of outgoes and income in the monetary terms of a rationalizing agricultural reformer (162, 163).[14] But he supplements the figures with two further sets of "results": a paragraph of practical advice for those who would plant beans, and a consideration of the moral lessons he has drawn from the process—the need to plant the seeds of virtues in "a new generation of men" (163, 164).

Such links between the spiritual and physical are one of Thoreau's major themes, of course. But the second does not simply dissolve into the first, as so often seems to happen in Emerson. The pond, like the bean field, serves as a mediating or connecting space—as a "field of water," "intermediate in its nature between land and sky" (188–89). The materiality of both sites is reinforced by the fact that Thoreau's relation to them is through physical labor—farming and fishing are both forms of work, ones that integrate the individual into the natural cycle (210).

At the beginning of "The Ponds," Thoreau describes himself "fishing from a boat by moonlight":

communicating by a long flaxen line with mysterious nocturnal fishes which had their dwelling forty feet below. . . . It was very queer, especially in dark nights, when your thoughts had wandered to vast and cosmogonal themes in other spheres, to feel this faint jerk, which came to interrupt your dreams and link you to Nature again. It seemed as if I might next cast my line upward into the air, as well as downward into this element which was scarcely more dense. Thus I caught two fishes as it were with one hook. (175)

Fishing and thinking are linked in this passage as analogous forms of communication with the natural. But just as Thoreau moves thematically between the physical and the spiritual, his writing moves from past to present tense, and from the first to the second person. "Your" present is silently joined to Thoreau's past experience. The two remain distinct, however, connected through similes ("as if," "as it were") rather than de-clared to be the same. Thoreau catches his reader with a syntactic hook. Such semantic shifts and transformations are, I would suggest, analogous to Whitman's manipulation of tense and syntax in "Crossing Brooklyn Ferry": in both cases, it is because the writer acknowledges the materiality of language that it can function as a mediating device.

One feature of Thoreau's text that distinguishes it from Whitman's is his wordplay and etymological exploration: "The ear of wheat, (in Latin *spica,* obsoletely *speca,* from *spe,* hope,) should not be the only hope of the husbandman; its kernel or grain (*granum,* from *gerendo,* bearing) is not all that it bears. How, then, can our harvest fail?" (166). Etymology (a kind of linguistic history) here enables Thoreau to find spiritual signif-icance within the physical, the movement taking place on the level of language itself. It also reveals a historicity within language, an evolution over time that generates a multiplicity or variation in meanings. In so doing, Thoreau's linguistic labor creates a conceptual space within his text—a space in which a flexibility or play between different meanings becomes possible.

Here and elsewhere, Thoreau uses such linguistic play to redefine terms like "account," "economy," and "foundation" through a gradual accretion of variant meanings. He criticizes Concord houses, for instance, because they lack true "foundations": "Before we can adorn our houses with beautiful objects," he says, "the walls must be stripped, and our lives must be stripped, and beautiful housekeeping and beautiful living be laid for a foundation" (38). But "foundation" quickly moves from the metaphorical or conceptual level to the immediate and practical: Thoreau begins his own house by digging a cellar "where a woodchuck had formerly dug his burrow" (44).

Similar shifts from the abstract to the physical run throughout the book. "Economy," for instance, systematically and doggedly insists on a return to the body as the ground for determining life's true "necessaries" (11). In "Where I Lived, and What I Lived For," Thoreau claims that "men establish and confirm their daily life of routine and habit every where, which still is built on purely illusory foundations" (96). His response is a call to "settle ourselves, and work and wedge our feet downward through the mud and slush of opinion, and prejudice, and tradition, and delusion, and appearance . . . till we come to a hard bottom and rocks in place, which we can call *reality,* and say, This is, and no mistake; and then begin, having a *point d'appui,* below freshet and frost and fire, a place where you might found a wall or a state" (97–98). This foundation is to be at once personal, political, and quite physical – both a literal and a figurative grounding for the social.

It is thus a whole complex of meanings that Thoreau invokes in his "Conclusion," when he calls upon his readers to "put the foundations under" their "castles in the air" (324). In a sense, Thoreau's years at the pond have been part of a foundational enterprise, one that yields the experiential basis for his text. His labor has been both physical and linguistic: he laments, for instance, his inability to "exaggerate enough even to lay the foundation of a true expression" (324). Here he plays upon the Latin root of "exaggerate" – to "pile up" – turning writing and building into inseparable aspects of a single project, one grounded in the natural and reaching rhetorically toward the social. He does not make the Whitmanesque claim that Walden and *Walden* are one and the same, but the latter is painstakingly drawn out of the former as its ultimate reality and *"point d'appui."* As Joan Burbick puts it, Thoreau has "found ground on which to build culture, connecting him with the human history of the soil and with the regenerative forces of nature."[15]

Thoreau, like Whitman, may look forward to the future, but he also knows that others have dug in this earth before him: "it appeared by the arrowheads which I turned up in hoeing, that an extinct nation had anciently dwelt here and planted corn and beans ere white men came to clear the land, and so, to some extent, had exhausted the soil for this very crop" (156). His native predecessors may be "extinct," but they have, perhaps, "exhausted the soil" before white agriculture even began. Here the conventional antebellum narrative of triumphant progress and modernity is reversed, with both Thoreau and his Concord neighbors consigned to economic and (agri)cultural belatedness.

Just as older meanings are already layered beneath nineteenth-century English like geological deposits, so human histories lie beneath the surface of the living landscape. "[W]ith my hoe, I disturbed the ashes of unchronicled nations," Thoreau says, "and their small implements of war and hunting were brought to the light of this modern day. They lay mingled with other natural stones, some of which bore the marks of having been burned by Indian fires, and some by the sun, and also bits of pottery and glass brought hither by the recent cultivators of the soil" (158–59). Unlike in the *Week*, Indian culture is not opposed to farming here. Artifacts old and new, red and white, are mingled with the "natural stones"; the bean field is the ground for linkages across the lines of time and race.

When Thoreau defines his relation to his neighbors in the village, he often casts himself as an Indian, a prior inhabitant with earlier and closer ties to nature. Rather than planting more popular cash crops like grain or English hay, he opts for beans, originally an Indian crop.[16] And he is ready to greet visitors from Concord with the cry " 'Welcome, Englishmen!' " supposedly the way in which the Pilgrims had been met on their arrival (154). He sees a continuity between his canoe and an old log one he has heard of, one that simply "belonged to the pond" (191). That canoe in turn "took the place of an Indian one of the same material but more graceful construction, which perchance had first been a tree on the bank" (191). Thoreau's labor—as farmer, fisherman, and then as writer—"brings to light" such historical and cultural connections as another of its (by)products.

The bean field thus has a rediscoverable history, but it is not the orthodox white narrative of conquest and displacement that Thoreau has attacked in the *Week*. As he "conjures up" the "Former Inhabitants" of the woods, Thoreau constructs an alternative, inherently oppositional version of the story of American settlement (256). It is a local, largely oral and unofficial history, democratic in both materials and method: pieced together out of archaeological and narrative fragments, built from "the memory of many of my townsmen," and filled with the "laugh and gossip" of ordinary life (256). In transcribing it, Thoreau "repeople[s]" the woods and recreates a varied and multiethnic, largely working-class community, with the bean field as its central reference point (264).

He begins "[e]ast of my bean-field, across the road," with "Cato Ingraham, slave of Duncan Ingraham, Esquire, gentleman of Concord village," but the language of legal documents soon turns more colloquial: "Some say that he was a Guinea Negro. There are a few who remember his little patch" (257). In this oral history, Cato links Concord to an African past, a darker alternative to its Puritan and revolutionary traditions. But all that remains of his house is a "half-obliterated cellar hole," "known to few," and filled with flowers (257). Cato's dwelling, like the others Thoreau describes here, is overgrown and nearly hidden. This may, on one hand, be a sign of failure; but it is also, in a sense, better than the graveyard memorials of the *Week*, for it reintegrates the human past into a living natural present. Thoreau compares the "cellar dents" he finds to "deserted fox burrows" (263).

"Here," Thoreau continues, placing the reader squarely within the space of the woods, "by the very corner of my field, still nearer to town, Zilpha, a colored woman, had her little house, where she spun linen for the townsfolk, making the Walden Woods ring with her shrill singing" (257). Racially, physically, and economically, she is consigned to the margins of the white community, and to what Thoreau terms "a hard life, and somewhat inhumane" (257). Her hut is burned by British troops during the War of 1812; Thoreau's paragraph, however, ends not with the historian's voice, but with her own, "muttering to herself over her gurgling pot, – 'Ye are all bones, bones!' " (257).

"Down the road," on "Brister's Hill," lived "Brister Freeman, 'a handy Negro,' slave of Squire Cummings" (257). In the Lincoln burial ground, his stone stands "a little on one side, near the unmarked graves of some British grenadiers who fell in the retreat from Concord" (258). But the apple trees he planted live on in the Walden woods, on the hill that bears his name – a domesticated species among the wild plants, and thus a living human presence among the natural. [17] Here and elsewhere, those cast aside or forgotten by official histories are central figures in the woods.

Thoreau closes his survey by moving "[f]arther in the woods than any of these," to where "Wyman the potter squatted, and furnished his townsmen with earthen ware" – a "fictile . . . art" that Thoreau sees as a predecessor to his own (261). Wyman lives outside the economic orders of both land ownership and taxation; the family was so poor that the sheriff simply " 'attached a chip,' for form's sake" (261). The potter is succeeded in his hut by Irishman Hugh Quoil, a soldier in Europe, perhaps, but only a "ditcher" suffering from delirium tremens in America (262).

In many respects, Thoreau is the inheritor of this countertradition. His manual labor as small-scale farmer and fisherman gives him a similar economic marginality; he too is a squatter in the woods, one who wishes to place himself outside the reach of the Concord tax gatherer. And his cabin is finished with boards from "the shanty of James Collins, an Irishman who worked on the Fitchburg Railroad" (43).

It is no accident, of course, that Thoreau takes up residence at the pond on July Fourth, but he intends to revise or replace, not just return to, the American revolutionary tradition (84). His version of that history begins with Indian artifacts and prerevolutionary slaves, after all – with the dark underside of the American past that his contemporaries would hide. And his list of visitors to the pond includes both figurative "runaway slaves" and a real one, whom Thoreau "helped to forward toward the northstar" (152).

Thoreau's project thus involves both geographical recentering and historical revision. His work amid the woods gives him a vantage point from which to mount a critique of the dominant social order – he is both physically distanced from it and aware of his place in an historically and economically marginalized tradition. He offers his work as a form of unalienated labor, one that reconnects the economic and the natural and contrasts sharply with that of his Concord neighbors.

When Thoreau, standing in his bean field, hears the town's "great guns" fired on "gala days," it comes as a disruption of nature's "sounds and sights" (159–60). The noise is reduced by the distance to that of a "puff ball," however; his townsmen may see it as "one of the *great* days," but "the sky had from my clearing only the same everlastingly great look that it wears daily, and I saw no difference in it" (160, 161).

Thoreau does find that martial music from a village band can be "really noble and inspiring": "I felt as if I could spit a Mexican with a good relish, – for why should we always stand for trifles? – and looked round for a woodchuck or skunk to exercise my chivalry upon" (160, 161). His disgust for the Mexican War is registered in both his comic deflation of its "chivalry" and his intensification of warfare into cannibalism, as he proposes to "spit" an enemy soldier like a slaughtered animal. It is an apt and carefully chosen image, for the Mexican War was one fought in support of proslavery interests, and the essence of slavery is, of course, the reduction of the slave to the level of the animal.

In "Brute Neighbors," Thoreau reintroduces slavery and the Mexican War as the historical context for his description of the battle of the ants: "The battle which I witnessed took place in the Presidency of Polk, five years before the passage of Webster's Fugitive Slave Bill" (232). It may be a conflict between "the red republicans on the one hand, and the black imperialists on the other," but Thoreau's primary concern is with American rather than European political conflict – by the end of the paragraph his main aim has become the satiric diminution of the battles of Concord and Bunker Hill (229–30).

Slavery is, for Thoreau, continuous with rather than opposed to the economic life of Concord village. New England's economic links to the South were many: thousands of Massachusetts farm women and children made palm-leaf hats under the outwork system, for example, many of them shipped south for use by Southern slaves.[18] In a single paragraph in "Economy," Thoreau speaks of factory workers, unemployed laborers, farmers, and "the laborers in our Southern States who produce the staple exports of this country, and are themselves a staple production of the South" (35). More problematically, he subsumes "the gross but somewhat foreign form of servitude called Negro Slavery" under the more general rubric of capitalist economic rationalization: "It is hard to have a southern overseer; it is worse to have a northern one; but worst of all when you are the slave-driver of yourself" (7).

The Northern worker has internalized the ideology of capitalist industrial regimentation, turning himself into another part of the market mechanism: "the laboring man has not leisure for a true integrity day by day; he cannot afford to sustain the manliest relations to men; his labor would be depreciated in the market. He has no time to be any thing but a machine" (6).[19] Such strict regulation and control of the labor process was characteristic of New England textile mills, which "organized production around elaborate divisions of labor" and "imposed novel time and work disciplines to insure . . . punctuality and sustained attentiveness."[20] But Thoreau sees these same qualities entering the economy of Concord as well: "Where is this division of labor to end?" he asks, "and what object does it finally serve?" (46). For him, both individual "integrity" and social relations are destroyed when bodily labor is quantified and regimented, the natural balance between labor and leisure turned from an alternation into an opposition.

If Southern slavery dehumanizes and commodifies its slave workers, Northern capitalism objectifies both Irish laborers and native railroad workers: "Did you ever think what those sleepers are that underlie the railroad?" Thoreau asks, "Each one is a man, an Irish-man, or a Yankee man. The rails are laid upon them" (92). Latent in Thoreau's wordplay, of course, is the possibility that some of these still sleeping and exploited workers will awake: "I am glad to know," he remarks, "that it takes a gang of men for every five miles to keep the sleepers down and level in their beds as it is, for this is a sign that they may sometime get up again" (93).

Thoreau is perfectly right to focus on the railroad as both the symbol and primary agent of change in the rural economy. For the decisive moment for Concord agriculture came in the 1840s, when a railroad link to

Boston was established. If Hawthorne is troubled, as we have seen, by the disorienting speed of the train's movement through the landscape, Thoreau seems more disturbed by its linearity and regimentation. The tracks cut into and across the countryside—Thoreau speaks several times of the railroad's "deep cut" (192, 304). The train's fixed schedule also imposes itself upon the farmer, and the temporality of the marketplace displaces that of the agricultural process.

Thoreau offers a contrast between nature's perpetual present and days that are "minced into hours and fretted by the ticking of a clock" (112). Human time can blend with the natural, as when the sound of Sunday church bells passes through the woods, setting off "a vibration of the universal lyre" and generating an echo that is "partly the voice of the wood" (123). And nature has its own temporality: the whippoorwills sing every evening "with as much precision as a clock, within five minutes of a particular time, referred to the setting of the sun" (124); and the pond has its own cycle of rises and falls, whose regularity Thoreau has not yet determined (180–81).

Concord life, however, is determined by the railroad timetable. The cars are more regular even than the sunrise (116), and the rattle and whistle of the train "penetrate" the woods all year round (115). The trains "go and come with such regularity and precision, and their whistle can be heard so far, that the farmers set their clocks by them, and thus one well conducted institution regulates a whole country. . . . Do they not talk and think faster in the depot than they did in the stage-office?" (117–18). A once natural process, farming, thus comes under the "regulation" of the market, and the rhythm of bodily labor is displaced by an abstract and quantified schedule. It is yet another way in which "We do not ride on the railroad; it rides upon us" (92).

It is this critique of Northern capitalism and its quantification and rationalization of life that Thoreau's work in the bean field makes possible—and to which it responds, offering a version of unalienated labor that retains contact with both the village and nature. In the unfinished essay "Reform and the Reformers," he speaks in praise of "the free labor of man": "We would have some pure product of man's hands," he says, "some pure labor, some life got in this old trade of getting a living – some work done which shall not be a mending, a cobbling, a reforming."[21] He sees such labor as a form of primary creation rather than secondary alteration, one in which "living" and "getting a living" are identical rather than opposed.

It is a vision not far from that of the early Marx in "The German Ideology." There Marx attacks "the distribution of labour" that forces "a particular, exclusive sphere of activity" on each individual; "in a communist society," he says, "each can become accomplished in any branch he wishes," making it possible "for me to do one thing today and another tomorrow, to hunt in the morning, fish in the afternoon, rear cattle in the evening, criticise after dinner, just as I have a mind, without ever becoming hunter, fisherman, shepherd or critic."[22] Except for the hunting and the livestock, perhaps, this seems not far from Thoreau's life in 1847, when he described himself to his Harvard class secretary as "a Schoolmaster – a private Tutor, a Surveyor – a Gardener, a Farmer – a Painter. I mean a House Painter, a Carpenter, a Mason, a Day-Laborer, a Pencil-Maker, a Glass-paper Maker, a Writer, and sometimes a Poetaster."[23]

Thoreau goes farther than Marx, however, in describing a mode of labor that combines different functions, rather than just the freedom to take on different roles in succession. He works barefoot, "dabbling like a plastic artist" in the sand (156). Labor, learning, art, and natural growth, no longer alienated from one another, become part of a single continuous process: "When my hoe tinkled against the stones, that music echoed to the woods and the sky, and was an accompaniment to my labor which yielded an instant and immeasurable crop" (159). Just as Whitman juxtaposes the contralto's voice with the lisp of the carpenter's plane, so Thoreau hears the sound of his hoe as an echoing "music." Such an aesthetic product is not just a byproduct or "accompaniment," however; it is a "crop" in and of itself, albeit an unquantifiable or "immeasurable" one.[24] Beyond this, it is also a music in harmony with nature, heard alongside the "Paganini performances" of the brown thrasher (158).

If Whitman's dominant image is of the skilled journeyman whose place was increasingly threatened by the new order of mass production, this was a position all too familiar to Thoreau. In the early 1840s he combined the roles of craftsman and engineer, working to refine the pencil-making processes used by his father's firm. By the time *Walden* appeared, however, "John Thoreau & Son" had abandoned pencil making in the face of a glutted market and was only grinding graphite powder for electro-typing.[25]

In *Walden,* Thoreau's model seems instead to be that of the journey-man farmer of a generation or two earlier, whose yeoman republican-ism was now threatened by economic rationalization and the forces of an expanded market. As several critics have pointed out, his bean field never made him economically self-sufficient—it had to be supplemented by work as a day laborer.[26] But this, along with the need to hire draft animals when necessary, had been true of many Concord farmers in earlier years.[27] And many other farm households depended upon additional income from weaving, hat making, or other putting-out activities.

Thoreau's objective is, finally, more than simply individual self-culture. He organizes his description of Walden's former inhabitants in spatial rather than temporal terms—from a surveyor's point of view, H. Daniel Peck suggests—and in so doing, he recasts them as contemporaries, as a single community.[28] "Former Inhabitants" may be largely mock-heroic in tone, but underneath it there remains a "continuing desire . . . to rebuild town society in his own terms."[29] "[T]his small village, germ of something more, why did it fail while Concord keeps its ground?" (264). Why, he wants to ask, has America not developed along the lines of this alter-native model? "Might not the basket, stable-broom, mat-making, corn-parching, linen-spinning, and pottery business have thrived here, making the wilderness to blossom like the rose, and a numerous posterity have inherited the land of their fathers? . . . Again, perhaps, Nature will try, with me for a first settler, and my house raised last spring to be the oldest in the hamlet" (264). Thoreau's image for his *Week* has been a woven basket (19), a product like those of the working people he describes here. He identifies himself with a community based on craft skills and arti-sanship, against the large-scale mills and factories spreading throughout the region.

Thoreau's is not simply an ahistorical or visionary conception. Antebellum New England was in transition, torn between conflicting but still coexisting versions of social and economic order. Mills and mill villages had cash economies based on rigid and rationalized control of their wage laborers. But alongside them remained another, less purely commercial model of communal life, one based on small-scale producers who might combine multiple economic roles or functions. Transactions between them were based less on cash than on barter, exchange, or a complex network of private debts and credits.[30]

Cooperative and communal practices were on the decline in Concord, replaced by a reliance on and exploitation of hired labor, but they remain visible in Thoreau's text.[31] On one hand, the village is a public space of gossip and talk, "a great news room," the sphere of town meeting and lyceum, in which the visitor is both a subject of discourse and a discursive subject himself (167). But it is also a collection of private, commercial enterprises, whose signs seek to "allure" the visitor, "some to catch him by the appetite, as the tavern and victualling cellar; some by the fancy, as the dry goods store and the jeweller's; and others by the hair or the feet or the skirts, as the barber, the shoemaker, or the tailor" (168). An older version of neighborliness and citizenship still struggles against an economic notion of the individual as isolated consumer. *Walden,* I am suggesting, is intended as an intervention in this conflict, a response to an ongoing process of economic and social change.

The re-emergence of a diverse, working-class community would be nature's work, Thoreau says, in which he sees himself as taking part. It is a history that "mak[es] the wilderness to blossom," instead of one that cuts into or across natural growth and development. Would nature's return in the form of this community be like the eventual return of the fish to the Musketaquid, a link to a level of history beneath the process of industrialization, one closer to the rhythms of natural time?

SEVEN

Division

and Revenge

Tucked away at the end of each volume of the Princeton edition of Thoreau's journals is a long list of cross-references linking passages from the journals to sections of his published works. These lists reveal an interesting pattern: Thoreau drew freely and widely from his journals for material for *Walden* and the *Week*, ranging across a decade's worth of entries; but he worked quite differently in composing his abolitionist essays. None of the journals from 1842–49 provides any material at all for "Resistance to Civil Government."[1] There are drafts of passages from "Slavery in Massachusetts" (in 1851 and 1854) and "A Plea for Captain John Brown" (in 1859), but these are discrete and self-contained segments, years (and hundreds of pages) apart.[2]

What this suggests is that Thoreau drafted his antislavery essays in a very different fashion than he did his first two books. The latter were carefully assembled and composed over a period of years. The former, on the other hand, were written much more quickly, in response to specific events, and primarily rather than secondarily for public delivery. They appear as breaks in or departures from the journal, neither parts of an organically developing whole nor the results of methodical construction. When Thoreau does generate multiple drafts for an essay, as with "Resistance to Civil Government," he does so outside the journal.[3]

If the abolitionist essays thus seem to abandon the compositional methods of *Walden*, they also reject its assumptions and results. *Walden*, I have suggested, creates a mediating space or middle ground between nature and society through self-conscious linguistic labor and construction. But Thoreau defines the slavery issue as one on which there is no middle ground and to which there can be no adequate linguistic or political response.

Such reservations about language have appeared earlier in his work: in the *Week,* for instance, Thoreau comments that "The word which is best said came nearest to not being spoken at all, for it is cousin to a deed which the speaker could have better done" (105), and he ends that book by praising silence as nature's primary and most eloquent state (391– 93). As he becomes more directly engaged in the political realm, this suspicion of language comes to the fore, and a split emerges in Thoreau's work, one that widens immensely as the Civil War approaches.

The central aim of "Resistance to Civil Government" is not connection but division: "Action from principle," Thoreau says, "changes things and relations; it is essentially revolutionary. . . . It not only divides states and churches, it divides families; aye, it divides the *individual,* separating the diabolical in him from the divine" (72). The essay works by drawing lines of opposition between categories, defining the differences between them as both qualitative and absolute.

Thoreau begins by separating cases subject to "the rule of expediency" from those to be decided according to conscience alone (65). "Government is at best but an expedient," according to Thoreau, but slavery, for him, is one of those matters "to which the rule of expediency does not apply, in which a people, as well as an individual, must do justice, cost what it may" (63, 68). Slavery is a matter of absolute justice, beyond measurement or calculation, beyond the discourses of either the marketplace or the statehouse: "This people must cease to hold slaves, and to make war on Mexico, though it cost them their existence as a people" (68).

Representative government and industrial capitalism blend together, as Thoreau speaks of government as a "machine" and of those who serve the state with their bodies as "machines" as well (67, 66). (In a sense, this parallels his argument in *Walden,* in which he linked the regimentation of Northern manual and factory labor to the dehumanizing effects of slavery.) Here, the political realm becomes an extension of the marketplace, with an array of "available" commodities–both candidates and voters, who make themselves "available" by their participation (70).

In many ways, Thoreau's rejection of politics resembles the stance of William Lloyd Garrison, but Thoreau's argument is, at bottom, the more radical of the two. Garrison attacks a political system irremediably corrupted by its acceptance of slavery, proclaiming, "NO UNION WITH SLAVEHOLDERS," but he does not reject representative government itself.[4] Thoreau, too, refuses to "recognize that political organization as *my* government which is the *slave's* government also" (67), but for him, all political representation–even under ideal conditions–remains fundamentally suspect.

"There are thousands," he says, "who are *in opinion* opposed to slavery and to the war, who yet in effect do nothing to put an end to them. . . . At most, they give only a cheap vote" (69). Expressing an opinion, either in speech or at the ballot box, is ultimately insignificant, for voting is no more than "a sort of gaming," "a playing with right and wrong, with moral questions; and betting naturally accompanies it. The character of the voters is not staked. I cast my vote, perchance, as I think right; but I am not vitally concerned that that right should prevail. I am willing to leave it to the majority. Its obligation, therefore, never exceeds that of expediency. Even voting *for the right* is *doing* nothing for it. It is only expressing to men feebly your desire that it should prevail" (69). Politics, insofar as it locates action within the sphere of representative processes and institutions, strips that action of its moral value. Opinions may be cheap or costly, but they can still be bought and sold, or gambled away in the political marketplace or gambling hall. Action that is mediated in any form, political or linguistic, cannot commit or express the character of the individual.

Thoreau's ideal government would, in the end, be entirely transparent: "this government never of itself furthered any enterprise, but by the alacrity with which it got out of its way," he claims, "The character inherent in the American people has done all that has been accomplished" (64). Underlying Thoreau's rhetoric are two quite radical assumptions: first, that character or thought can produce action directly, without the mediating structures of linguistic or political representation; and, second, that truly meaningful action is possible only to the extent that it remains unmediated.

At first glance, this view seems more than compatible with Whitman's vision of pure democracy in the 1855 *Leaves*. But Thoreau's radicalism leads in the opposite direction from Whitman's—not toward integration into a collective whole but away from it. Thoreau's charge to his readers is simply to "withdraw their support, both in person and in property, from the government of Massachusetts" (74). "[I]f *one* HONEST man," he says, "*ceasing to hold slaves,* were actually to withdraw from this copartnership, and be locked up in the county jail therefor, it would be the abolition of slavery in America" (75). This claim can be read in two different ways: on one hand, if one man were to renounce slavery in this way, it might begin a series of such withdrawals, and then the gradual abandonment of slaveholding throughout the nation; alternatively, if one man withdrew from partnership in the national commitment to slave owning, America would lose its absolute status as a "slave State." The first reading offers a vision of incremental change—it thus belongs, one might say, to the realm of expediency; the latter, based on a set of absolute categories and bypassing questions of representation, is more in keeping with the terms of the essay as a whole.

In all three essays, Thoreau figures moral oppositions in geographical terms; the result is two opposed and mutually exclusive spaces—those of slavery and of freedom. So long as the state condones slavery, the only place of freedom is within its own "peculiar institution," the jail (82). There is no territory left for negotiation or neutrality.

Here, however, we have reached perhaps the central difficulty for Thoreau: "Resistance to Civil Government" is, of course, itself an exercise in linguistic representation, a piece of political rhetoric. One might advance an argument for the lyceum or town meeting as a democratic space for public deliberation, the exercise of which might lead to moral action—but Thoreau has hardly done so.[5] The essay thus works to undermine its own efficacy and legitimacy. Is Thoreau's alternative to representation no more than nominal change, a mere shift in descriptive categories?

When Thoreau decides to follow his night in jail by joining a "huckle-berry party," it is a rejection of political parties and an attempt to escape the political altogether, to reach a point where "the State was nowhere to be seen" (84). In so doing, he may be said to demonstrate the limits of state power, but such a spiritual or even physical withdrawal remains an individual gesture, one with limited physical or moral effect. Unlike Thoreau's re-creation of an alternative history and community in Walden woods, this turn to the woods seems only to mark rather than to resolve a moral impasse.

"Slavery in Massachusetts," written six years after "Resistance to Civil Government," begins at the same point, but takes its argument a step or two further—to the very edge of violence. Speaking at a July Fourth meeting in Framingham, Thoreau once again begins by insisting on the "impertinence" of law in relation to the moral issue of slavery (92). The law is concerned with "expediency" (103); committing a matter to the courts is like voting: "the judge may decide this way or that; it is a kind of accident, at best" (97). Thoreau's call is thus again for "each inhabitant of the State [to] dissolve his union with her, as long as she delays to do her duty" (104).

In this essay, Thoreau links politics, the marketplace, and the dehumanizing impact of slavery even more forcibly. The political discourse of the Boston newspapers is "a leaf from the gospel of the gambling-house, the groggery and the brothel, harmonizing with the gospel of the Merchants' Exchange" (101–2). Most men, Thoreau insists, "are not men of principle"; their politics is just another kind of property management (102). And judges who follow the Constitution alone "are merely the inspectors of a pick-lock and murderer's tools" (98).

It is just this reduction of the moral to the economic or criminal, the human to the commodity, that is the essence of slavery: "If I were seriously to propose to Congress to make mankind into sausages, I have no doubt that most of the members would smile at my proposition. . . . But if any of them will tell me that to make a man into a sausage would be much worse,—would be any worse, than to make him into a slave,—than it was to enact the Fugitive Slave Law, I will accuse him of foolishness, of intellectual incapacity, of making a distinction without a difference" (96–97). Both sausages and slaves are commodities, objects traded and then consumed by the plantation economy. Northern supporters of the Fugitive Slave Law are parties to this commodification, which, in Thoreau's image, becomes an act of cannibalism. His technique, as in *Walden,* is to bring an abstraction down to the level of the body: there, his goal was to provide a ground for positive spiritual values; here, the result is a physical immediacy that repulses rather than uplifts.

If "Slavery in Massachusetts" rejects the American political present, it veers still further away from *Walden* in its treatment of the revolutionary past. Only a week after the Sims case had been decided in 1851, according to Thoreau, the inhabitants of Concord celebrated "their liberty – and the courage and love of liberty of their ancestors who fought at the bridge. As if *those* three millions had fought for the right to be free themselves, but to hold in slavery three million others" (95). Present-day Americans would try to ground the antebellum status quo in the revolutionary tradition; to do so, Thoreau charges, is to make 1776 into a slaveholders' revolt.[6] Nowadays, he laments, the Massachusetts militia trains "merely to rob Mexico, and carry back fugitive slaves to their masters" (95).

From his position in his Walden bean field, Thoreau could both acknowledge the pull of patriotism and attempt to build an alternative historical tradition, one that would include rather than suppress African and Native Americans. Now, however, he demands a radical break from the past: "The question is not whether you or your grandfather, seventy years ago, did not enter into an agreement to serve the devil, and that service is not accordingly now due; but whether you will not now, for once and at last, serve God" (103). In "Resistance to Civil Government," he had criticized lawyers and politicians for their allegiance to "consistency" or precedent rather than truth (87). Now he declares it to be "no time . . . to be judging according to . . . precedents, but to establish a precedent for the future" (97). At this same Independence Day meeting, Garrison destroyed a copy of the Constitution, a gesture very much in the spirit of Thoreau's remarks. For in "Slavery in Massachusetts," both the Constitution as a legal document and the nineteenth century's link to the revolutionary past are to be discarded, politics and history both to be subsumed by the absolute moral conflict of the present.

The Sims and Anthony Burns cases had both shown the impossibility of using legal discourse to further the antislavery cause. After 1850, all of the fugitives who escaped capture in Massachusetts did so through either physical flight or the threat or actual use of violence, and Thoreau himself had become a participant in the Underground Railroad.[7] In this context, it is not surprising that Thoreau should pose the issue in such stark terms, and reject both legal and political discourse and action. He declares himself willing to accept and practice violence: "I need not say what match I would touch, what system endeavour to blow up, – but as I love my life, I would side with the light, and let the dark earth roll from under me, calling my mother and my brother to follow" (102). To specify a particular act would be almost to neutralize it, by converting it into discourse; Thoreau speaks only of a total, potentially annihilating gesture. "My thoughts are murder to the State," he says, once again leaping directly from thought into violent action, without the intermediate step of representation or expression (108).

The image with which Thoreau brings his essay to a close, "a white water-lily" (108), is a complex and deceptive one. Lawrence Buell finds both it and the "huckleberry party" of "Resistance to Civil Government" "disturbing" in "the insouciance with which the persona turns away from social confrontation for the sake of immersion in a simplified green world."[8] But while the lily may be an "emblem of purity" for Thoreau, it is hardly a symbol of delicacy or passivity: "It reminds me that nature has been partner to no Missouri Compromise. I scent no compromise in the fragrance of the water-lily. It is not a *Nymphoea Douglassi*" (108). Unlike in the soon-to-be-published *Walden,* the turn to nature here is not toward a middle ground, whose virtues may be rediscovered and then reinfused into the social. Both natural and moral purity are "wholly sundered" from the political, from slavery, servility, and death (108).

Thoreau ends not with a reimmersion in the pastoral but with a renewed insistence on absolute oppositions – between good and evil, light and dark. For him, Massachusetts clearly belongs to the latter realm: he has surrendered "the illusion that my life passed somewhere only *between* heaven and hell, . . . now I cannot persuade myself that I do not dwell *wholly within* hell" (106).

"A Plea for Captain John Brown" is composed later and under different conditions than *Walden,* of course, but it only continues and intensifies the divergences we have already seen.[9] A single image may be enough to show the distance Thoreau has traveled between 1854 and 1859: "in the moral world," he says, "when good seed is planted, good fruit is inevitable, and does not depend on your watering and cultivating; . . . when you plant, or bury, a hero in his field, a crop of heroes is sure to spring up" (119). Both literally and figuratively, Thoreau has abandoned his bean field and the work of cultivation. There does remain a level of historical and literary allusion embedded in his writing here, but it is just this kind of attention to language as a medium that the essay will most forcefully and insistently reject.

John Brown has risen above "the trivialness and dust of politics," Thoreau says (125). He is like the Puritans, who "were neither Democrats nor Republicans, . . . not making many compromises, nor seeking after available candidates" (113–14). His "appointment" does not come from a president or a political party: "he did not set up even a political graven image between him and his God" (120). The result, for Thoreau, is a figure far beyond a merely "representative" status (125).

For Thoreau, the government is no more than a "counterfeiting law-factory, standing half in a slave land and half in a free" (137). At this point, representation can only be falsification, for the slavery issue has long passed beyond the limits of the political and discursive. He intensifies his image of totalizing spatial enclosure still further, comparing America to a vast slave ship; he derides the idea of reform through " 'the quiet diffusion of the sentiments of humanity,' " turning the "diffusion of humanity" into a euphemism for casting overboard the corpses of dead slaves (124). What is needed is not political reform, but the cleansing violence of revolt.

Men without a cause or commitment like Brown's, Thoreau says, are no more than "stupid and timid chattels" (117)–not participants in the economic order but objects manipulated by it. Brown does not conceive of his action in economic terms at all: "I don't suppose he could get four-and-sixpence a day for being hung, take the year round; but then he stands to save a considerable part of his soul—and *such* a soul!—when *you* do not. No doubt you can get more in your market for a quart of milk than for a quart of blood, but that is not the market that heroes carry their blood to" (119). Thoreau has always insisted that the moral and the economic are incommensurable, but here his language not only implies that the New England farmer is a dealer in human blood rather than just milk (in other words, a slave trader), but that he is also in a sense a consumer of it. Brown's execution once again becomes an act of cannibalism.

"A Plea for Captain John Brown" thus sweeps away all mediating institutions, political or economic, far more brutally than the earlier essays. They may have implied a rejection of language in their leap from thought to action, but the later essay makes that attack an explicit one. Brown is "[a] man of rare common sense and directness of speech, as of action"; he "par[es] away his speech," and is "not in the least a rhetorician" (115). He answers his interrogators with "truth, clear as lightning, crashing into their obscene temples" (126). Thoreau later speaks of the "indignation that is said to have cleared the temple once" (133), but in this earlier passage, it is not clear whether Brown's words destroy institutions or individuals. In either case, speech is the equivalent of action—but its power is only a destructive one.

Brown's speech is "a Sharps' rifle," his words as direct as bullets, Thoreau implies (127). But the essayist's words are not similarly fatal. In *Walden,* he had expressed the wish to "speak somewhere without bounds," with enough "extravagance" to achieve his desired effect (324). In his "Plea," on the other hand, he praises Brown for speaking "within bounds," without overstatement or eloquence—now effectiveness depends upon reticence and restraint (115). In a telling aside, Thoreau notes that Brown posed as a surveyor in order to scout his enemies in Kansas (115–16). Thoreau, however, is just a surveyor, his words only words. And he goes on to turn those words against themselves and against their author: in Brown "there is no idle eloquence, no made, nor maiden, speech,"

Thoreau insists (127). No wordplay like this very sentence, in fact—Thoreau's pun indicts its own construction, the very fact of its "making" as language.[10] Ultimately, he defers the hope of adequate representation indefinitely, turning the last page of the essay into little more than a commentary on Brown's own words.[11]

Thoreau can "foresee the time when the painter will paint that scene [the settlement of the slavery question]," but such a picture will only "be the ornament of some *future* national gallery, when at least the present form of Slavery shall be no more here" (138; emphasis added). It will take an eradication of slavery—indeed, an apocalyptic transformation—before an adequate representation of freedom will be possible. That moment, however, will bring only grieving and destruction: "We shall then be at liberty to weep for Captain Brown. Then, and not till then, we will take our revenge" (138).

By the time America reaches the Civil War, Thoreau has forsaken politics and public speech almost completely. He is left reaching for a transformation that will occur, not through language, but through its displacement and supersession, in an apocalyptic revelation.

These three essays are, perhaps, the most overtly political and insurrectionary—and the least literary and ambiguous—of all the texts I have discussed. So it is ironic that they should increasingly fall back upon the terms of the jeremiad tradition that Sacvan Bercovitch has described.[12] In their insistent individualism and their recourse to the revolutionary founding fathers as standards for judgment, they come closest to the kind of dissent that Bercovitch sees as so easily recontained within American pluralism. On the other hand, the nineteenth-century Whig version of the jeremiad, according to Bercovitch, was designed to moderate the revolutionary impulse into continuity and consensus.[13] But Thoreau, along with many others in the abolitionist movement, had been moving ever closer toward an open endorsement of violent resistance to the state. Nowhere, perhaps, can we find a more radical *rejection* of the very idea of consensus than in "Slavery in Massachusetts" or "A Plea for Captain John Brown." With the rejection of discourse as a value, pluralism would seem to become an impossibility.

Thoreau's work almost explodes under the pressure of the slavery issue. Nature and society, language and moral action—the terms that *Walden* struggles to bring together—are cast asunder with the utmost possible force. The antislavery essays end by emptying out the middle landscape of pastoral, leaving a nonhuman wilderness set against an all-too-human world of social corruption. The result, at its darkest, is a longing to escape from history itself, a desire for cleansing annihilation.

~

Civil Wars

If, as I have argued, Thoreau's "Plea for Captain John Brown" looks toward the Civil War as an apocalyptic transformation, Hawthorne sees the war in cataclysmic terms as well. In the preface to *Our Old Home,* he uses the image of a "hurricane," whose force compels him to abandon romance writing altogether: it is "sweeping us all along with it, possibly, into a Limbo where our nation and its polity may be as literally the fragments of a shattered dream as my unwritten Romance."[1] Romance and political reality come together here, but in a disastrous mutual disintegration. For Hawthorne, too, there is no more "neutral territory" left; as the rising violence makes even political institutions seem illusory, imagination itself becomes "a kind of treason."[2]

By the end of the 1850s, then, Hawthorne, Whitman, and Thoreau had all been forced to abandon their projects of literary mediation or transformation. Each had sought to fashion a new version of community in response to the nation's economic and racial divisions. But those conflicts had intensified to the point that no adequate means of representation seemed to remain—a view confirmed by the South's refusal to recognize the results of the 1860 elections.

For other writers, however, such a plunge into direct conflict might open new textual possibilities, rather than just foreclosing old ones. To Margaret Fuller and Louisa May Alcott, wartime meant a liberation from conventional categories of difference, whether of gender, race, or literary genre. In this conclusion, I briefly set their responses against those of Hawthorne and Whitman—to give a sense, I hope, of both the limits and the remaining potential of mid-nineteenth-century American writing.

In some ways, Fuller's dispatches from Italy for the *New York Tribune* (1847–50) are direct antecedents for Hawthorne's *Marble Faun* (1859). Her "letters" display not just a newly radical political perspective but a comparable shift in form as well. Fuller begins to interweave her aesthetic and political responses into reports that go beyond the boundaries of even her own earlier travel writing, becoming, as Larry J. Reynolds has suggested, sketches for a radical history of the Roman Republic.[3] A decade later, the revolutionary political culture that inspired Fuller had been long suppressed, but it and she both seem to hover over Hawthorne's romance, unquiet spirits that he can neither accept nor expel.

The Civil War did not silence Whitman as it did Hawthorne; "When Lilacs Last in the Dooryard Bloom'd" (1865) does, however, show major changes in his poetic practice, signs of the cost he pays for his reassertion of a poetic voice. Louisa May Alcott's story "My Contraband" (1863/1869), on the other hand, confronts such issues of literary authority and complicity quite directly, foregrounding its own generic and political compromises. And in so doing, it offers a skeptical challenge to the nationalistic model of heroic sacrifice on which Whitman's elegy depends.

Italy

From August 1846 through June 1850, Margaret Fuller contributed a series of reports to Horace Greeley's *New York Tribune* under the heading "Things and Thoughts in Europe." The first group of dispatches, from England and Scotland, seem by and large the notes of an intellectual tourist, mixing conversations with writers such as Wordsworth and Carlyle with stops at literary and historical sites. But when Fuller reaches the Continent, she begins to leave the conventions of travel writing behind, first widening her focus to cover politics and social issues, and then reshaping her work entirely, into a fluid blend of aesthetic and political commentary.[4]

This change in Fuller's interests and technique is visible in letter 13, written from Naples in early 1847 but looking back on her journey from Paris. At Lyons, her party sets out to "visit some of the garrets of the weavers," and a "sweet little girl" offers to guide them, leading the group "by a weary, winding way, whose pavement was much easier for her feet in their wooden *sabots* than for ours in Paris shoes."[5] It is a conventional contrast: a simple, friendly child in primitive but practical garb vs. the impractically fashionable tourists. The image, however, is soon altered: "My sweet little girl turned out to be a wife of six or seven years' standing, with two rather sickly looking children" and a household desperate for work in order to stave off eviction. By the end of a single long paragraph, Fuller's sympathetic description has modulated into a direct attack on the exploitation of working-class women like her guide.

Worth noting here is not just Fuller's politicized response but the fact that she describes her initial, perhaps patronizing, assumptions as well. The result is both a demonstration of her own shift in perspective and a critique of the tourist's detached, aestheticized viewpoint, from which local inhabitants appear only as picturesque objects. Fuller quotes her guide directly, acknowledging her voice even as she emphasizes the woman's lack of political and economic agency.

Fuller's next letter, written from Rome in May 1847, illustrates the way in which she begins to merge aesthetic and political matters in her dispatches.[6] She opens with an attack on the "vulgarity" of English tourists, which "talks of *'managing'* the Colosseum by moonlight, – and snatches *'bits'* for a *'sketch'* from the sublime silence of the Campagna" (132). Her aim, she implies, is to craft a response that will neither segment and commodify the experience of Italy nor reduce it to "bits" and "sketches" on the page.

Fuller goes on to comment on the work of both expatriate artists and the Italian masters, an impressionistic survey that is finally concerned more with her responses than with the works themselves. She seems doubtful, in fact, that any commentary can do justice to the daily reality of Rome: "I have heard owls hoot in the Colosseum by moonlight, and they spoke more to the purpose than I ever heard any other voice upon that subject. I have seen all the pomps and shows of Holy Week in the church of St. Peter, and found them less imposing than an habitual acquaintance with the place" (135–36). Already, perhaps, one senses Fuller moving away from the tourist's emphasis on passing visits and spectacular events toward an expatriate's comparatively fixed or "habitual" view.

In her next report, written from Milan, she remarks that "Every stone has a voice, every grain of dust seems instinct with spirit from the Past, every step recalls some line, some legend of long-neglected lore" (140). For her, the historical and literary past is a continuous and invigorating daily presence.

The topic of church ceremonies brings her to the Pope, public festivals, and the world of Italian politics. The street culture of nineteenth-century Rome is a key ingredient here, for it provides space for religious processions, popular celebrations, and political demonstrations alike. Indeed, in the months that follow, these forms will often blend together, as in Vaclav Havel's Prague, both in the street and on Fuller's page. "Festivities," she writes in a later dispatch, "have been of great importance [in Italy], since for a century or two back, the thought, the feeling, the genius of the people have had more chance to expand, to express themselves, there than anywhere else" because of government censorship (180). In this instance, she describes a torchlight procession, "a river of fire" moving through the streets to thank the Pope for his support of a representative council: "The stream of fire advanced slowly with a perpetual surge-like sound of voices; the torches flashed on the animated Italian faces. I have never seen anything finer. Ascending the Quirinal they made it a mount of light. Bengal fires were thrown up, which cast their red and white light on the noble Greek figures of men and horses that reign over it" (136–37). Fuller's response is a dual one, to the demonstration's political content and to the sheer visual spectacle of the scene, the play of colored light on classical sculpture. The moment seems to contain all the liberating promise of "My Kinsman, Major Molineux" with none of Hawthorne's ambivalence.

In an October report, she speaks of "laborers of the lowest class" "marching home at night; keeping step as if they were in the National Guard, filling the air and cheering the melancholy moon, by the patriotic hymns sung, with the mellow tone and in the perfect time that belongs to Italians. I would describe the extempore concerts in the streets, the rejoicings at the theatres, where the addresses of liberal souls to the people, through that best vehicle, the drama, may now be heard" (160). Here the daily movement of the urban crowd blends with more formal political and cultural activity to create an atmosphere of revolutionary ferment.[7]

This interplay reaches its climax at the time of Carnival, in March 1848. This year, Fuller notes, Romans dedicated the candlelight festivity of the Moccoletti "in honor of the Revolutions of France and Austria, and nothing could be more beautiful": "Here and there danced men carrying aloft *moccoli,* and clanking chains, emblem of the tyrannic power now vanquished by the people. The people, sweet and noble, who, in the intoxication of their joy, were guilty of no rude or unkindly word or act, and who, no signal being given as usual for the termination of their diversion, closed, of their own accord and with one consent, singing the hymns for Pio [the Pope], by nine o'clock" (211). The "play of Carnival" (210) becomes first a revolutionary gesture and then the momentary vehicle of a new community; the next year, she will again emphasize the democratic, egalitarian nature of the festival (248). Fuller closes this section of her letter with an impassioned declaration of her own political allegiance, to "the true aristocracy of a nation, the only really noble–the LABOURING CLASSES" (211).

By this point, Fuller has largely abandoned the role of traveling observer in favor of that of an expatriate–and, soon, an open partisan. She would no longer speak *for* her readers as their representative abroad, but instead speak *to* them from a position external–and increasingly opposed–to their own. In some ways, the individualism that structures a travel narrative is also gone, or at least sharply diminished: Fuller begins to quote speeches in their entirety, making her text into a vehicle for the ideas of Mazzini and others. And, as the previous quotation suggests, her own critical voice is often subordinated to a description of "the people" as primary historical agent.[8]

The dispatches are, by this point, difficult for a twentieth-century reader to classify: they are neither conventional history, nor purely political commentary, nor just sketches of landscape and culture. They offer subjective responses at times, but hardly a personal narrative: the crucial events in Fuller's private life–her marriage to Giovanni Ossoli and her pregnancy and motherhood–are never mentioned, becoming visible only inferentially and in hindsight, as explanations for the gaps between dispatches.[9] Reynolds is right to call the letters a "coherent and powerful rhetorical construct," but it is a construct of Fuller's own devising, a fluid bricolage of themes and styles that reflects the complexity of her position and the power of her now revolutionary socialism.[10]

Fuller's position is that of a self-conscious intermediary between na-tions, cultures, and different modes of cultural activity. Her knowledge of Italian enables her to bridge the gulf between English-speaking vis-itors and artists and the culture around them. When, for example, she accompanies an American artist to the ceremony at which the Roman Republic is proclaimed, her companion "remained impassive": "Passing the Winter in Rome to study Art, he was insensible to the artistic beauty of the scene—insensible to this new life of that spirit from which all the forms he gazes at in galleries emanated" (257, 258). For Fuller, on the other hand, the moment is one of simultaneous political, spiritual, and artistic rebirth. The political act becomes beautiful in itself—because its spirit is the same as that which informs artistic creation.

This fusion between the political and the aesthetic runs through her dispatches, even during the siege of Rome and after the fall of the repub-lic. She begins her description of the departure of Garibaldi's troops by wishing that Sir Walter Scott could see "a sight so beautiful, so romantic and so sad":

> Whoever knows Rome knows the peculiar solemn grandeur of [the piazza of St. John Lateran], scene of the first triumph of Rienzi, the magnificence of the "mother of all churches," the Baptistery with its porphyry columns, the Santa Scala with its glittering mosaics of the early ages. . . . The sun was setting, the crescent moon rising, the flower of the Italian youth were marshaling in that solemn place. . . . They had all put on the beautiful dress of the Garibaldi legion, the tunic of bright red cloth, the Greek cap, or else round hat with Puritan plume, their long hair was blown back from resolute faces. (304)

The richness of this passage comes not just from its dramatic framing, but from the way it combines an awareness of current political history with a complex sense of place. It is the setting that enables Fuller to summon up both the historical echoes of Rienzi's fourteenth-century republican revolt and the sacred meaning of the Santa Scala, as parts of the dense cultural heritage – pagan and Catholic, ancient and modern, popular and elite – of the city Garibaldi leaves behind. To these she adds her own passionate response, both personal and political, to the beauty and the pathos of the figures before her.[11]

Ironically, the richness and power of Fuller's authorial voice can seem even greater in defeat. Her letter from Florence dated June 6, 1850, speaks with a grim confidence: "The next revolution, here and elsewhere, will be radical" and its eventual outcome assured: "the struggle that is now to begin will be fearful, but even from the first hours not doubtful. . . . Men shall now be represented as souls, not hands and feet, and governed accordingly" (321, 322). Six months before her death, Fuller is already reaching for mythic stature.

By the late 1850s, Hawthorne had been responding to Fuller and her work for more than two decades – ever since their days at Brook Farm. His reaction had always been ambivalent but powerful, and her final incarnation – as a combination of radical socialist and feminist, journalist and historian, wife and mother – clearly disturbed him most.

In a now notorious entry in his *Italian Notebooks,* dated April 3, 1858, Hawthorne records some gossip he has heard about her in Rome, stories remarkable not just for their scurrility but also for Hawthorne's apparent readiness – even eagerness – to accept them. According to his informant, American sculptor Joseph Mozier, "poor Margaret" remained in Rome during the fighting of 1849 only because of her "purely sensual" attraction to Giovanni Ossoli.[12] Ossoli himself is described as no more than a handsome, barely literate servant, "half an idiot, and without any pretensions to be a gentleman" (14:155). Fuller "was a great humbug," Hawthorne decides; he repeats Mozier's charge that she "had quite lost all power of literary production," and that her "History of the Roman revolution" simply "never had existence" (14:156).

The notebook entry thus mounts two different attacks on Fuller, but the charges are, for Hawthorne, intimately related. First, her decision to remain in Rome was based, he says, on personal or private concerns, not political or intellectual ones. And those private concerns – marriage and motherhood—are labeled as "purely sensual," a submission to what he calls her "strong and coarse" sexual nature (14:155). Second, such an access to or expression of feminine sexuality inevitably—indeed, *necessarily,* for Hawthorne—means a loss of the presumably masculine "power of literary production": "she proved herself a very woman, after all, and fell as the weakest of her sisters might" (14:156, 157).

What Hawthorne suppresses, of course, is any mention of Fuller's *Tribune* dispatches. Their very existence—their successful transgression of the generic and gender boundaries that he would impose—refutes his charges and assumptions. What the notebook passage shows, finally, is Hawthorne's own intense anxieties about female authorship and, at this point in his career, his own inability to lend political and historical resonance to his own romance.

In *The Marble Faun,* Hawthorne returns to the impasse glimpsed at the end of *The House of the Seven Gables,* in which the revisionary potential of the romance comes to threaten the textual structures on which it depends. He thematizes problems of representation, but in this text he fragments and disperses the elements of his earlier moonlight scenes: the plot does not build toward a single act of rebellion—this occurs barely a third of the way through—but instead explores its aftermath. The most Hawthorne can do is to gather together (and then surrender) his different strands at the close—in another unsettling moment of public theater.

Hawthorne's subtitle is "The Romance of Monte Beni," not "A Romance of Rome"—this points away from issues of art and representation, back toward the questions of genealogical continuity and inheritance that constitute the "romance" of *The House of the Seven Gables.* From this perspective, then, the "romance" of *The Marble Faun* lies in the faunlike innocence Donatello has inherited from his Monte Beni ancestors. The genealogy of Monte Beni, like that of the Maules, is a matter of "tradition" rather than "written record."[13] But, in contrast to the earlier novel, this romance does not act to historicize the Italian present; it instead only mythologizes and mystifies origins, leading the "romancer . . . into a region of old poetry"—back to the Golden Age (4:231).

The historicizing force in *The Marble Faun* lies not in the romance plot, but in its realistic Roman setting: the narrator's aim, he says, is "not to meddle with history – with which our narrative is no otherwise concerned, than that the very dust of Rome is historic, and inevitably settles on our page" (4:101). Fuller speaks of such "dust" as "instinct with spirits from the past," but Hawthorne finds it only deadening. The landscape he describes is that of an irretrievably fallen world: "no land of dreams, but the broadest page of history, crowded so full with memorable events that one obliterates another; as if Time had crossed and re-crossed his own records till they grew illegible" (4:101). History, in this formulation, is not an ongoing process, but a long-completed text – indeed, a work so often revised that the layers of representation only obscure their original referents. And the weight of such a history can only be more oppressive because of its inaccessibility. The result is a text suffused by a sense of belatedness and cultural decline.

In an outburst reminiscent of Holgrave, the narrator wishes that "[a]ll towns should be made capable of purification by fire, or of decay within each half-century. Otherwise, they become the hereditary haunts of vermin and noisomeness . . . we may build almost immortal habitations, it is true; but we cannot keep them from growing old, musty, unwholesome, dreary, full of death-scenes, ghosts, and murder-stains" (4:301, 302). The force of history turns the thrust of the romance away from a critique of the present, which seems "pressed down or crowded out," and toward a desire to simply erase or "white-wash" the text of the past (4:6, 303).

As the story begins, Miriam is "haunted" by a figure from that past, a representative of patriarchal and legal authority whom she resists – but also takes as her artistic model (4:32). This mix of resistance and creative dependence echoes Hawthorne's description of his own work in "The Custom-House." She and her friends define their work, however, not in terms of a political or historical past, but in relation to a primarily artistic or literary one. Their themes and subjects most often come from classical and Renaissance art, not from the people and places around them. Its art-historical content may be revisionary, but Miriam's work, like Kenyon's and Hilda's, has little reference beyond the aesthetic.

Hawthorne's expatriate artists stroll through Rome, taking in "some of those scenes of ruin, which produced their best effects under the splendour of the Italian moon" (4:141). This search for "effects" is symptomatic of the way in which Kenyon and his colleagues see Italy and its inhabitants in almost exclusively aesthetic terms, as " 'the Pictorial Land' " (4:371). The work of wine making, for instance, is said to be "unlike other toil," for it has "a flavour of poetry" about it (4:275). And Kenyon "delight[s] in . . . picturesque bits of rustic character," such as women working in the fields and, "more agreeable" still, a girl bearing an enormous burden of twigs and shrubs (4:290–91). The picturesque and the poetic are here clearly opposed to the hard economic facts of daylight labor.

The operation of Kenyon's studio is built upon just such a split between the intellectual "work" of artistic perception and the physical production of sculpture as commodity. The studio may look like "a stone-mason's workshop," but the sculptor's involvement in the process extends only to the making of a clay model, which is his "intimate production . . . moulded throughout with his loving hands, and nearest to his imagination and heart" (4:114). The actual work in marble is left to "a class of men [with] merely mechanical skill," mere "instruments," "nameless machine[s] in human shape" (4:115). Unlike Holgrave's photography or Blithedale's ideal of aesthetic labor, this is not a process that integrates or unifies the manual and the intellectual. Instead, it separates and hierarchizes conception and execution, artist and craftsman, the aesthetic and the economic – mystifying the process with a language of organic growth and emergence, in which "the figure is imbedded in the stone" and needs only to be "freed from its encumbering superfluities" (4:115).[14]

The fatal confrontation between Miriam, Donatello, and her Model comes as the climax of a "moonlight ramble," in which a group of artists wanders across the city (4:142). Roman moonlight has a problematic effect, however – unsettling, but neither aestheticizing nor transformative. The first thing the company sees as they leave a party is the front of the palace opposite, where the moonlight reveals "the iron-barred basement-windows, that gave such a prison-like aspect to the structure, and the shabbiness and squalor that lay along its base" (3:142). If anything, this light makes more visible the grim realities of urban Rome – its working classes (a cobbler and a cigar vendor), a French soldier on patrol, and even "a homeless dog" (3:142).

In the Coliseum, the group seeks to "partake . . . in the thin delights of moonshine and romance," but as "the moonlight filled and flooded the great empty space," it again makes the interior "too distinctly visible," taking away "that inestimable effect of dimness and mystery, by which the imagination might be assisted to build a grander structure" (4:155, 153). Here moonlight works *against* the imagination; it is this opposition, not an interpenetration, that yields a more accurate picture of reality.[15]

The excursion culminates at the Tarpean Rock, at midnight. This is one of those liminal points essential to the romance: "as the Italian moonlight fell a-down the height, it scarcely showed what portion of it was man's work, and what was Nature's, but left it all in very much the same kind of ambiguity and half-knowledge, in which antiquarians generally leave the identity of Roman remains" (4:168). We stand, at this moment, on the line between history and nature, but this point, in *The Marble Faun,* is "the edge of [a] precipice" (4:169). There is no neutral ground where nature and human history intermingle, just as there are no fauns to combine human and animal characteristics.

What follows is a momentarily static tableau—Miriam kneeling as Donatello and the Model struggle at the edge of the cliff—while Hilda watches from the courtyard below. Her spectatorial presence confirms the moment's theatrical quality. As in others of Hawthorne's works, this scene contains the potential for both rebellion and repetition. The murder of the Model is Donatello's attempt to free Miriam from her past, a past whose return threatens to end her career as an artist. The result, however, is that if their past now seems "remote," it is because they have joined "an innumerable confraternity of guilty ones" (4:174, 177). For this is also the rock from which the Romans threw political criminals, and Miriam and Donatello have joined a history of murderers.

In *The House of the Seven Gables,* Hawthorne allowed Holgrave to avoid the temptation of such destructive repetition, but in *The Marble Faun,* the attempt to escape from history only precipitates a fall deeper into it. Donatello, according to Evan Carton, "assumes the role of the model, whose mysterious bond to Miriam is repeatedly suggested to involve a bloody deed of which he was the author and she was—or appeared to be—indirectly guilty."[16] The Model had threatened to take Miriam away from Rome and to separate her from Donatello, but it is the murder that actually does so.

The lovers are enabled to return—to each other, and then to Rome—only through an act of symbolic submission to paternal authority. Kenyon leads Donatello to Miriam in the market square at Perugia, beneath the "patriarchal majesty" of the statue of Pope Julius III (4:314). As a "guilty and repentant pair," they receive the statue's "benediction" (4:323). The tableau is designed as the exact opposite of the one at the Tarpean Rock—it is noon rather than midnight, the pair look up at the statue in repentance rather than down at their victim in defiance, and Kenyon, not Hilda, acts as witness.

Unlike the noontide scaffold scenes in *The Scarlet Letter,* however, this moment is only superficially a public one. The lovers' submission is at this point *merely* symbolic. And in the Rome of *The Marble Faun,* the moral or religious cannot be distinguished from the legal, as Hilda discovers when she enters the confessional at St. Peter's. It is the conjoined forces of church and state that hold Hilda prisoner after her trip to the Palazzo Cenci. And her release comes only with Donatello's surrender, amid the apparent disorder of Carnival.

In *The Scarlet Letter,* popular festivals show the survival and continued vitality of English village culture in Puritan Boston and provide an occasion for the symbolic inclusion of outsiders—sailors, Indians, etc. Roman Carnival may once have served as such an expression of a popular culture outside or beneath official structures of power. Certainly, in Fuller's dispatches of 1848 and 1849, the celebration takes on a barely concealed subversive force.

For Hawthorne, though, Carnival has lost its character as a participatory and creative, truly popular celebration: Now it is "traditionary, not actual" (4:436). "The populace look on with staid composure," while tourists do the celebrating, an audience drawn into the spectacle designed for its consumption (4:437). The festival has been reabsorbed and neutralized by the dominant economic and political order. Where lovers once picked flowers to toss at their beloveds, now these favors are purchased from vendors, who then gather them off the street and resell them, soiled and wilted as they may be: "These venal and polluted flowers . . . are types of the small reality that still subsists in the observance of the Carnival" (4:441). Such debased signs of the natural are circulated and recirculated in the festive marketplace.

Nevertheless, the Corso is full of signs of legal and military force – police, Papal dragoons, and French infantry as well. Soldiers have stood in the background elsewhere in Hawthorne's Rome, as intermittent reminders of 1848, the Roman revolution, and the subsequent reaction (4:142, 161). Now, "making its way right through the masquerading throng," there comes "a full band of martial music, reverberating, in that narrow and confined, though stately avenue, between the walls of the lofty palaces, and roaring upward to the sky, with melody so powerful that it almost grew to discord" (4:442). It is official power, not a rebellious mob, that produces discord here, as it heralds the appearance of the civic authorities and their military escort. Hawthorne has returned to the images of "My Kinsman, Major Molineux," but in this "feverish dream" the poles have been reversed (4:446).[17]

It is at this moment that Kenyon first sees the masked figures of Miriam and Donatello. For both pairs of lovers, Carnival theater has ceased to offer a liberating alternative to the established order. Its theatricalization of excess and popular expression is only an empty performance, another forum for the exercise of political and military control. Donatello's seizure by a group of soldiers becomes just another "bustle" that goes unnoticed, another " 'frolic of the Carnival' " (4:450, 451).

Hilda reappears at the moment Donatello surrenders; the forms of popular culture now serve as just another mode in which people and objects can circulate within the closed economic, legal, and religious order of the law. If the Roman people retain any power, it is only that of restraint, as they "let loose their mirthful propensities, while muzzling those fiercer ones that tend to mischief" (4:441). The street theater of Carnival has seen its revolutionary promise corrupted and denied; this is romance as ritual surrender.[18]

Hawthorne builds his description of the Carnival from two contrasting sets of notebook entries. The first, from February 1858, shortly after his arrival in Rome, are darker and more critical, and it is these that set the tone for this section of the novel. The second group comes from March 1859 and presents a warmer and more good-natured view of the festival, making no mention of a police or military presence.

The key difference, Hawthorne concludes in 1859, is between the perspectives of the spectator and the participant: "If you merely look at [the celebration], it depresses you; if you take even the slightest share in it, you become aware that it has a fascination, and you no longer wonder, at last, that the young people take such delight in plunging into this mad river of fun, that goes roaring through the heart of solemn old Rome" (14:503–4). The previous year, Hawthorne and his family had ridden in a carriage through the Corso, taking the role of aristocratic spectators and becoming the targets of what Hawthorne describes as a predominantly lower-class crowd (14:68). In 1859, however, he joined in the festivities from both balcony and street level, throwing confetti and taking part in a "civil war," in which different groups tried to extinguish each other's torches (14:504).

In *The Marble Faun,* Kenyon's shift in perspective is the opposite of Hawthorne's – a happy participant one year, he is a disillusioned spectator the next (4:437–38). One possible explanation for the reversal may lie in a comment Hawthorne makes repeatedly in the 1859 notebook entries – that the scene is impossible to remember and describe clearly: "the spectacle is strangely like a dream, in respect to the difficulty of retaining it in the mind and solidifying it into a description" (14:501; see also 14:500). For Hawthorne, popular or collective expression seems to escape from rather than animate or enable authorship. Margaret Fuller's finest writing may have come from her immersion in just such a political culture, but for Hawthorne, the artist must pull back from participation in either carnival or civil war, into a darker and more distanced role, if he is to write at all.

America

"When Lilacs Last in the Dooryard Bloom'd" depends upon a similar withdrawal – a separation of poetry from public life that becomes, paradoxically, the precondition for its claim to representative status. "Song of Myself" treats death and life simply as aspects of a continuous whole, the line between them erased by the shift from individual to collective experience. "Lilacs," on the other hand, struggles to "pass beyond" that difference. Its achievement, finally, is to refigure death as redemptive individual sacrifice, a notion antithetical to the collective vision of the 1855 *Leaves*.[19]

The poem offers dual narratives – of individual and national mourning – but it juxtaposes rather than merges them. The former appears first only in compressed and fragmentary form (sections 2 and 8), but it is ultimately given precedence, once it has been recast as a narrative of poetic composition, as the story of "Lilacs" itself and the ground for Whitman's response to the larger national crisis.

Whitman begins by privileging selected objects as symbols, but the very choice of symbolism as a technique has important implications. His focus on particular images – lilac, western star, thrush, and "thought of him I love" – marks a renunciation of both the catalog and its democratic poetics in favor of a more traditional and politically conservative one.[20]

Lincoln's death appears initially as a singular moment of discontinuity and rupture, set against the cyclical movement of "ever-returning spring" (2:529). So too does mourning seem a static or repetitive condition: "I mourn'd . . . and yet shall mourn" (2:529, ellipsis in original). Grief enters the poem, in section 2, as, in fact, a blockage of expression, in a series of ejaculations that split Whitman's lines in two and deny them either rhythmic or syntactical completion:

> O shades of night! O moody, tearful night!
> O great star disappear'd! O the black murk that hides the star!
> O cruel hands that hold me powerless! O helpless soul of me! (2:529)

Thus blocked from utterance, the poet turns to nature for an adequate representation or response: from the lilac bush, "A sprig, with its flower, I break" (2:530). But such a gesture is, again, only a repetition of loss, another "break" in the living whole.

Section 6 describes the public response to the passage of Lincoln's funeral train, but the poet remains unable to do more than "give you [the coffin] my sprig of lilac" (2:531). He wishes to "chant a song for you, O sane and sacred death," but he can only generalize his response by expanding or multiplying his earlier destructive gesture, in a line that seems to stutter in its repetition: "Copious, I break, I break the sprigs from the bushes" (2:531).

The process of regeneration and recovery begins not with the poet, but with the movement of the coffin itself:

> Over the breast of the spring, the land, amid cities,
> Amid lanes, and through old woods, (where lately the violets peep'd from the
>   ground, spotting the gray debris;)
> Amid the grass in the fields each side of the lanes – passing the endless grass;
> Passing the yellow spear'd wheat, every grain from its shroud in the
>   dark-brown fields uprising;
> Passing the apple-tree blows of white and pink in the orchards;
> Carrying a corpse to where it shall rest in the grave,
> Night and day journeys a coffin. (2:530)

It is as if the coffin's passing is itself a generative force, bringing forth flowers from debris, grains of wheat from their shrouds – exactly the opposite of the poet's gesture. The coffin holds a body, of course, but it also symbolizes the absence of the living president – an absence to which the resurrection of the wheat is read as response and recompense.

Sections 10 and 11 give voice to the poet's desire to "warble myself for the dead one there I loved" (2:533). How, he asks, "shall I deck my song for the large sweet soul that has gone?" (2:533). The very utterance of these questions, the poet's admission of powerlessness, now seems to generate answers, just as the journeying coffin seemed to generate new life:

> Pictures of growing spring, and farms, and homes . . .
> And the city at hand, with dwellings so dense, and stacks of chimneys,
> And all the scenes of life, and the workshops, and the workmen homeward
>   returning. (2:533)

This recovery of poetic voice is, of course, achieved only in the act of commemoration, at the cost of the life of "him I love."

The coffin has taken both poet and poem out from the dooryard, into first a rural landscape and then an urban space of public mourning. Public or communal speech is what is missing here, but the poem's response is precisely to turn away from the public and political. The poet is drawn instead toward the natural—not to the open vistas of sections 5 and 11, but to a realm of "secluded recesses," toward the "hermit" thrush, "withdrawn to himself, avoiding the settlements" (2:530). It is the thrush who sings "Death's outlet song of life," a song inseparable from life itself, like breath and speech in "Song of Myself" (2:530). But his is a "solitary" song, sung only "by himself" in the swamp, in the liminal space of "In Paths Untrodden."

This becomes the characteristic movement of "When Lilacs Last in the Dooryard Bloom'd"—a response to public and collective loss made possible only by the poet's withdrawal as an individual from the public sphere: "I fled forth to the hiding receiving night, that talks not" (2:535). The poet is to listen in silence and be "charm[ed]" by nature's organic fusion of life and death, a fusion seemingly no longer possible within the social order or, even, within the poem—except, that is, insofar as projected outside it (2:536).

The regenerative process begun by the coffin's passage is completed by the song of the thrush, which echoes 1860's "A Word Out of The Sea" in its dominant image, of the maternal ocean as death itself. In the earlier poem, the ocean only whispered the word "Death," giving the listening boy access to language but leaving him in a state of perpetually unsatisfied desire. Here, on the other hand, the bird's song expresses a desire for death, to which death comes as a fulfillment. Where the poet began as "rapt" by the bird's "carol," merely "tall[ying] the song of the bird" (2:536), by the end of the song their positions are reversed, as the bird "kept up" "to the tally of my soul" (2:537).

Whitman has never mentioned the violent moment of Lincoln's death, but now he is able to confront the human wreckage of the Civil War as a whole:

> I saw battle-corpses, myriads of them,
> And the white skeletons of young men—I saw them,
> I saw the debris and debris of all dead soldiers. (2:538)

These are the "debris" only alluded to parenthetically in section 5 ("spotting the gray debris"), the dead only referred to as "you" in section 7. The dark masses of mourners of section 6 are also further individualized:

> The living remain'd and suffer'd – the mother suffer'd,
> And the wife and the child, and the musing comrade suffer'd,
> And the armies that remain'd suffer'd. (2:538)

Both the dead and the grieving mass of the nation are brought into the field of poetic speech, in preparation for the poem's final resolution.

The first stanza of section 16, like "A Word out of the Sea," uses participial phrases to compress a series of actions into a single extended present state, but here it is a condition of transcendence:

> Passing the visions, passing the night;
> Passing, unloosing the hold of my comrades' hands;
> Passing the song of the hermit bird, and the tallying song of my soul. (538)

Whitman passes beyond grief, into a renewed sense of his role as poet. His response has risen from the individual to the national level, as he comes to address the country's collective loss. But he has done so as a solitary elegist, alone in a natural landscape that has displaced the political and social.[21] Whitman's final stanza gathers in the symbols of the poem, leaving him "in the fragrant pines, and the cedars dusk and dim" (2:539). He stands "in the midst" of "comrades," but the hands holding his are those of the "knowledge" and the "thought of death" (2:535). Theirs is a chilling touch indeed.

Compared to the radical physicality of Whitman's earlier poems, "When Lilacs Last in the Dooryard Bloom'd" seems strikingly abstract, almost disembodied in its imagery. It is not Lincoln's wounded body that travels across the landscape; it is "a coffin," a structure that contains but also withholds the corpse from view, replacing it as an object of public mourning (2:530). And the bodies of the war dead appear only near the poem's end, as "white skeletons" and "debris" (2:538).

Such abstraction, as Timothy Sweet has noted, is part of a larger dehistoricizing movement, one that does much to sever the poem from Whitman's own experience.[22] His service as a wartime nurse in Washington hospitals had brought him into immediate and quite physical contact with devastated male bodies, and in *Drum Taps* he had fashioned out of that contact a persona for himself as "wound dresser." But here, rather than follow the spirit of Lincoln's second inaugural and "bind up" national as well as individual wounds, Whitman retreats from such a public role and setting.

Above all, perhaps, what is effaced from Whitman's elegy are the bodies over which the war was fought – the black bodies of American slaves. It is with these wounded, racially marked bodies that Louisa May Alcott's "My Contraband" begins. How, she asks, can they be brought into narrative and given voice? What literary conventions might prove adequate to address the complexities of race in America? Alcott's story thematizes these issues, as it foregrounds and interrogates the process of its own inscription. She deploys several generic possibilities, first the sentimental and then the gothic, before folding them, as Whitman does, into a narrative of national reconciliation through legitimized violence and sacrifice.

For six weeks in 1862, Alcott served as a nurse in Washington's Union Hotel Hospital before being invalided home with typhoid fever. The experience led to the writing of *Hospital Sketches* (1863), her first literary success, and then to a commitment to writing as a career. Over the next few years, Alcott published a string of anonymous or pseudonymous "thrillers" before the publication of *Little Women* in 1868.

"My Contraband" first appeared in November 1863, under the title "The Brothers," in the decidedly middle- or highbrow context of the *Atlantic Monthly,* alongside poems by Longfellow and Lowell and essays by Francis Parkman, Henry David Thoreau, Louis Agassiz, and Charles Sumner. It is, however, a somewhat unsettling inclusion among historical studies and appeals to Boston's revolutionary heritage – for one of the burdens of Alcott's tale is an implicit critique of white northern liberalism. She had tested the limits of the *Atlantic*'s editorial policy a year before with "M.L.," a tale about miscegenation that had been rejected.[23] Her return to such issues in "The Brothers" is thus inevitably self-conscious – at once carefully judged and even more subversive.

Alcott's experimentation with genre is begun by her narrator, Nurse Dane, as she contemplates the mulatto slave, or "contraband," who has been assigned as her assistant: "He sat on his bed doing nothing; no book, no pipe, no pen or paper anywhere appeared, yet anything less indolent or listless than his attitude and expression I never saw. Erect he sat, with a hand on either knee, and eyes fixed on the bare wall opposite, so rapt in some absorbing thought as to be unconscious of my presence."[24] He is still, but not purposeless, so absorbed in interior thought that his expression seems "blank" to the observer. He is a figure both self-possessed and inscrutable, racially marked but otherwise almost an emblem of the opaque and other. The man's mixed race only intensifies his exoticism—and his "comeliness" and attraction—for Nurse Dane (585). Her desire is expressed, however, not in a further attempt to "read" his features, but in her projection onto them of an explanatory narrative. She explains his "passionate melancholy," for example, as "a mute protest against the broken law that doomed [him] at [his] birth" (585). In so doing, she renders the opaque and "blank" body transparent, the mute vessel of a narrative of sexual and racial transgression.

"What could he be thinking of?" she asks, before imagining a series of possible answers: "I wondered if it were some deep wrong or sorrow, kept alive by memory and impotent regret; if he mourned for the dead master to whom he had been faithful to the end; or if the liberty now his were robbed of half its sweetness by the knowledge that someone near and dear to him still languished in the hell from which he had escaped" (585). These are fragments of sentimental fictions, summoned up from a distance. Each places him in a conventional role—as a mourner, as a faithful servant or lover or child—in any of these, he becomes a passive object for Dane "to know and comfort" (585). And each scenario also takes for granted the detachment and superiority of the white observer, whose privileged position allows her to script the life of the black subject before her.

Such narrative structures prove all too fragile, however, breaking even as she touches the man's shoulder: "the man vanished and the slave appeared. . . . [with his] obsequious 'Yes, Ma'am,' any romance that had gathered round him fled away, leaving the saddest of all sad facts in living guise before me" (585). But what are the "facts" that Dane opposes to her earlier "romance"? On the one hand, there is the "ghastly wound" (585) on the man's face, now visible as he turns. And there is also his demeanor as a contraband, which highlights the larger "fact" of the master/slave relation: Dane says she had intended "to offer comfort as a friend," but finds herself giving "an order as a mistress" (585). Her opposition between "friend" and "mistress" is an illusory one, however. For the impulse to friendship springs from Dane's own "romance," and the position of romancer depends on an assertion of narrative power analogous to that of a "mistress." Dane claims that she tries "to teach the men self-respect by treating them respectfully," specifically by calling her attendants by their last names (586). But her power over "Bob" cannot be disguised in this way: "'I'ses got no other [name], Ma'am [he tells her]; we have our masters' names, or do without. Mine's dead, and I won't have anything of his about me'" (586). The nurse's egalitarian efforts cannot simply undo slave history through a renaming; she cannot confer or reassert an identity that has been so systematically denied.

The wounded body and spirit of the slave can neither be woven back into the sentimental fabric of Dane's "romance" nor enfolded in a mystified "equality" between white nurse and black attendant. "Robert's" behavior, in fact, soon turns inexplicable and threatening. He is more of a "gentleman" than the Confederate officer Dane attends, but the contraband falls into "black moods," "which began to disturb me, because I had no power to lighten them" (587). One night, Dane awakes to find that he has discarded the officer's medicine, and intends to let him die. She can only describe this as the "mad act" of someone "out of his head" (588, 589).

Dane cannot comprehend such hatred—unless, that is, the man had been Robert's owner—but that is not the story she finds herself in the midst of: "'He's my brother,'" Robert tells her (589). She appeals to him on these specific grounds, only to be shaken once again by the response:

"I'm not like to forget that, Ma'am, when I've been thinking of it all this week. I knew it when they fetched him in, an' would 'a' done it long 'fore this, but I wanted to ask where Lucy was; he knows,—he told to-night,—an' now he's done for."

"Who is Lucy?" I asked hurriedly . . .

> With one of the swift transitions of a mixed temperament like this, at my question Robert's deep eyes filled, the clenched hands were spread before his face, and all I heard were the broken words, –
>
> "My wife – he took her." (589)

Betsy Klimasmith has described the "mixed" mulatto body as the point at which the gothic and sentimental modes intersect in Alcott's work, as female desire transgresses the limits of orthodox domesticity.[25] In this case, Robert's responses hardly enable Dane to revive her earlier sentimental "romance"; instead, they precipitate the breakdown of narrative altogether, into "broken words" to which she can offer no reply. Alcott's story begins its own "swift transition," spiraling toward the gothic, a mode based on a logic of revenge rather than reconciliation.

This is Robert's narrative territory, however, over which Dane no longer has control. He and the officer, " 'Marster Ned,' " had the same father, but Ned " 'always hated me, I looked so like old Marster: he don't, – only the light skin and hair" (590). Their antagonism leads to Ned's seizure and rape of Robert's wife, Lucy, and her eventual suicide. The tale could not be further from Dane's romanticized version of the master/slave relation; its combination of miscegenation and incestuous rivalry works to entangle and confuse all lines of difference – racial, genealogical, or economic. And it can end only as it began – with the violence it shows to be the core of slavery itself.[26]

The oppression of American race slavery may not, perhaps, be narratable at all, for it is already brutally encrypted on the slave body itself:

> "Yer thought I was a white man once [Robert exclaims]: – look here!"
>
> With a sudden wrench he tore the shirt from neck to waist, and on his strong brown shoulders showed me furrows deeply ploughed, wounds which, though healed, were ghastlier to me than any in that house. I could not speak to him. (590)

For the light-skinned Robert, it is not color that determines race, but these marks of enslavement. The scars of the lash are imaged as ploughed furrows, as twisted counterparts of the slave's own labor – "ghastlier" than war wounds, because they are signs of subordination rather than a conflict between equals.

"The Brothers'" plunge into the gothic has obviously made a simple return to the sentimental mode impossible, but its regression into wordless violence leaves the story at an impasse. How is it possible to speak of American race slavery without either sentimentalizing its cruelties or reinscribing and deepening its wounds? Dane sees herself as trapped, "locked up with a dying man and a lunatic" (590), and struggles desperately to improvise a resolution. Finally, she convinces Robert to let the captain live, in hope that " 'the Lord will give me back my Lucy' ": " 'As surely as there is a Lord,' " Dane tells him, " 'you will find her here or in the beautiful hereafter, where there is no black or white, no master and no slave' " (591). Such a vision, based on Christian forgiveness and reconciliation, is possible only if one posits the transcendence of racial and economic difference altogether. It may be enough to lead Robert to relent and eventually depart, but it is clearly no more than a psychological (and narrative) ploy, one that cannot bring his story – or Alcott's – to a satisfactory close.

It requires a larger national narrative of wartime sacrifice and reconciliation for the gothic violence of slavery to be resolved and recontained. After a break, Dane returns to nursing following the Union attack on Fort Wagner, South Carolina. She finds Robert among the wounded, recognizing him only by the scar on his cheek and the name over his bed, "Robert Dane" (594). The change of name may suggest a union between the two figures, but it also reinscribes her position of power, with her name replacing his master's and her voice taking final possession of his story.

In battle, Robert has been able to attack the recovered "Marster Ned" directly, his suicidal rage turned to sacrificial valor, fratricide made symbolic rather than actual. Ned gives his brother a fatal wound, but one of Robert's companions, a freeman Dane calls "black as the ace of spades," kills the rebel officer in turn (594). The result is the hospital scene with which the story closes: "the dark freeman looked at the white slave with the pitiful, yet puzzled expression I have so often seen on the faces of our wisest men, when this tangled question of Slavery presented itself, asking to be cut or patiently undone" (594). Alcott confronts the impasse of race slavery once again, but the war has turned the vengeful energy of the gothic against itself. Robert dies, and his place is taken up by his free, but dark-skinned, comrade. His story dissolves into a master narrative of national strife and reunification, but such political and geographical healing requires the lines of racial difference to be drawn once more, and perhaps with even greater strength.[27]

The subversive force of Alcott's story comes from the way in which she pits literary genre and ideology against each other, revealing narrative's potential for both resistance and containment. She invokes the structures of popular literary conventions, only to destabilize them and undermine her readers' sense of security within them. The result is a powerful critique of unifying visions such as Whitman's: on the one hand, they may be no more than a new set of sentimental illusions; on the other, they perform a key ideological function in containing violence and restructuring difference. Alcott takes pains to emphasize both the corrosive violence of race slavery and the wartime sacrifices of African Americans in particular. She clearly implicates herself as writer, as well, both through her narrative persona and her revised title of 1869.[28] Republishing the story as "My Contraband," Alcott foregrounds the issue of authorial power: if Robert is Dane's "contraband" or property, then her authority, as both nurse and narrator, is linked to that of the slave master; and if, in another sense, the tale is Alcott's "contraband," an illicit possession, then narrative itself becomes part of a potentially corrupt system of property relations. The white writer may—indeed must—attempt to confront racism, to speak for black as well as white, but Alcott cannot let the ideological implications of the process go unnoted or unchallenged. Her very decision to republish "The Brothers" in 1869—after emancipation, after the Fourteenth and Fifteenth Amendments—reopens the racial questions that her readers might have wished to consider closed.

It is, I would argue, precisely literature's self-interrogating critical potential that makes a project like Alcott's possible. Alcott deliberately turns literary convention against itself to reveal fissures in the national discourse on race; in the same way, Fuller's aesthetic awareness enables her to see both the potential radicalism of Carnival and the falsity of the "actors" in the "comedy" of bourgeois politics.[29] In both cases, their work is empowered, not undermined or vitiated, by its "literary" or "aesthetic" aspects.

Nor do Hawthorne's romance and Whitman's poems operate in a separate, mystified realm somehow different from that of Thoreau's abolitionist essays or Marx's historical analyses—or from that of twenty-first-century cultural criticism. Whitman's postwar writing does attempt to refashion a consensus on more conservative lines, but Hawthorne's romance, even in *The Marble Faun,* remains sharply critical of any drive toward ideological cohesion—"always historicize" is as much his motto as it is Frederic Jameson's.

My aim throughout this book has been to highlight what I see as moments of energizing, even daring, political imagination: Hawthorne's opening of the romance to progressive politics in *The House of the Seven Gables;* Whitman's democratic poetics of 1855; Thoreau's linguistic and imaginative labor in the woods and pages of *Walden;* Fuller's cultural and political commentary; and Alcott's subversion of the popular genres in which she works. All these texts push against the envelope of representation (and, in Whitman's case, beyond it), reaching toward revolutionary transformation in ways that even Marx cannot.

Texts have different uses—and limitations—at different historical moments. Their political and cultural work may be indirect, but it is nonetheless substantial: the democratic inclusiveness of Whitman's earlier work retains its force even today for movements of resistance and liberation, while Thoreau's "Resistance to Civil Government" has been a central text in the struggles of both colonized peoples and persons of color. Each historical conjuncture calls forth different modes of political and cultural resistance. We can look back in historical retrospect and see the ideological contexts in which such discourses come into being, but if we take them to be wholly determined by those contexts, then we simply join in the process of recontainment and denial.

Revolutionary action, if it is to be more than pure, directionless violence, must attempt some expression of its revolutionary content—and thus reenter the discursive realm it would transform. But is "revolutionary discourse" simply a contradiction in terms, as Sacvan Bercovitch and others would suggest? It is not just a rhetorical question, but it is not finally an answerable one either. As long, however, as a Prague Spring of 1968 can be followed, even decades later, by a Velvet Revolution, art will have the potential–and the obligation–of speaking moonlight truths to power.

NOTES

Introduction. The Eighteenth Brumaire and the Magic Lantern

1. Bercovitch, *The Office of the Scarlet Letter,* 89.

2. George Levine mounts an inquiry slightly different from mine in "Reclaiming the Aesthetic," his introduction to *Aesthetics and Ideology:* "I am trying," he says, "to imagine the aesthetic as a mode engaged richly and complexly with moral and political issues, but a mode that operates differently from others" (3). Levine is interested in the aesthetic as a "utopian space" of "almost free play," in which "connections with the political and the ideological are at least partly short circuited" (17). Where he describes the aesthetic as a mode of disengagement from the political, my study attempts to move in the opposite direction.

3. I quote here from Terry Eagleton's paraphrase in *Marxism and Literary Criticism,* 29.

4. Eagleton, *Marxism and Literary Criticism,* 30.

5. Karl Marx, "The Eighteenth Brumaire of Louis Bonaparte," 436.

6. Greenblatt, *Renaissance Self-Fashioning: From More to Shakespeare,* 5.

7. Hawthorne, *The Scarlet Letter,* 2:36.

8. This argument is made most fully and explicitly in chapter 1 of Bercovitch, *The Office of the Scarlet Letter,* "The A-Politics of Ambiguity" (1–31).

John Carlos Rowe offers a somewhat different response to Bercovitch in *At Emerson's Tomb.* He describes "the Emersonian tradition of aesthetic dissent" as assuming "that rigorous reflection on the processes of thought and representation constitutes in itself a critique of social reality and effects a transformation of the naive realism that confuses truth with social convention" (1). His book seeks to resituate such texts in the context of the political and social reform movements of their time. My argument is that Hawthorne, Whitman, and Thoreau all attempt to redefine or move beyond such a version of dissent.

9. Terdiman, *Discourse/Counter-Discourse,* 79.

10. Terdiman, *Discourse/Counter-Discourse,* 79, 71.

11. Terdiman, *Discourse/Counter-Discourse,* 80, 202.

12. Carton, *The Rhetoric of American Romance,* 1, 168.

13. de Man, "The Resistance to Theory," 18.

14. de Man, "Resistance to Theory," 20. Such a reflexive, self-critical dimension may be a form of co-optation for Bercovitch, but it is also a distinguishing feature of Marx's proletarian revolutions, which "criticize themselves constantly" (433).

15. Macherey, *A Theory of Literary Production,* 61, 64.

16. Macherey, *A Theory of Literary Production,* 78, 79.

17. Raymond Williams, *Marxism and Literature,* 113, 112.

18. Bhabha, "The Commitment to Theory," 115.

19. Bhabha, "The Commitment to Theory," 117.

20. Laclau and Mouffe, *Hegemony and Socialist Strategy,* 2.

21. Whitman, according to Betsy Erkkila, "would not have understood" the New Critical opposition between politics and aesthetics (*Whitman the Political Poet,* 7).

22. Benjamin, "The Author as Producer," 225, 228.

23. Ash, "The Revolution of the Magic Lantern," 42–51. On the Situationist International, see "Lipstick Traces (On a Cigarette)" in Greil Marcus's *Lipstick Traces,* 343–431.

24. Stokes, *The Walls Came Tumbling Down,* 154.

25. Wheaton and Kavan, *The Velvet Revolution,* 53, 54. The overlap between the political and the theatrical was again visible at a mass meeting of 750,000 on a Prague parade ground, which featured both political speakers and "theater sketches" (91).

26. Havel, *Open Letters,* 333.

27. Havel, *Open Letters,* 332.

28. Havel, *Open Letters,* 276–77.

29. Havel, *Open Letters,* 277.

30. Havel, *Open Letters,* 283.

31. F. O. Matthiessen makes this observation, but he does not go on to build on it, as I do (*American Renaissance,* 281).

32. *Walt Whitman's "Leaves of Grass": The First (1855) Edition,* 5. As Matthiessen notes, Hawthorne's "desire to provide a neutral ground 'where the Actual and Imaginary may meet' happens to contrast significantly with a note of Whitman's that 'imagination and actuality must be united'" (*American Renaissance,* 264).

One. Hawthorne's Drama of Revolt

1. Beyond his description of the romance in "The Custom-House" (*The Scarlet Letter*, 1:35–36), see also *The House of the Seven Gables* (2:213, 281) and *The Marble Faun* (4:155). Unless otherwise noted, all further references to Hawthorne's work are to volumes in the Centenary Edition, with volume numbers followed by page numbers.

2. Brodhead, *Hawthorne, Melville, and the Novel*, 24.

3. Carton, *The Rhetoric of American Romance*, 247.

4. Bercovitch, *The American Jeremiad*, 143.

5. In *The Province of Piety*, Michael Colacurcio offers an extended reading of Hawthorne's tales based on a view of Hawthorne as a critic of the Whig history to which Bercovitch has him subscribing.

6. Colacurcio identifies this as Boston's First Church (*The Province of Piety*, 146). It may not be the heart of rebellion in the colony—that would be the Old South Church, according to Colacurcio (147)—but it remains central to the patriarchal tradition in New England.

7. Peter Shaw sees the mob's action as having a similarly ambiguous status: "The crowd, having fixed on Major Molineux as the representative of the authority it has grown ready to overthrow, enacts a scapegoat ritual that predicts but is not yet an actual act of revolution" (*American Patriots and the Rituals of Revolution*, 20).

8. Jeffrey Richards suggests that eighteenth-century "street protests and demonstrations take on a formalized character something like that of the stage play, but with far different implications. Because the rituals and theatricalized challenges take place in public streets and squares, spaces where people expect theatrical behavior only as part of a politically neutral social aesthetic, protest takes on symbolic meaning by converting the world into stage and the actors into world-players. . . . these street challenges lead ultimately to a theater larger than that of the playhouse, to a self-proclaimed play of revolution with serious, real-world consequences" (*Theater Enough*, 201, 202).

Richards goes on to show how the rhetoric of theatrical performance and display permeates political discourse of the revolutionary period. My focus—and Hawthorne's as well, I think—is on theatricality itself rather than just the *images* of it that Richards cites. Hawthorne's allusion to comedy rather than tragedy is characteristic of Tory rather than Whig writers, according to Richards (226); this suggests Hawthorne's considerable ambivalence about the relation between politics and theater.

9. Q. D. Leavis conveys a fine sense of the complexity of this moment, its fusion of politics, theater, and dream: "The colonists . . . have secretly planned to throw off British rule, or at any rate to rid themselves of Major Molineux, a symbolic action which, performed in the street outside the church at midnight and before the innocent eyes of the mystified youth, takes the form of something between a pageant and a ritual drama, disguised in the emotional logic of a dream" ("Hawthorne as Poet," 200).

10. I am drawing here primarily from Glenn Hughes, *A History of the American Theater,* 174, 185, and elsewhere.

11. Kurt Eisen discusses this tale in the context of what he sees as the ambiguous moral status of theater in Hawthorne's work ("Hawthorne's Moral Theaters and the Post-Puritan Stage," 257–59).

12. Hughes, *A History of the American Theater,* 174.

13. David Reynolds, *Walt Whitman's America,* 163.

14. Along with David Reynolds, see Wilentz, *Chants Democratic,* 259, 265, and Meserve, *Heralds of Promise,* 33.

15. See Greenblatt, *Shakespearean Negotiations,* 1–20.

16. Colacurcio sees the "Legends" as offering "an ironic commentary on the pattern of emerging American historiography" (392), a view seconded by Frederick Newberry in *Hawthorne's Divided Loyalties,* 59–61.

17. Carton describes this aspect of the "Legends" in more negative terms. The sequence, he says, shows that "history is art's construct as well as its subject, and art not only makes history but is made by it. The price of this recognition is the relinquishment of fixed boundaries between event and representation, between past and present, even between the actual and the imaginary" (*Rhetoric,* 170).

Two. Mauling Governor Pyncheon

1. Hawthorne, *The Scarlet Letter,* 1:35, 36.

2. Berlant, *The Anatomy of National Fantasy,* 183.

3. Hawthorne, *The House of the Seven Gables,* 2:1, 2.

4. As Michael Davitt Bell puts it, "the imaginative action of 'The Custom-House' is never incorporated into the historical action of *The Scarlet Letter*" (*The Development of American Romance,* 181). Bell goes on to argue that Hawthorne's attempt to join imagination and history in *The House of the Seven Gables* is a failure (184–85).

Brook Thomas, on the other hand, discusses *The House of the Seven Gables* as a blend of romance and novel whose ostensibly imaginary elements are often derived from the actualities of nineteenth-century Salem (*Cross-Examinations of Law and Literature*, 83).

5. The Nietzschean version of genealogy I have in mind here is that invoked by Michel Foucault in his "Nietzsche, Genealogy, History" (*Language, Counter-memory, Practice*, 161).

6. Hawthorne's addition of the letter *w* to the family name of "Hathorne" becomes especially significant in this context. The new name sounds nearly identical to the old, while looking quite different *in print*.

7. See, for instance, Matthiessen, *American Renaissance*, 341–42; Turner, *Nathaniel Hawthorne*, 230; and Gilmore, *American Romanticism and the Marketplace*, 101.

8. Both the Hathornes and the Pyncheons also claimed tracts of land in Maine (2:xxiii). Hawthorne's mother's family, the Mannings, did in fact own land in Maine (Turner, *Nathaniel Hawthorne*, 15).

9. Michaels, "Romance and Real Estate," 159.

10. Brook Thomas also notes the dependence of the Pyncheon claims on a chain of legal documents and texts (*Cross-Examinations of Law and Literature*, 53). Gilmore suggests, on the other hand, that the primary distinction for Hawthorne is between public and private rather than between writing and speech (Gilmore, *American Romanticism and the Marketplace*, 98).

11. For a reading of such legends as an alternative, subversive form, see Susan Mizruchi, *The Power of Historical Knowledge*, 131–34.

Joel Pfister describes the gothic as a "means of dismantling . . . unjust social reality," but he sees Hawthorne's text as seeking to transcend the form, as Phoebe's middle-class domesticity "degothicizes Holgrave, domesticates him, and ushers him out of his identification with his working-class ancestors, the Maules, and into the rising middle class" (*The Production of Personal Life*, 146, 156).

12. Richard Chase notes that in his career as one of Hawthorne's "rustic jacks-of-all-trade," Holgrave embodies "the succession of a capitalist order to an agrarian one" (*The American Novel and Its Tradition*, 76).

13. Alice's entrapment in her chair echoes that of Milton's Lady in *Comus*. But the lady can tell her captor, "Thou canst not touch the freedom of my mind / With all thy charms, although this corporeal rind / Thou hast immanacled, while Heav'n sees good" (*Complete Poetical Works of John Milton*, 130, lines 663–65). Alice, on the other hand, has been stripped of precisely this freedom. (Hawthorne makes a direct allusion to Comus's chair later, in "Governor Pyncheon" [2:274].)

14. Hawthorne returns to the subject of mesmerism in the figure of Westervelt in *The Blithedale Romance.* But it has disturbed him for over a decade, as an 1841 letter to Sophia Peabody, his then-fiancée, attests: if she were to allow herself to be hypnotized, he says, "there would be an intrusion into thy holy of holies – and the intruder would not be thy husband!" (quoted in *The Blithedale Romance,* 242).

In more general terms, Hawthorne has long been concerned with the problem of a storyteller's potential manipulation of his audience – see, for example, the story "Alice Doane's Appeal," which Emily Miller Budick discusses in *Fiction and Historical Consciousness,* 99–102.

15. Frederick Crews describes this novel as " 'about' the risks of artistic imagination, which are simply the risks of seizure by unconscious wishes" (*The Sins of the Fathers,* 173). A Freudian reading might well describe the urge to repetition in such scenes as unconscious compulsion.

16. Michaels describes Alice Pyncheon as already reduced to the status of property, her "self" already alienated and commodified by the market (*The American Renaissance Reconsidered,* 177–78).

17. Laurence Holland offers a more positive reading of this scene: "Though Holgrave draws back from subduing Phoebe to his mastery, his abstention and the verbal repudiation of his story-telling do not cancel out or invalidate his effort, for the scene portends the consummation of their union: together the effort and the restraint constitute, by prefiguring, the reciprocal and authentic bond of intimacy that will eventually mature between them" ("Authority, Power, and Form: Some American Texts," 9).

For another reading largely congruent with my own, but coming to a more sanguine conclusion about both Hawthorne's moonlight scenes and the larger issue of the novel's ability to generate a new cultural center, see Richard Millington, *Practicing Romance,* 105–53, and especially 136–45.

Gordon Hutner, on the other hand, suggests that Holgrave's "triumph" is achieved at the cost of Phoebe's "truncation," as her development is "submerged" into a secondary plot that "perpetuates the diminishment of females and their own quest for power" (*Secrets and Sympathy,* 72–73). See also 83–88 for an elaboration of Hutner's critique.

18. Crews captures the complexity of the chapter's tone when he speaks of "the clogged passion, the vindictive pleasure, expressed in that extraordinary chapter (18) which is given over to a fearful taunting of Jaffrey's corpse" (*The Sins of the Fathers,* 175).

19. Evan Carton describes Hawthorne as "the ultimate avenging Maule here,"

who "performs a wild rhetorical witch dance around [the] corpse" (*The Rhetoric of American Romance,* 223, 221). But he sees the intensity and excess of the chapter as "more desperate than triumphant," an attempt to revive the sadly declined Pyncheon family as a target (223).

20. Millington describes this speech as evidence of a "cultural immaturity" and merely personal anxiety in Holgrave (*Practicing Romance,* 133). This is, I think, to underestimate the degree to which Hawthorne participates in the feelings expressed here. The speech is, in fact, drawn directly from a notebook entry of 1844; it is not simply created as part of Holgrave's characterization (see *The American Notebooks,* 8:252).

21. Quoted in Matthiessen, *American Renaissance,* 214n. For the full text, see Ephraim London, ed., *The Law as Literature,* 406–39.

22. Hawthorne's association of moonlight with the romance predates the White case, of course, appearing as early as "My Kinsman, Major Molineux," written in the late 1820s.

23. Hawthorne's family was, in fact, linked by marriage to the two Crowninshield brothers charged with committing the murder (Turner, *Nathaniel Hawthorne,* 6).

24. As Brook Thomas notes, in the White case, the Whig Webster was opposed by Democratic lawyer Robert Rantoul for the defense—the case thus involved both political and legal conflict (*Cross-Examinations of Law and Literature,* 59).

25. Brook Thomas dwells on the parallels between the Judge and Justice Joseph Story, but we never see the Judge acting in any *legal* capacity; he appears only as speculator and politician. This is one reason I have chosen to emphasize the political rather than the legal context of Hawthorne's tale.

For a reading of Hepzibah's shop as *representative* of nineteenth-century consumer capitalism, see Mizruchi, *The Power of Historical Knowledge,* 85–87.

26. See Dale Baum, *The Civil War Party System,* 28. Charles Swann assumes that the novel is set in 1848, but he only does so in order to place the text in a generalized revolutionary context (*Nathaniel Hawthorne: Tradition and Revolution,* 97).

27. See Formisano, *The Transformation of Political Culture,* 329–36.

28. Formisano describes incidents of this kind in Boston during the later 1830s and 1840s (*The Transformation of Political Culture,* 327–29).

29. Hawthorne, *Life of Franklin Pierce,* 113–14. As president, Pierce sought to placate Southern Democrats; it was his administration that forced Massachusetts Democrats to end their alliance with the Free Soilers (Baum, *The Civil War Party System,* 29–30).

30. Leo Marx, *The Machine in the Garden*, 180. It is worth noting that Hawthorne describes the railroad from the perspective of the *traveler* here, not that of the stationary observer in a pastoral landscape. For an analysis of the latter situation, as depicted in the *American Notebooks*, see Marx, 13–17, 23–24.

31. The phrase belongs to John Ruskin (*Complete Works*, 8:159), quoted in Schivelbusch, *The Railway Journey*, 54.

32. Schivelbusch, *The Railway Journey*, 37–38.

33. Leo Marx, *The Machine in the Garden*, 214.

34. See, for instance, Leo Marx's discussion of two 1847 speeches by Daniel Webster (*The Machine in the Garden*, 209–14).

35. See Oscar Handlin and Mary Flug Handlin, *Commonwealth*, 211–12.

36. For more on the effects of rail travel on nineteenth-century perceptions of space and time, see Schivelbusch, *The Railway Journey*, 33–44.

37. See Arlin Turner, *Nathaniel Hawthorne*, 223–25.

38. Quoted in the introduction by William Charvat to *The House of the Seven Gables*, 2:xxii.

39. See Shloss, *In Visible Light*, 31–33.

40. Richard Millington suggests that the book begins with this fusion rather than achieving it through the romance (*Practicing Romance*, 109).

41. The narrative voice preserves the ironic bite of "Governor Pyncheon" in the book's final chapter: "The sudden death of so prominent a member of the social world, as the Honorable Judge Jaffrey Pyncheon, created a sensation (at least, in the circles more immediately connected with the deceased) which had hardly quite subsided in a fortnight" (2:309). It is from this point that he proceeds to give a definitive explanation for the deaths of both Jaffrey Pyncheon and his uncle.

42. As Kenneth Dauber puts it, the "function" of Hawthorne's speech "is not to synthesize, but to serve as a locus of association" (*Rediscovering Hawthorne*, 19).

43. Bell, *The Development of American Romance*, 14.

Three. Moonshine and Masquerade

1. Hawthorne, *The Blithedale Romance*, 3:2. Hawthorne's sense of the unreality of Brook Farm is not the product of time and distance: in a letter dated September 3, 1841, written to Sophia Peabody after only a few days' absence from the farm, he comments, "my life there was an unnatural and unsuitable, and therefore an unreal one. It already looks like a dream behind me" (15:566).

2. Quoted in Spann, *Brotherly Tomorrows,* 62.

3. Richard Brodhead discusses the Veiled Lady in connection with changes in antebellum theatrical and literary production in chapter 2 of his *Cultures of Letters,* 48–68.

4. Kurt Eisen discusses both Margaret Fuller and Fanny Kemble as sources for Zenobia's character in "Hawthorne's Moral Theaters and the Post-Puritan Stage," 273.

5. Dana Brand takes both the lyceum's list of attractions and Coverdale's description of the crowd as "rather suburban than rural" (3:197) as signs of a growing cultural cosmopolitanism and spectatorship in the period (*The Spectator and the City in Nineteenth-Century American Literature,* 123–24).

6. Nina Baym offers a fine discussion of the tension between spirituality and physical possession, idealization and exploitation in Westervelt's exhibition of the Lady in "*The Blithedale Romance:* A Radical Reading," 360–65.

7. Gillian Brown describes Coverdale's voyeurism as a kind of "utopian consumerism," linking his aesthetic detachment to the economic relation between audience and performer (*Domestic Individualism,* 120).

8. Brand argues that the urbanites at Blithedale are merely adopting temporary roles, never abandoning the urban cosmopolitanism that privileges both fluidity of identity and the spectatorial detachment cultivated by Coverdale (*The Spectator and the City in Nineteenth-Century American Literature,* 137–41).

9. Hawthorne, *The American Notebooks,* ed. Randall Stewart, 78. All further references to these notebooks are to this edition.

10. See Hawthorne, *The French and Italian Notebooks,* 14:155–56; this entry is discussed in greater detail in my conclusion.

11. Roy Male takes this scene as an attack on both Fuller's feminism and her character (*Hawthorne's Tragic Vision,* 150).

12. See Halttunen, *Confidence Men and Painted Women,* 156.

Robert S. Levine takes an opposite view of this scene, emphasizing the subversive, even satanic overtones of the masquerade and placing it in a tradition of Protestant revolution; he links Coverdale as observer to Robin Molineux (*Conspiracy and Romance,* 151–53).

13. Richard Francis offers a far more positive reading of masquerade at both Blithedale and Brook Farm; he emphasizes the liberating aspect of its role-playing and subversion of social hierarchies. See his *Transcendental Utopias,* 53–65. My main point about Blithedale's theatricality, on the other hand, is its superficial and temporary nature, the way it substitutes, in Hawthorne's eyes, for real changes in social hierarchy and power.

14. George Ripley to Ralph Waldo Emerson, 9 November 1840, in Sams, ed., *Autobiography of Brook Farm,* 6. To some extent, Coverdale's experience echoes Hawthorne's as surveyor in the Salem Custom-House.

15. Bromell, *By the Sweat of the Brow,* 11.

16. Spann, *Brotherly Tomorrows,* 56.

17. For Hawthorne's comments on the deadening effects of labor at Brook Farm, see his letters to Sophia Peabody of June 1 and August 12, 1841 (15:545, 558).

18. See Spann, *Brotherly Tomorrows,* 61–62.

19. Irving Howe makes a similar point about the novel as a whole: "If Hawthorne criticizes the utopian impulse on the ground that it does not really succeed in avoiding the evil of the great world, he also implies that another trouble with utopianism is that it does not bring its followers into sufficiently close relation with the evil of the great world" ("Hawthorne: Pastoral and Politics," 292).

20. Male also notes these foreshadowings (*Hawthorne's Tragic Vision,* 141–42, 144).

21. Joel Pfister suggests that Zenobia's suicide is in fact a gesture of resistance to the stereotypical images of beautiful female death that Coverdale would impose on it (*The Production of Personal Life,* 94–95).

22. Hawthorne, *The American Notebooks,* 113–14.

Four. Whitman in 1855: Against Representation

1. As Larry J. Reynolds points out, Whitman's response as journalist to the French revolution of 1848 involved a particular focus on Lamartine and especially on the way in which he combined the roles of writer and political leader (*European Revolutions and the American Renaissance,* 134–36).

2. From Whitman's review of *Napoleon,* by William Hazlitt, quoted in Brasher, ed., *Whitman as Editor of "The Brooklyn Daily Eagle,"* 100.

3. *Collected Writings of Walt Whitman: The Early Poems and the Fiction,* 40.

4. *Walt Whitman's "Leaves of Grass": The First (1855) Edition,* 134, lines 31–36; ellipses in original. All further references to the 1855 edition are to this text and are in parentheses. References to the preface correspond to page numbers, those to the poetry to line numbers.

5. David Reynolds, *Beneath the American Renaissance,* 107.

6. Erkkila, *Whitman the Political Poet,* 26–27.

M. Wynn Thomas *(The Lunar Light of Whitman's Poetry)* offers an economic reading that dovetails with my own in many respects, but his focus, like Erkkila's, is usually on the content rather than the form or methods of the poetry. I concentrate on the differences between various versions of *Leaves of Grass,* while Thomas tends to disregard or de-emphasize them.

One critic who does treat both the social and economic contexts of Whitman's work and some of its formal features is Robert Shulman in *Social Criticism and Nineteenth-Century American Fictions.* He sees Whitman as responding to the divisive pressures of market society, countering them with a fluid, egalitarian poetics; finally, however, Shulman regards Whitman as failing to provide an adequate vision of the social or to take account of the power of the nineteenth-century industrial order.

7. For Erkkila's discussion of these issues, see *Whitman the Political Poet,* 86–93.

More recently, Wai Chee Dimock has spoken of the "intimate connection between Whitman's poetic language and political philosophy," a formulation that links, but still distinguishes between, the two ("Whitman, Syntax, and Political Theory," 71).

Kerry Larson focuses directly on Whitman's attempt to bring the reader into the work of the poem, the generation of a "consensual framework" that is the poem's subject as well as its main objective (*Whitman's Drama of Consensus,* xiv.) Larson goes on to emphasize the tensions between poet and reader; he finds these elements in the 1856 and 1869 editions in particular, but sees them as characteristic of Whitman's work as a whole (18–19).

8. Cantor, *The Space Between,* 21. Tenney Nathanson describes this quality of Whitman's writing in largely nonpolitical terms, as an aspiration toward a kind of "word magic" (*Whitman's Presence,* 6–9 and elsewhere).

9. According to Karen Sánchez-Eppler, "Whitman proposes in *Leaves of Grass* that the divisions in the social fabric, the nature of identity, and the relation of the poet's word to the external world are not simply analogous, but finally identical questions" ("To Stand Between," 945). Sánchez-Eppler argues, however, that Whitman's attempt to create both a poetry of the body and a poetics of merger is inevitably self-contradictory, forced to replicate the differences it would overcome.

In *Disseminating Whitman,* Michael Moon describes Whitman as attempting "to project actual physical presence" into his texts, but falling back upon a strategy of "substitution" (5, 6). Moon also focuses on the fluidity and indeterminacy that characterizes Whitman's work, but largely restricts his discussion to issues of homoeroticism and the male body.

M. Jimmie Killingsworth comes closer to my position in his description of Whitman's "physical eloquence," which yields a "poetry of the body" that "opens out into potential physical action" ("Whitman's Physical Eloquence," 71). For Killingsworth, Whitman's writing awakens a "sympathetic desire for physical contact which reading cannot finally satisfy" (71); I take this more limited view of language and textuality to be characteristic of the second and later editions of *Leaves of Grass,* but not of that of 1855.

10. David Simpson notes many of the stylistic features I discuss later, but he goes no further ("Destiny Made Manifest," 179–81). Allen Grossman, on the other hand, does note the hierarchical implications of poetic representation: "Hierarchy (the defeat of equality) is the sufficient condition of (poetic) representation, as it is of any *actual* state of affairs (social, linguistic, or perceptual)" ("Whitman's 'Whoever You Are Holding Me Now in Hand,'" 114).

11. Dimock, "Whitman, Syntax, and Political Theory," 71, 73.

12. Michael Warner is quite blunt in his rejection of this view of Whitman as "a prophet of the 'liberal self,' a self that regards itself as universal, that does not recognize 'difference' . . . in every major poem he wrote, Whitman tries out an enormous range of strategies for frustrating the attempt to 'self' his language" ("Whitman Drunk," 40). I differ from Warner in differentiating between the poems of 1855 and Whitman's later work, which I see as moving closer to conventional notions of selfhood.

13. Anderson, *The Imperial Self,* 96, 107.

14. Pearce, *The Continuity of American Poetry,* 169.

15. Philip Fisher has described the nineteenth-century American conception of "democratic space" as "identical from place to place," such an identity being required for both political and literary representation. His definition has three other components: democratic social space is also unbounded; it is transparent and intelligible; and it denies the possibility of an observer or oppositional perspective. These last three points seem to me to apply to Whitman, but the first, based as it is on the process of representation, fits "Song of Myself" less well ("Democratic Social Space," 75, 76).

16. Cowley makes this argument in his introduction to *Walt Whitman's "Leaves of Grass": The First (1855) Edition,* x. Ivan Marki takes a similar position in *The Trial of the Poet,* 2–3.

17. As I have noted, the poems in the 1855 edition do not have titles or section

numbers; for purposes of discussion, however, it seems best to refer to them by their final titles, and to use section numbers in dealing with "Song of Myself."

18. My description here and throughout is based on Walt Whitman, *Leaves of Grass: A Facsimile of the First Edition.*

19. Erkkila, in a reading otherwise largely consonant with my own, does not hesitate to make these connections: "the portrait is a construct, an invention of the poet as the representative American who emerges in the poems" (*Whitman the Political Poet*, 4). It is the conflation of names and images into a single representative figure that Whitman is working against, I argue.

Terry Mulcaire places the 1855 *Leaves* in the context of nineteenth-century debates over copyright and the ongoing commodification of the literary marketplace in "Publishing Intimacy in *Leaves of Grass*," 471–501.

20. For a discussion of the careers of Irving and Cooper, see Ezra Greenspan, *Walt Whitman and the American Reader,* 16–21.

David Reynolds offers a dizzying list of the papers and magazines for which Whitman wrote during this period (*Walt Whitman's America*, 83–84). Shelley Fisher Fishkin finds elements of "Song of Myself" foreshadowed even in Whitman's earliest editorial work—for the *New York Aurora* in 1842—in its use of a spectatorial persona and catalogs of ordinary objects and persons (*From Fact to Fiction*, 15–18).

21. See Erkkila, *Whitman the Political Poet*, 53–59.

22. For a reader anticipating poetry, the preface may even seem to block access to the book per se. This is the view of Richard Bridgman in his introduction to *Leaves of Grass: A Facsimile of the First Edition,* xxxi.

23. David Reynolds describes the book's exterior as designed for the middle-class parlor, in contrast to the newspaper-style text within: "Everything about the book manifested Whitman's interest in dissolving boundaries between different cultural levels" (*Walt Whitman's America*, 313).

24. *Collected Writings of Walt Whitman: Notebooks and Unpublished Prose Manuscripts,* 165.

25. The editor, Edward F. Grier, comments about an earlier notebook, "It is not surprising to find such mundane matters intermingled with intense private outpourings, for WW put everything and anything into his notebooks (and memorandum books)" (*Notebooks*, 1:54).

26. At first glance, Whitman's words may seem to echo Emerson's declaration in "The Poet" that "America is a poem in our eyes" (Emerson, *Selected Essays,* 281). But there is a key difference: Emerson's phrase makes the nation's poetic status

dependent on the viewer, on the poet's own "tyrannous eye" (281). Whitman, on the other hand, calls the nation's poetry "essential" and inherent. He may build on Emerson's vision of the American poet, on his notion that "words are also actions" (263), but the younger man's words serve a poetic and political project quite different from his predecessor's.

27. Mark Bauerlein describes Whitman's objective as the restoration of language to a "natural" status: "if the word can be made contiguous or coexistent with the event, the poems would be spontaneously deictic, not distantly representational" (*Whitman and the American Idiom,* 5). I differ from Bauerlein in emphasizing Whitman's view of writing as action, and as political action at that.

28. It is this convention that allows Erkkila to make a distinction between "The Sleepers" and "Song of Myself." She can thus accept the former's "radically democratic and carnivalesque landscape in which the hierarchy and polarity of the daytime world give way to the erotic flow of night" but deny such a destabilizing impact or intention to the latter (*Whitman the Political Poet,* 119).

29. *Life Illustrated,* August 9, 1856. Reprinted in *New York Dissected: A Sheaf of Recently Discovered Newspaper Articles by the Author of "Leaves of Grass,"* 120. All further references to these essays are to this edition and are given parenthetically.

30. See the introduction by Emory Holloway and Ralph Adimari in *New York Dissected,* 3.

31. Warner sees Whitman as demonstrating "the impossibility of selfing" ("Whitman Drunk," 40). The poet exploits "the special discursive conventions of print-mediated publicity," which are based on "the necessary anonymity and mutual nonknowledge of writer and reader, and therefore on the definitional impossibility of intimacy" (40).

32. Greenspan argues that Whitman, in both his poetry and his earlier journalism, constructs an egalitarian rhetorical relationship between himself and his reader (*Walt Whitman and the American Reader,* 107). He later speaks of a "conflation" of text, reader, and poet, but then reiterates his view of Whitman's poetry as one of "mediation" or "matching" rather than fusion (118). My reading of these lines, on the other hand, emphasizes the way in which Whitman challenges such differences or oppositions.

33. It is, ultimately, the voice, and not words, that functions as the guarantor of physical presence: "Not words, not music or rhyme I want . . . . not / custom or lecture, not even the best, / Only the lull I like, the hum of your valved voice" (lines 75–77). Whitman's demand here is for the flowing presence of sound itself, as the ground out of which words, music, and rhyme may be differentiated.

34. M. Wynn Thomas, *The Lunar Light of Whitman's Poetry,* 154.

35. Edward K. Spann describes the city's "vibrant street life" as "an expression of urban community" (*The New Metropolis,* 156).

Donald Pease points out the importance of the urban crowd for Whitman in particular: "Like the multiple impulses surging up in a person, urban crowds are transitory sources of energy. For Whitman, crowds extinguish differences among persons: in the electric suddenness of movement in and among crowds persons encounter equality as an everyday experience" (*Visionary Compacts,* 110).

36. Ryan, *Civic Wars* 51.

37. As Whitman puts it in "A Song for Occupations," "[I] send no agent or medium . . . . and offer no representative of value – but offer the value itself" (line 47).

38. Buell, *Literary Transcendentalism,* 167.

39. See Spann, *The New Metropolis,* 100–114.

40. See Spann, *The New Metropolis,* 35–37.

41. Alan Trachtenberg speaks of Whitman's "mode of procession," which "constructs itself as a recounted movement through city space, a passage which attempts to comprehend a whole in its parts" ("Whitman's Lesson of the City," 170).

42. According to F. O. Matthiessen, Whitman described himself as "a jour printer" (*American Renaissance,* 531). Fishkin offers a fine reading of this section, emphasizing the continuity between the activities described and the work of the poet (*From Fact to Fiction,* 38–40).

43. Bromell, *By the Sweat of the Brow,* 11, 29.

44. See Sean Wilentz, *Chants Democratic* 4–5. M. Wynn Thomas emphasizes this context for Whitman's poetry (*The Lunar Light of Whitman's Poetry,* 81–82), but seems to waver in his estimation of Whitman's focus on artisans and craft values: "Whitman's kosmos," he says, "stands in opposite and corrective relationship to the actual New York society of its time, [but it also] approximates that society's most favorable (mis)conception of itself" (85). For him, Whitman's poetry is simultaneously transformative and mystifying.

45. See David Reynolds, *Beneath the American Renaissance,* 170.

46. Sánchez-Eppler suggests that "merger depends upon the arresting of narrative and its replacement with the atemporality of the lyric" ("To Stand Between," 934).

47. The catalog "associates" them, Pease suggests, rather than separating them as discrete "representations" (*Visionary Compacts,* 139).

48. Whitman makes this particular choice in 1855, after Texas's admission to the Union as a slave state and after the Mexican War. The ironies deepen further when one considers that the Texans' conflict with Mexico sprang, at least in part, from their desire to continue holding slaves after slavery had been abolished under the Mexican constitution. Fannin, in particular, had been a slave trader before the war began (Long, *Duel of Eagles,* 199).

The point is not that Whitman plays fast and loose with historical details (the massacre took place not in "early summer" [line 877], for instance, but on Palm Sunday, March 27, according to Long [282]) but that he offers a deliberately refashioned and selective version of history.

49. Fishkin compares this section to one of Whitman's Brooklyn *Eagle* editorials urging war with Mexico; she emphasizes the poem's straightforward description compared to the editorial's abstract and conventionally heightened rhetoric (*From Fact to Fiction,* 47–49). Erkkila sees Whitman's omission of names as part of his effort to turn "history into national myth" (*Whitman the Political Poet,* 110).

50. Once again, Whitman's concern is less with historical accuracy than with dramatic force. He moves John Paul Jones's famous "I have not yet begun to fight" from a point early in the fight to a later, more desperate one, for example. For a more accurate version, see Morison, *John Paul Jones: A Sailor's Biography,* 240.

51. Trachtenberg describes this moment in terms of Whitman's fluctuating relation to the crowd: "The poet comes to himself through the intermediary of the crowd; the call emerges from and expresses the oneness of being close and being distant" ("Whitman's Lesson of the City," 170).

52. David Reynolds, *Walt Whitman's America,* 156–58, 171–72.

53. Wilentz, *Chants Democratic,* 259.

Five. 1856 and After

1. Whitman, *"Leaves of Grass": A Textual Variorum of the Printed Poems,* 1:159. All references to poems added in 1856 are to the original versions as given in this edition.

2. Quentin Anderson notes this shift, but in rather different terms: "In this poem the bullying persona of the poet is absent; . . . When the poet is present, the whole question of the struggle to attain his all-inclusive consciousness is ignored; he simply has it and invites the reader to enjoy it" (*The Imperial Self,* 122). As Betsy Erkkila describes it, "Whereas in 1855 he envisioned the poet as an

incarnator of the nation, in 1856 he moves toward an emphasis on the poet as fuser of the nation" (*Whitman the Political Poet,* 133).

3. Terry Mulcaire reads both "Crossing Brooklyn Ferry" and the "Calamus" poems of 1860 (and, indeed, all of *Leaves of Grass*) as approaching the reader through the crucial mediating process of publication ("Publishing Intimacy in *Leaves of Grass*," 485–97).

4. M. Wynn Thomas, for instance, sees signs of strain in the 1860 edition, but claims that it was "after the Civil War that the extreme social consequences of industrial and commercial capitalism seriously came to occupy Whitman's conscious attention," changing the shape and content of his work (*The Lunar Light of Whitman's Poetry,* 149).

5. During the period in which he was composing the poems of the 1856 edition, Whitman was also at work on a prose political tract, *The Eighteenth Presidency!* This division, in both form and content, suggests an even more radical separation between poetry and the political than is implied within the second *Leaves* itself.

6. Whitman, *Leaves of Grass,* 736. All further references to Whitman's letter are to this edition.

7. M. Wynn Thomas does not make the distinction between the 1855 and 1856 editions that I am offering here; he takes the poem's anger as an indication of Whitman's critical view of American capitalist society throughout his early work (*The Lunar Light of Whitman's Poetry,* 7–9).

8. Ryan, *Civic Wars,* 151–57.

9. Killingsworth, "Whitman's Physical Eloquence," 73.

10. *Collected Writings of Walt Whitman: Notebooks and Unpublished Prose Manu-scripts,* 227–37.

11. See Ryan, *Civic Wars,* 144–45, 152.

12. Thomas sees such a conflation of present and future in the 1860 *Leaves* as enabling Whitman to minimize "the trauma of revolutionary historical change" ("Whitman and the Dreams of Labor," 141).

13. Whitman, *"Leaves of Grass": A Textual Variorum of the Printed Poems,* 2:344. All references to poems from the 1860–61 and 1867 *Leaves* are to the original versions as given in this edition.

14. The difference is marked even more forcefully in the original edition, in which this line is followed by a subtitle rendered in capitals: "REMINIS-CENCE" (2:344).

15. Dana Brand speaks of the Calamus poems as utopian in spirit, but also describes them as "a response to an awareness of time, death, and loss" (*The Spectator and the City,* 179).

16. Greenspan, *Walt Whitman and the American Reader* (New York: Cambridge University Press, 1990), 197. Greenspan also notes Whitman's growing conservatism and distaste for the urban masses in his period as editor of the *Brooklyn Times* in 1857–59 (184–87).

Erkkila has revised her position in a more recent essay, arguing against a split between public political poet and private poet of same-sex love between men ("Whitman and the Homosexual Republic," 159).

17. Grossman, "Whitman's 'Whoever You Are Holding Me Now in Hand,'" 121.

18. Grossman calls "Calamus" a "new pastoral . . . exploratory of presence unmediated by representation" ("Whitman's 'Whoever You Are Holding Me Now in Hand,'" 117).

Six. *To Reconcile the People and the Stones*

1. Thoreau, *Walden,* 19.

2. For a description of Thoreau's compositional practices, see the historical introduction to *Journal,* vol. 2, especially 454–59.

3. Thoreau, *A Week on the Concord and Merrimack Rivers,* 5.

4. Lawrence Buell suggests that the *Week*'s opening chapter "acts out [the] paradox of timelessness versus time"; he suggests that the poem that follows this passage, for instance, creates "the sense of . . . an escape from time altogether into the timeless world of meditation" (*Literary Transcendentalism,* 209, 210). Joan Burbick, on the other hand, argues that Thoreau tries to reconcile or evade such a paradox by integrating history and nature, "reaching for the sacred in an uncivil version of historical time" (*Thoreau's Alternative History,* 5).

5. The intensity and bitterness of the subject for Thoreau are even clearer in earlier drafts; there, he seems almost obsessed by the contrast between stone monuments and decomposing flesh: "Instead of a stinking graveyard, let us have blooming and fertile fields," he says. "These condemned, these damned bodies. Think of the living men that walk on this globe, and then think of the dead bodies that lie in graves beneath them, carefully pact away in chests as if ready for a start! Whose idea was that to put them there?" (Linck C. Johnson reproduces these passages in *Thoreau's Complex Weave,* 458–59.)

6. At the end of Dustan's story, Thoreau looks back to Lovewell's, thus clearly connecting the two (324).

7. Elsewhere, Thoreau sounds almost like Whitman when he speaks of poetry: as a "song" that is "a vital function like breathing" (91).

8. For an examination of the ways in which Thoreau mines and revises his sources, see Johnson's chapter "The Uses of the Past" (*Thoreau's Complex Weave,* 122–62).

9. Sayre, *Thoreau and the American Indians*; Sayre offers a summary of "savagism" as an ideology on 4–6. The term itself he takes from Pearce, *Savagism and Civilization.*

10. Another apple tree serves to mark both the highest water level of a 1785 freshet and the site of an earlier killing of a friendly Indian by others of his tribe (356).

11. Gilmore's argument is put forward in *American Romanticism and the Marketplace,* 35–51. He uses "mediation" in a more narrowly economic sense than I do, and, I suggest, also conflates the positions of *Walden* and "Resistance to Civil Government" in a way that I argue against.

For a response to Gilmore that examines Thoreau's actual relations to the literary and intellectual marketplace of his day, see Steven Fink, *Prophet in the Marketplace.*

12. Leo Marx, *The Machine in the Garden,* 256.

13. Leo Marx notes that "Of themselves the facts do not, cannot, flower into truth; they do not show forth a meaning" (*The Machine in the Garden,* 259). What I have sought to emphasize is the centrality of *labor* in the process Thoreau describes of *generating* or *making* meaning; this work is both physical and verbal, but not simply "figurative" or imaginative, as Marx suggests (262).

14. Thoreau plays on the different meanings of "account" and "accounting" at several other points in *Walden* as well – most obviously in "Economy," a chapter whose title works in the same fashion (see 48–61).

Robert A. Gross reads "The Beanfield" as a direct parody of Colman and other reformers; see his "The Great Beanfield Hoax," 483–97.

15. Burbick, *Thoreau's Alternative History,* 82.

16. Gross, "The Great Beanfield Hoax," 493.

17. H. Daniel Peck makes this point in *Thoreau's Morning Work,* 139. He offers a fuller reading of "Former Inhabitants" than I do here; it is also a darker one, for Peck sees the chapter as introducing the possibilities of failure and death into Thoreau's text.

See also Peck's "The Crosscurrents of *Walden*'s Pastoral," 74–75.

18. See Dublin, "Women and Outwork in a Nineteenth-Century New England Town," 52.

19. Thoreau's language is both an uncanny echo and an inversion of that of agricultural reformers. Gross quotes "a New Hampshire writer" on New England

farmers: "they have not time to make the necessary retrenchments and improvements: but continue (to use the common expression) 'slashing on, heels over head,' without consideration – zeal without improvement; thus they make perfect slaves of themselves, and never reform, pass through the world without enjoying the sweets of living" ("Culture and Civilization," 53).

20. Prude, "Town-Factory Conflicts in Antebellum Rural Massachusetts," 78.

21. Thoreau, *Reform Papers,* 188.

22. Karl Marx, "The German Ideology," 124.

23. Quoted by Henry Petroski in "H. D. Thoreau, Engineer," 8.

24. Thoreau's description of himself in the bean field is reminiscent of Longfellow's description of Goethean self-culture: Goethe "became like the athlete of ancient story, drawing all his strength from earth. His model was the perfect man, as man; living, moving, laboring upon earth in the sweat of his brow" (quoted in Richardson, *Henry Thoreau: A Life of the Mind,* 55).

25. Petroski, "H. D. Thoreau, Engineer," 10–11, 14.

26. Leo Marx makes this point in *The Machine in the Garden,* 257.

27. See Gross, "Culture and Cultivation," 45.

28. Peck, *Thoreau's Morning Work,* 136.

29. Buell, *New England Literary Culture,* 333.

30. See Prude, "Town-Factory Conflicts," 75–76; and Dublin, "Women and Outwork," 55–56.

31. See Gross, "Culture and Cultivation," 51–52.

Seven. Division and Revenge

1. Robert Sattelmeyer cites pages 262–64 of the Berg Journal as containing ideas that would lead to "Resistance to Civil Government," but the passage does not seem to be conceived as a draft or even as notes for an essay (Thoreau, *Journal,* 2:461).

2. The journal material on slavery and the Sims case appears on 3:203–9 of Thoreau, *Journal.* Wendell Glick discusses the journal sources for all three essays in his general introduction to Thoreau, *Reform Papers,* 228–31.

3. See Glick's historical introduction to Thoreau, *Reform Papers,* 228.

Robert C. Albrecht discusses the ways in which Thoreau reshaped journal entries on John Brown in constructing his "Plea" for a Concord audience. His main point, however, is that these are *tactical* changes, designed to increase the lecture's rhetorical effectiveness, not an evolution of development of its ideas ("Thoreau and His Audience," 393–402).

Robert D. Richardson Jr. makes a similar observation about "Slavery in Massachusetts" and its relation to journal entries of 1854 (*Henry Thoreau*, 315).

4. For a statement of Garrison's position, see "No Union with Slaveholders," reprinted from the May 31, 1844, edition of the *Liberator,* in Frederickson, ed., *William Lloyd Garrison,* 52–55.

5. In "Slavery in Massachusetts," Thoreau does speak of a rural town meeting as "the true Congress" (99), but this is only an aside in the midst of an extended attack on the established institutions of Boston.

6. Thoreau's journal drafts of April 1851 draw a much sharper contrast between the revolutionary era and its leaders and the politicians of the 1850s, "men not descendants of the men of the revolution . . . [but] men born to be slaves" (*Journal,* 3:203). The journal entry employs a jeremiad structure, but this is considerably diminished in the published version of four years later.

7. See Schwartz, "Fugitive Slave Days in Boston," 192–212.

8. Buell, *The Environmental Imagination,* 38.

9. Both Raymond D. Gozzi and Richard Lebeaux, in psychoanalytic essays on Thoreau, focus on his father's death in early 1859 as a crucial event that accounts at least in part for the intensity of Thoreau's response to Brown: they see Thoreau as identifying with Brown as oedipal rebel against the paternal state. See Gozzi, "A Freudian View of Thoreau," 14–16, and Lebeaux, "Identity Crisis and Beyond," 49–53.

10. Albrecht notes that the pun did not appear in Thoreau's original journal entry, but was added later – as, I suggest, a deliberate denigration of the lecture's status as speech instead of action ("Thoreau and His Audience," 396).

11. Gregory Eiselein discusses Brown's attack on "talk" as a substitute for action (and Thoreau's endorsement of it) as less a critique of language per se than a sign of a crisis in the conception of humanitarian reform (*Literature and Humanitarian Reform in the Civil War Era,* 17–38).

12. See, for instance, pages 111 and 113 of "A Plea." Bercovitch's treatment of the jeremiad tradition in the nineteenth century can be found in chapter 5 of *The American Jeremiad,* 132–75). He discusses *Walden* on 185–90.

The language of the jeremiad was used by many in the antislavery movement. See, for instance, the 1850 letter of Theodore Parker's quoted by Schwartz ("Fugitive Slave Days in Boston," 194).

13. Bercovitch, *The American Jeremiad,* 134.

Conclusion. Civil Wars

1. Hawthorne, *Our Old Home,* 5:4.

2. Hawthorne's "Chiefly about War-Matters"; see Masur, ed., *The Real War Will Never Get in the Books,* 168.

3. Larry J. Reynolds, *European Revolutions and the American Literary Renaissance,* 57.

4. Fuller does note instances of urban poverty in Britain, but these remain only isolated observations. While Larry J. Reynolds describes the change in Fuller's writing as a political radicalization, I want to stress the ways in which her dispatches begin to *combine* the aesthetic and the political rather than just displacing one with the other.

5. Fuller, *"These Sad But Glorious Days,"* 127.

6. Jeffrey Steele also notes these shifts in Fuller's writing, but he takes as his primary example a later dispatch, letter 18, written in December 1847 (*The Essential Margaret Fuller,* xlii–xliii).

7. Of the crowd, Fuller remarks that "their conduct is like music" (160).

8. See also, for instance, 229, 245.

9. Fuller's letters reveal a network of friends and family, but there is little overlap between them and her dispatches. On the few occasions when public events appear in the letters, they do so in quite different form from that of the published versions. See, for example, her descriptions of the Rossi assassination in a letter to her mother and of a battle in a letter to Emelyn Story (*The Letters of Margaret Fuller,* 5:146–47, 238, and *"These Sad But Glorious Days,"* 239–40, 292–93).

10. Larry J. Reynolds, *European Revolutions and the American Literary Renaissance,* 57.

11. Steele describes a decline in Fuller's use of allusion in these dispatches compared to *Woman in the Nineteenth Century* or *Summer on the Lakes* (*The Essential Margaret Fuller,* xliv); she replaces a literary context with a historical or political one, he suggests. My point here is that it is her immediate experience of Rome *as place* that makes this possible. Larry J. Reynolds discusses this passage, but omits precisely the sections on which I focus here (*European Revolutions and the American Literary Renaissance,* 71–72).

12. Hawthorne, *The French and Italian Notebooks,* 14:155.

13. Hawthorne, *The Marble Faun,* 4:232.

14. Richard Brodhead places the art in *The Marble Faun* in the context of the new aesthetics of the 1850s, "in which art has been strongly reidentified not with the work of making but with a canon of masters and masterpieces" (*The School of Hawthorne,* 73).

For an account of the costs of operating a Roman studio in this period, see Fuller's letter 29, in which she seeks to explain the costs of (and the prices charged by) American artists (*"These Sad But Glorious Days,"* 272).

15. The stroll has begun at the Trevi fountain, where Miriam looks for her "reflected image" in the water but sees only shadows: " 'There they lie on the bottom, as if all three were drowned together' " (4:146). Both the absence of a reflecting mirror and the mention of drowning echo *The Blithedale Romance,* here also signaling a breakdown in imaginative power.

A link between Miriam and Zenobia again appears when the narrator compares the mention of her name to "bringing up a drowned body" (4:229).

16. Carton, *The Marble Faun: Hawthorne's Transformations,* 39.

17. In his notebooks, Hawthorne describes the procession bearing "the heads of the Roman police" as "the most effective masque of the day," a shallow imitation of authority that parallels the illusory freedom of the crowd (14:71).

18. In the notebooks, Hawthorne calls "the chained tiger-cat" of "the Roman populace . . . a very harmless brute" (14:70). For Leonardo Buonomo, Hawthorne does not see the French troops as invaders, but as "a natural manifestation of the moral malady of the city," whose inhabitants "find in their state of subjection and mutual mistrust their natural condition" (*Backward Glances,* 54, 55).

For a reading of the carnival scene as a restaging and recontainment of the revolutionary energies of 1848–50, see Robert S. Levine, " 'Antebellum Rome' in *The Marble Faun,*" 25–31.

19. My reading of "Lilacs" is heavily indebted to the work of Allen Grossman, especially to a seminar delivered at Johns Hopkins University on March 16–18, 1983. My approach to the 1855 *Leaves* has been largely defined against the positions taken by Grossman in those talks, but my view of "Lilacs" derives in many ways from his.

20. Whitman, *"Leaves of Grass": A Textual Variorum of the Printed Poems,* 2:529. All references to poems from the 1865–66 "Sequel to Drum-Taps" are to the original versions as given in this edition.

21. Whitman finds himself, in Grossman's words, "at the greatest distance . . . from the social world in which alone his intention can have meaning" ("The Poetics of Union in Whitman and Lincoln," 202).

22. Sweet focuses on the way in which "Lilacs" displaces human objects in favor of an idealized natural landscape, in a "pastoral evasion of history" (*Traces of War,* 67; see also 67–77).

23. See Stern's introduction to *Louisa May Alcott: Selected Fiction,* xix. Stern sug-

gests that the piece had been rejected because of its abolitionist position; to me it seems the treatment of miscegenation is the more likely cause.

24. Alcott, "The Brothers," 585. All further references to the story are to this first edition, except as noted.

25. Klimasmith, "Slave, Master, Mistress, Slave," 115–35.

26. Teresa Goddu reads Alcott's gothic mode as performing a demystifying role in relation to the sentimental. Her focus is on the way in which it "unveils" the penetration of the domestic sphere by the forces of the marketplace; my point is a parallel one – that the gothic reveals the essential violence of race slavery beneath its veneer of sentimental paternalism. See her *Gothic America,* 117–30.

27. Mark Patterson emphasizes the construction of black masculinity through Civil War service in his reading of the story; for him, African American masculinity is made visible in the text, but finally normalized – "whitened," feminized, even disembodied ("Racial Sacrifice and Citizenship," 147–66). I take Alcott to be more self-conscious and self-critical about this process than he does, I believe.

28. Other changes in the 1869 edition involve the correction of historical errors and the replacement of references to the ongoing war effort of 1863 with ones to the eventual Union victory. Also included, though, is a more systematic racial coding of African American speech ("Missis" replaces "ma'am," for example), the effect of which is to reconfirm the lines of racial difference that the earlier version had called into question. This is one reason I have chosen to quote from the *Atlantic Monthly* version.

Alcott comments on some of these matters in a letter of November 12, 1863, to Thomas Wentworth Higginson, who had written her from South Carolina about the story (*Selected Letters of Louisa May Alcott,* 96–97).

29. Fuller, *"These Sad But Glorious Days,"* 237, 285. Fuller's comments on French politics as empty theater *precede* Marx's.

BIBLIOGRAPHY

Albrecht, Robert C. "Thoreau and His Audience: 'A Plea for Captain John Brown.'" *AL* 32 (1961): 393–402.

Alcott, Louisa May. "The Brothers." *Atlantic Monthly* 12 (November 1863): 584–95.

————. *Louisa May Alcott: Selected Fiction*. Ed. Daniel Shealy, Madeleine B. Stern, and Joel Myerson. Boston: Little, Brown, 1990.

————. *Selected Letters of Louisa May Alcott*. Ed. Joel Myerson, Daniel Shealy, and Madeleine B. Stern. Boston: Little, Brown, 1987.

Anderson, Quentin. *The Imperial Self: An Essay in American Literary and Cultural History*. New York: Knopf, 1971.

Ash, Timothy Garton. "The Revolution of the Magic Lantern." *New York Review of Books* 36, nos. 21–22 (January 18, 1990): 42–51.

Bauerlein, Mark. *Whitman and the American Idiom*. Baton Rouge: Louisiana State University Press, 1991.

Baum, Dale. *The Civil War Party System: The Case of Massachusetts, 1848–76*. Chapel Hill: University of North Carolina Press, 1984.

Baym, Nina. "*The Blithedale Romance:* A Radical Reading." Hawthorne, *Blithedale Romance,* ed. Gross and Murphy 351–68.

Bell, Michael Davitt. *The Development of American Romance*. Chicago: University of Chicago Press, 1980.

Benjamin, Walter. "The Author as Producer." *Reflections*. Trans. Edmund Jephcott. Ed. Peter Demetz. New York: Harcourt, Brace, 1978. 220–38.

Bercovitch, Sacvan. *The American Jeremiad*. Madison: University of Wisconsin Press, 1978.

————. *The Office of the Scarlet Letter*. Baltimore: Johns Hopkins University Press, 1991.

Berlant, Lauren. *The Anatomy of National Fantasy*. Chicago: University of Chicago Press, 1991.

Bhabha, Homi K. "The Commitment to Theory." *Questions of Third Cinema*. Ed. Jim Pines and Paul Willeman. London: BFI, 1989. 111–32.

Brand, Dana. *The Spectator and the City in Nineteenth-Century American Literature.* Cambridge: Cambridge University Press, 1991.

Brasher, Thomas L., ed. *Whitman as Editor of the "Brooklyn Daily Eagle."* Detroit: Wayne State University Press, 1970.

Brodhead, Richard. *Cultures of Letters: Scenes of Reading and Writing in Nineteenth-Century America.* Chicago: University of Chicago Press, 1993.

———. *Hawthorne, Melville, and the Novel.* Chicago: University of Chicago Press, 1976.

———. *The School of Hawthorne.* New York: Oxford University Press, 1986.

Bromell, Nicholas. *By the Sweat of the Brow: Literature and Labor in Antebellum America.* Chicago: University of Chicago Press, 1993.

Brown, Gillian. *Domestic Individualism: Imagining Self in Nineteenth-Century America.* Berkeley: University of California Press, 1990.

Budick, Emily Miller. *Fiction and Historical Consciousness.* New Haven: Yale University Press, 1989.

Buell, Lawrence. *The Environmental Imagination: Thoreau, Nature Writing, and the Formation of American Culture.* Cambridge, Mass.: Harvard University Press, 1995.

———. *Literary Transcendentalism: Style and Vision in the American Renaissance.* Ithaca, N.Y.: Cornell University Press, 1973.

———. *New England Literary Culture: From Revolution through Renaissance.* Cambridge: Cambridge University Press, 1986.

Buonomo, Leonardo. *Backward Glances: Exploring Italy, Reinterpreting America (1831–1866).* Madison, N.J.: Fairleigh Dickinson University Press, 1996.

Burbick, Joan. *Thoreau's Alternative History: Changing Perspectives on Nature, Culture, and Language.* Philadelphia: University of Pennsylvania Press, 1987.

Cantor, Jay. *The Space Between: Literature and Politics.* Baltimore: Johns Hopkins University Press, 1981.

Carton, Evan. *The Marble Faun: Hawthorne's Transformations.* New York: Twayne, 1992.

———. *The Rhetoric of American Romance.* Baltimore: Johns Hopkins University Press, 1985.

Chase, Richard. *The American Novel and Its Tradition.* New York: Doubleday, 1957.

Colacurcio, Michael. *The Province of Piety.* Cambridge, Mass.: Harvard University Press, 1984.

Crews, Frederick. *The Sins of the Fathers.* New York: Oxford University Press, 1966.

Dauber, Kenneth. *Rediscovering Hawthorne.* Princeton: Princeton University Press, 1977.

de Man, Paul. "The Resistance to Theory." *Yale French Studies* 63 (1982): 3–20.

Dimock, Wai Chee. "Whitman, Syntax, and Political Theory." Erkkila and Grossman 62–79.

Dublin, Thomas. "Women and Outwork in a Nineteenth-Century New England Town." Hahn and Prude 51–70.

Eagleton, Terry. *Marxism and Literary Criticism.* Berkeley: University of California Press, 1976.

Eiselein, Gregory. *Literature and Humanitarian Reform in the Civil War Era.* Bloomington: Indiana University Press, 1996.

Eisen, Kurt. "Hawthorne's Moral Theaters and the Post-Puritan Stage." *Studies in the American Renaissance.* Ed. Joel Myerson. Charlottesville: University of Virginia Press, 1993. 255–73.

Emerson, Ralph Waldo. *Selected Essays.* Ed. Larzer Ziff. New York: Penguin, 1982.

Erkkila, Betsy. "Whitman and the Homosexual Republic." Folsom 153–71.

———. *Whitman the Political Poet.* New York: Oxford University Press, 1989.

Erkkila, Betsy, and Jay Grossman, eds. *Breaking Bounds: Whitman and American Cultural Studies.* New York: Oxford University Press, 1996.

Fink, Steven. *Prophet in the Marketplace: Thoreau's Development as a Professional Writer.* Princeton: Princeton University Press, 1992.

Fisher, Philip. "Democratic Social Space: Whitman, Melville, and the Promise of American Transparency." *Representations* 24 (1988): 60–101.

Fishkin, Shelley Fisher. *From Fact to Fiction: Journalism and Imaginative Writing in America.* Baltimore: Johns Hopkins University Press, 1985.

Folsom, Ed, ed. *Walt Whitman: The Centennial Essays.* Iowa City: University of Iowa Press, 1994.

Formisano, Ronald P. *The Transformation of Political Culture: Massachusetts Parties, 1780s–1840s.* New York: Oxford University Press, 1983.

Foucault, Michel. *Language, Countermemory, Practice.* Ed. Donald F. Bouchard. Trans. Donald F. Bouchard and Sherry Simon. Ithaca, N.Y.: Cornell University Press, 1987.

Francis, Richard. *Transcendental Utopias: Individual and Community at Brook Farm, Fruitlands, and Walden.* Ithaca, N.Y.: Cornell University Press, 1997.

Frederickson, George M., ed. *William Lloyd Garrison.* Englewood Cliffs, N.J.: Prentice-Hall, 1968.

Fuller, Margaret. *The Letters of Margaret Fuller.* Vol. 5, *1848–49.* Ed. Robert N. Hudspeth. Ithaca, N.Y.: Cornell University Press, 1988.

———. *"These Sad but Glorious Days": Dispatches from Europe, 1846–1850.* Ed. Larry J. Reynolds and Susan Belasco Smith. New Haven: Yale University Press, 1991.

Gilmore, Michael. *American Romanticism and the Marketplace.* Chicago: University of Chicago Press, 1985.

Goddu, Teresa. *Gothic America.* New York: Columbia University Press, 1997.

Gozzi, Raymond D. "A Freudian View of Thoreau." Gozzi, *Thoreau's Psychology* 1–18.

———, ed. *Thoreau's Psychology: Eight Essays.* Lanham, Md.: University Press of America, 1983.

Greenblatt, Stephen. *Renaissance Self-Fashioning: From More to Shakespeare.* Chicago: University of Chicago Press, 1980.

———. *Shakespearean Negotiations.* Berkeley: University of California Press, 1988.

Greenspan, Ezra. *Walt Whitman and the American Reader.* Cambridge: Cambridge University Press, 1990.

Gross, Robert A. "Culture and Cultivation: Agriculture and Society in Thoreau's Concord." *Journal of American History* 63, no. 1 (June 1982): 42–61.

———. "The Great Beanfield Hoax." *VQR* 61 (1985): 483–97.

Grossman, Allen. "The Poetics of Union in Whitman and Lincoln: An Inquiry toward the Relationship of Art and Policy." Michaels and Pease 183–208.

———. "Whitman's 'Whoever You Are Holding Me Now in Hand': Remarks on the Endlessly Repeated Rediscovery of the Incommensurability of the Person." Erkkila and Grossman 112–22.

Hahn, Steven, and Jonathan Prude. *The Countryside in the Age of Capitalist Transformation: Essays in the Social History of Rural America.* Chapel Hill: University of North Carolina Press, 1985.

Halttunen, Karen. *Confidence Men and Painted Women: A Study of Middle-Class Culture in America, 1830–1870.* New Haven: Yale University Press, 1982.

Handlin, Oscar, and Mary Flug Handlin. *Commonwealth: A Study of the Role of Government in the American Economy, Massachusetts, 1774–1861.* Rev. ed. Cambridge, Mass.: Harvard University Press, 1969.

Havel, Vaclav. *Open Letters: Selected Writings, 1965–1990.* Ed. Paul Wilson. New York: Knopf, 1991.

Hawthorne, Nathaniel. *The American Notebooks.* Ed. Randall Stewart. New Haven: Yale University Press, 1932.

————. *The American Notebooks*. Ed. Claude M. Simpson. Vol. 8 of *The Centenary Edition*.

————. *The Blithedale Romance*. Ed. Seymour Gross and Rosalie Murphy. New York: Norton, 1978.

————. *The Blithedale Romance*. 1852. Ed. William Charvat et al. Vol. 3 of *The Centenary Edition*. 1–298.

————. *The Centenary Edition of the Works of Nathaniel Hawthorne*. Ed. William Charvat et al. 20 vols. to date. Columbus: Ohio State University Press, 1962–.

————. *The French and Italian Notebooks*. Ed. Thomas Woodson. Vol. 14 of *The Centenary Edition*.

————. *The House of the Seven Gables*. 1851. Ed. William Charvat et al. Vol. 2 of *The Centenary Edition*.

————. *The Letters, 1813–1843*. Ed. Thomas Woodson et al. Vol. 15 of *The Centenary Edition*.

————. *Life of Franklin Pierce*. 1852. Reprint, N.Y.: Confucian Press, 1981.

————. *The Marble Faun*. 1860. Ed. William Charvat et al. Vol. 4 of *The Centenary Edition*.

————. *Our Old Home*. 1863. Ed. William Charvat et al. Vol. 5 of *The Centenary Edition*.

————. *The Scarlet Letter*. 1850. Ed. William Charvat et al. Vol. 1 of *The Centenary Edition*.

————. *The Snow-Image and Uncollected Tales*. Ed. William Charvat et al. Vol. 11 of *The Centenary Edition*.

————. *Twice-Told Tales*. 1837. Ed. William Charvat et al. Vol. 9 of *The Centenary Edition*.

Holland, Laurence. "Authority, Power, and Form: Some American Texts." *Yearbook of English Studies* 8 (1978): 1–14.

Howe, Irving. "Hawthorne: Pastoral and Politics." Hawthorne, *Blithedale Romance,* ed. Gross and Murphy 288–97.

Hughes, Glenn. *A History of the American Theatre, 1700–1950*. New York: French, 1951.

Hutner, Gordon. *Secrets and Sympathy*. Athens: University of Georgia Press, 1988.

Johnson, Linck C. *Thoreau's Complex Weave: The Writing of "A Week on the Concord and Merrimack Rivers."* Charlottesville: University Press of Virginia, 1986.

Killingsworth, M. Jimmie. "Whitman's Physical Eloquence." Folsom 68–78.

Klimasmith, Betsy. "Slave, Master, Mistress, Slave: Genre and Interracial Desire in Louisa May Alcott's Fiction." *ATQ* 11, no. 2 (June 1997): 115–35.

Laclau, Ernesto, and Chantal Mouffe. *Hegemony and Socialist Strategy.* London: Verso, 1985.

Larson, Kerry. *Whitman's Drama of Consensus.* Chicago: Chicago University Press, 1988.

Leavis, Q. D. "Hawthorne as Poet." *Sewanee Review* 59 (spring and summer 1951): 179–85, 198–205, 456–58.

Lebeaux, Richard. "Identity Crisis and Beyond: Eriksonian Perspectives on the Pre-Walden and Post-Walden Thoreau." Gozzi, *Thoreau's Psychology* 19–66.

Levine, George. *Aesthetics and Ideology.* New Brunswick, N.J.: Rutgers University Press, 1994.

Levine, Robert S. " 'Antebellum Rome' in *The Marble Faun*." *ALH* 2, no. 1 (spring 1990): 19–38.

———. *Conspiracy and Romance: Studies in Brockden Brown, Cooper, Hawthorne, and Melville.* Cambridge: Cambridge University Press, 1989.

London, Ephraim, ed. *The Law as Literature.* Vol. 2 of *The World of Law.* New York: Simon and Shuster, 1960.

Long, Jeff. *Duel of Eagles: The Mexican and U.S. Fight for the Alamo.* New York: Morrow, 1990.

Macherey, Pierre. *A Theory of Literary Production.* Trans. Geoffrey Wall. London: Routledge, 1978.

Male, Roy. *Hawthorne's Tragic Vision.* New York: Norton, 1957.

Marcus, Greil. *Lipstick Traces: A Secret History of the Twentieth Century.* Cambridge, Mass.: Harvard University Press, 1990.

Marki, Ivan. *The Trial of the Poet: An Interpretation of the First Edition of "Leaves of Grass."* New York: Columbia University Press, 1976.

Marx, Karl. "The Eighteenth Brumaire of Louis Bonaparte." Tucker 436–525.

———. "The German Ideology." Tucker 110–64.

Marx, Leo. *The Machine in the Garden.* New York: Oxford University Press, 1964.

Masur, Louis, ed. *The Real War Will Never Get in the Books: Selections from Writers during the Civil War.* New York: Oxford University Press, 1993.

Matthiessen, F. O. *American Renaissance: Art and Expression in the Age of Emerson and Whitman.* New York: Oxford University Press, 1941.

Meserve, Walter J. *Heralds of Promise: The Drama of the American People during the Age of Jackson, 1829–1849.* New York: Greenwood, 1986.

Michaels, Walter Benn. "Romance and Real Estate." Michaels and Pease 156–82.

Michaels, Walter Benn, and Donald Pease, eds. *The American Renaissance Reconsidered.* Baltimore: Johns Hopkins University Press, 1985.

Millington, Richard. *Practicing Romance.* Princeton: Princeton University Press, 1991.

Milton, John. *Complete Poetical Works.* Ed. Douglas Bush. Boston: Houghton Mifflin, 1965.

Mizruchi, Susan. *The Power of Historical Knowledge.* Princeton: Princeton University Press, 1988.

Moon, Michael. *Disseminating Whitman: Revision and Corporeality in "Leaves of Grass."* Cambridge, Mass.: Harvard University Press, 1991.

Morison, Samuel Eliot. *John Paul Jones: A Sailor's Biography.* Boston: Little, Brown, 1959.

Mulcaire, Terry. "Publishing Intimacy in *Leaves of Grass.*" *ELH* 60 (1993): 471–501.

Nathanson, Tenney. *Whitman's Presence: Body, Voice, and Writing in "Leaves of Grass."* New York: New York University Press, 1992.

Newberry, Frederick. *Hawthorne's Divided Loyalties.* Rutherford, N.J.: Fairleigh Dickinson University Press, 1987.

Patterson, Mark. "Racial Sacrifice and Citizenship: The Construction of Masculinity in Louisa May Alcott's 'The Brothers.' " *SAF* 25, no. 2 (autumn 1997): 147–66.

Pearce, Roy Harvey. *The Continuity of American Poetry.* Princeton: Princeton University Press, 1969.

———. *Savagism and Civilization.* Baltimore: Johns Hopkins University Press, 1965.

Pease, Donald. *Visionary Compacts: American Renaissance Writing in Cultural Context.* Madison: University of Wisconsin Press, 1987.

Peck, H. Daniel. "The Crosscurrents of *Walden*'s Pastoral." Sayre, *New Essays* 73–94.

———. *Thoreau's Morning Work: Memory and Perception in "A Week on the Concord and Merrimack Rivers," the Journal, and "Walden."* New Haven, Conn.: Yale University Press, 1990.

Petroski, Henry. "H. D. Thoreau, Engineer." *American Heritage of Invention and Technology* 5, no. 2 (fall 1989): 8–16.

Pfister, Joel. *The Production of Personal Life: Class, Gender, and the Psychological in Hawthorne's Fiction.* Stanford: Stanford University Press, 1991.

Prude, Jonathan. "Town-Factory Conflicts in Antebellum Rural Massachusetts." Hahn and Prude 71–102.

Reynolds, David. *Beneath the American Renaissance.* Cambridge, Mass.: Harvard University Press, 1989.

———. *Walt Whitman's America: A Cultural Biography.* New York: Vintage, 1996.

Reynolds, Larry J. *European Revolutions and the American Literary Renaissance.* New Haven: Yale University Press, 1988.

Richards, Jeffrey. *Theater Enough.* Durham, N.C.: Duke University Press, 1991.

Richardson, Robert D., Jr. *Henry Thoreau: A Life of the Mind.* Berkeley: University of California Press, 1986.

Rowe, John Carlos. *At Emerson's Tomb: The Politics of Classic American Literature.* New York: Columbia University Press, 1997.

Ryan, Mary. *Civic Wars: Democracy and Public Life in the American City during the Nineteenth Century.* Berkeley: University of California Press, 1997.

Sams, Henry W., ed. *Autobiography of Brook Farm.* Englewood Cliffs, N.J.: Prentice-Hall, 1958.

Sánchez-Eppler, Karen. "To Stand Between: A Political Perspective on Whitman's Poetics of Merger and Embodiment." *ELH* 56 (1989): 923–49.

Sayre, Robert F. *Thoreau and the American Indians.* Princeton: Princeton University Press, 1977.

———, ed. *New Essays on "Walden."* Cambridge: Cambridge University Press, 1992.

Schivelbusch, Wolfgang. *The Railway Journey.* Berkeley: University of California Press, 1986.

Schwartz, Harold. "Fugitive Slave Days in Boston." *NEQ* 27 (1954): 192–212.

Shaw, Peter. *American Patriots and the Rituals of Revolution.* Cambridge, Mass.: Harvard University Press, 1981.

Shloss, Carol. *In Visible Light.* New York: Oxford University Press, 1987.

Shulman, Robert. *Social Criticism and Nineteenth-Century American Fictions.* Columbia: University of Missouri Press, 1987.

Simpson, David. "Destiny Made Manifest: The Styles of Whitman's Poetry." *Nation and Narration.* Ed. Homi K. Bhabha. London: Routledge, 1990. 177–96.

Spann, Edward K. *Brotherly Tomorrows: Movements for a Cooperative Society in America 1820–1920.* New York: Columbia University Press, 1989.

———. *The New Metropolis: New York City, 1840–57.* New York: Columbia University Press, 1981.

Steele, Jeffrey, ed. *The Essential Margaret Fuller.* Burlington, N.J.: Rutgers University Press, 1992.

Stokes, Gale. *The Walls Came Tumbling Down: The Collapse of Communism in Eastern Europe*. New York: Oxford University Press, 1993.

Swann, Charles. *Nathaniel Hawthorne: Tradition and Revolution*. Cambridge: Cambridge University Press, 1991.

Sweet, Timothy. *Traces of War: Poetry, Photography, and the Crisis of the Union*. Baltimore: Johns Hopkins University Press, 1990.

Terdiman, Richard. *Discourse/Counter-Discourse: The Theory and Practice of Symbolic Resistance in Nineteenth-Century France*. Ithaca, N.Y.: Cornell University Press, 1985.

Thomas, Brook. *Cross-Examinations of Law and Literature*. Cambridge: Cambridge University Press, 1987.

Thomas, M. Wynn. *The Lunar Light of Whitman's Poetry*. Cambridge, Mass.: Harvard University Press, 1987.

———. "Whitman and the Dreams of Labor." Folsom 133–52.

Thoreau, Henry David. *Journal*. Vol. 2, *1842–48*. Ed. Robert Sattelmeyer. Princeton: Princeton University Press, 1984.

———. *Journal*. Vol. 3, *1848–51*. Ed. Robert Sattelmeyer et al. Princeton: Princeton University Press, 1990.

———. *Reform Papers*. Ed. Wendell Glick. Princeton: Princeton University Press, 1973.

———. *Walden*. Ed. J. Lyndon Shanley. Princeton: Princeton University Press, 1971.

———. *A Week on the Concord and Merrimack Rivers*. Ed. Carl F. Hovde et al. Princeton: Princeton University Press, 1980.

Trachtenberg, Alan. "Whitman's Lesson of the City." Erkkila and Grossman 163–73.

Tucker, Robert C., ed. *The Marx-Engels Reader*. New York: Norton, 1972.

Turner, Arlin. *Nathaniel Hawthorne*. New York: Oxford University Press, 1980.

Warner, Michael. "Whitman Drunk." Erkkila and Grossman 30–43.

Wheaton, Bernard, and Zdenek Kavan. *The Velvet Revolution: Czechoslovakia, 1988–1991*. Boulder, Colo.: Westview, 1992.

Whitman, Walt. *Collected Writings of Walt Whitman: The Early Poems and the Fiction*. Ed. Thomas L. Brasher. New York: New York University Press, 1963.

———. *Collected Writings of Walt Whitman: Notebooks and Unpublished Prose Manuscripts*. Vol. 1. Ed. Edward F. Grier. New York: New York University Press, 1984.

———. *Leaves of Grass*. Ed. Sculley Bradley and Harold W. Blodgett. New York: Norton, 1973.

———. *Leaves of Grass: A Facsimile of the First Edition*. Ed. Richard Bridgman. San Francisco: Chandler, 1968.

———. *"Leaves of Grass": A Textual Variorum of the Printed Poems*. Vol. 1, *Poems, 1855–56*. Ed. Sculley Bradley et al. New York: New York University Press, 1980.

———. *"Leaves of Grass": A Textual Variorum of the Printed Poems*. Vol. 2, *Poems, 1860–67*. Ed. Sculley Bradley et al. New York: New York University Press, 1980.

———. *New York Dissected: A Sheaf of Recently Discovered Newspaper Articles by the Author of "Leaves of Grass."* Ed. Emory Holloway and Ralph Adimari. New York: Rufus Rockwell Wilson, 1936.

———. *Walt Whitman's "Leaves of Grass": The First (1855) Edition*. Ed. Malcolm Cowley. New York: Viking, 1959.

Wilentz, Sean. *Chants Democratic: New York City and the Rise of the American Working Class, 1788–1850*. New York: Oxford University Press, 1984.

Williams, Raymond. *Marxism and Literature*. Oxford: Oxford University Press, 1977.

Wright, Gordon. *France in Modern Times*. 2d ed. Chicago: Rand McNally, 1974.